Love Rules

D1520676

Love Rules

SILENT HOLLYWOOD
AND THE
RISE OF THE
MANAGERIAL CLASS

Mark Garrett Cooper

University of Minnesota Press

Minneapolis / London

An earlier version of chapter 1 was published in *Cultural Critique* 39 (1998). Reprinted here with permission.

Published by the University of Minnesota Press
111 Third Avenue South, Suite 290
Minneapolis, MN 55401-2520
http://www.upress.umn.edu

Library of Congress Cataloging-in-Publication Data

Cooper, Mark Garrett.
    Love rules : silent Hollywood and the rise of the managerial class / Mark Garrett Cooper.
        p.   cm.
    Includes bibliographical references and index.
    ISBN 0-8166-3752-0 (alk. paper) — ISBN 0-8166-3753-9 (pbk. : alk. paper)
        1. Love in motion pictures.   2. Silent films—United States—History and criticism.   3. Motion picture audiences.   4. Race relations in motion pictures.   I. Title.
    PN1995.9.L6 C66 2003
    791.43'63543—dc21
                                                                2002152229

Printed in the United States of America on acid-free paper

The University of Minnesota is an equal-opportunity educator and employer.

12 11 10 09 08 07 06 05 04 03   10 9 8 7 6 5 4 3 2 1

For Thomas E. Roberts

Contents

Acknowledgments

This book would not have been possible without the resources of a number of archives and the expertise of those who run them. I thank Richard Manning, keeper of the Brown University Film Archives; Edward Stratmann and the George Eastman House; the gracious staff of the Margaret Herrick Library of the Academy of Motion Picture Arts and Sciences, especially Barbara Hall; Charles Silver of the Museum of Modern Art's Film Study Center; the always helpful staff of the Library of Congress (Motion Picture, Broadcasting, and Recorded Sound Division); and the Baker Library of the Harvard Business School. A summer grant and a semester's teaching leave from the College of Arts and Sciences at Florida State University facilitated the completion of the project.

Several readers have left their mark on the text over the years. The adroit guidance of Philip Rosen sustained the project from the beginning, and the critical acumen of Neil Lazarus kept it on track. The argument took shape through invaluable readings by and discussions with Nathan Angell, Laura Briggs, Mary Anne Doane, Melani McAlister, Jessica Shubow, Ezra Tawil, Khachig Tölölyan, Elizabeth Weed, Kristen Whissel, and the participants of the 1995–96 seminar of Brown University's Pembroke Center for Teaching and Research on Women. In later phases, R. M. Berry, Barry J. Faulk, and Ellen Rooney lent their considerable talents to the introduction. Jennifer L. Fleissner convinced me that chapter 1 was finally finished, while

Josh Kates performed an equally admirable feat by showing why chapter 2 had a draft yet to go. W. T. Lhamon's expertise aided the revision of chapter 4, and I have Leonard Tennenhouse to thank for noticing at the outset that the subject of that chapter (the movie mogul) would be a key link in my argument. The text assumed its final form through the keen advice of Paula Rabinowitz, who showed me how I might best knit together its various components. I am grateful to them all.

I owe a special acknowledgment to Nancy Armstrong. From start to finish, her dedication to the project far exceeded what any young scholar has a right to expect. At every turn, she met my conviction that cinema's role in U.S. culture had yet to be explained with the demand that I actually explain it. While my success will be for others to judge, I wish to record my admiration for the one who taught me to relish the attempt.

Among the many who have helped to write this book, there are two who might be said to have lived with it. John Marx and Jennifer Ting will no doubt discern the traces they have left on each of the following pages. I will simply say that I am proudest of the passages to which they have most contributed.

I received my early education from the excellent public school teachers of Littleton, Colorado. This book is dedicated to one among them, for the basic and invaluable lesson that not all ideas are thinkable at all times.

Introduction

The lovers find one another at last. Their eyes meet and remain locked in a mutual stare as they are drawn together through the frame. Speech cannot render the depth of emotion this image implies. True love beams from the faces that fill the screen. Although this is their first real meeting, the permanence of the couple's union appears self-evident.

Despite its inevitability, this ending arrives as if by magic. Indeed, from the very beginning of the film, those situations that suggest a bond between the partners also imply that only superhuman coordination will make it secure. At first the entire span of the United States separates Sam from Annie. His voice travels from the West Coast through the ether to emerge from her car radio on the East Coast. Although she cannot see him and he does not know she exists, the manner in which each looks longingly out of frame demonstrates that neither can be complete without the other. A sense of destiny develops as the two strive in vain to see one another across highway traffic, as Sam lingers atop one New York City skyscraper toward which Annie gazes from another, and, finally, as her elevator ascends that skyscraper at the very instant his descends it. Precisely by holding Sam and Annie apart, the film makes everything depend on getting the two together. To connect them is simultaneously to guarantee personal happiness, secure the nuclear family, and unite America's opposite shores.

Such a high-stakes meeting cannot be achieved simply by setting Sam and Annie on a collision course. Rather, it requires an ability to represent their togetherness as desirable because difficult, to throw obstacles in the path of reciprocal movement and mutual recognition, and to convince audiences that such obstacles can and will be removed. *Sleepless in Seattle* conjures obstructions only to make them vanish; the look of love appears eternal by comparison. No doubt, the makers of this popular 1993 romantic comedy anticipated correctly that viewers would instantly recognize its concluding images as signs of true love. To endow such images with the power of resolution, they reprised the formula of connection, separation, and reunion that had delivered the Hollywood happy ending for more than eighty years. The magic of love hardly depends on an ad hoc agreement between the film's producers and its consumers. It occurs within habitual practices and expectations. Yet it is far from self-evident why filmmakers and audiences have delighted in the repetition of this particular visual pattern to the point of endowing it with the mystical aura of fate. The explanation requires nothing short of a history of cinematic culture.

The form now known simply as "the movies" became a defining characteristic of American life during the 1910s and 1920s. To be sure, the conventions of the feature film owe a good deal to shorter films produced during the first decade of the century and were significantly altered by the introduction of sound in the late 1920s. Nonetheless, the year 1909 marks the end of the brief, transitional nickelodeon period, during which one-reel films came to be understood as something more than a series of local attractions, and the very beginning of the feature film era, during which longer narratives plainly addressed a heterogeneous national viewership in a manner standardized through central control of production, distribution, and exhibition.[1] Around 1907, domestic filmmakers and critics began to decry the foreign threat posed by the films of the French company Pathé, which dominated the U.S. nickelodeon market between 1905 and 1908. This was a vigorous campaign to establish that motion pictures should be distinctly American in origin and content.[2] A very different sort of argument prevailed by 1915, when the National Association for the Advancement of Colored People chose *The Birth of a Nation* as the target of its first nationwide protest.[3] By that time, it could be assumed that a movie might represent America to itself, as various groups vied to assert just what that representation would be and who would regulate it. With increasing vociferousness during the 1920s, all manner of discourses marveled at the popularity of American motion pictures, their national character, and their potential, for good or ill, to influence the individuals their audience comprised. By 1928, splendid movie palaces and myriad smaller theaters sold perhaps sixty-five million tickets per week.[4] That same year, former postmaster general and industry spokesman Will Hays declared Hollywood motion pictures "the epitome of civilization and the quintessence of what we mean by 'America'." It must have been difficult for his readers to remember that the movies had not existed a scant twenty years earlier.[5]

To address the nation through movies presupposed not just a particular sort of film, but an increasingly complex division of labor and the escalating participation of finance capital. In this, the developing motion picture industry had a good deal in common with other lines of business. Nonetheless, the division of labor that characterizes mature Hollywood production cannot be said to precede the feature film. It did not exist in 1915 when D. W. Griffith and former insurance man Harry Aitken formed their own company to produce *The Birth of a Nation*.[6] Its rudiments did exist by 1919, when Famous Players–Lasky floated a $10 million public stock offering to finance the purchase of a string of theaters and became the prototype of the fully integrated movie corporation. The director-supervisor gave way to a hierarchy of specialized workers headed by a producer. These management hierarchies increasingly answered to commercial banks and shareholders. By 1930, six fully integrated studios and two smaller firms constituted an oligopoly in the film industry.[7] The rapid rise of the Hollywood studios was neither the triumph of cinematic technology per se nor the inevitable result of capitalism. Rather, it was a process whereby diverse viewers came to appreciate a certain kind of movie as capable of representing the nation to itself, while filmmakers and financiers developed institutions capable of mass producing that kind of movie for a profit.

The visual love story enabled this process. In order to produce the form known as Hollywood cinema, filmmakers working in nearly every genre repeatedly demonstrated that in order to be safe, happy, and capable of forming a family, a particular kind of couple had to be located in a particular kind of space. Unfaithful spouses, intrusive black men, criminal masterminds, and perilous settings galore threatened the romantic couple. They did so to comical as well as tragic effect. No matter the nature of the threat, however, the rising feature film promised to make love secure by constituting a well-illuminated space. Great distances, rapidly moving objects, strong shadows, and innumerable barriers introduced a separation; they prevented the lovers' mutual recognition and allowed a villain or rival to intrude upon them. Togetherness therefore required the abolition of distance, the cessation of motion, even illumination, and the collapse of barriers. Out of heterogeneous spaces, silent features crafted a homogeneous space surrounding a white man and woman—exactly the process *Sleepless in Seattle* reiterates when it eliminates the final obstacle to the look Sam and Annie seem destined to share. To be sure, Hollywood does not always keep its promise of a happy ending. The doom of heartbreak may instantly be recognized in the failure to restore the lovers' shared eyeline, a disappointment to which the persistence of a cluttered, opaque, or gloomy setting invariable contributes. More typically, however, obstructions yield to a space of order and light with a happy couple at its core. Through the repetition and extension of this pattern, the love story established itself as the commonsense form of Hollywood narrative. In the process, it envisioned not only America but the entire world as a disparate and often conflicting series of spaces, any one of which could potentially be made safe for the romantic couple and the American family it founded.

To set in place the basic components of the family thus depends on a narrative agent capable of differentiating, juxtaposing, transforming, and reconciling diverse spaces. This organizing perspective has no location in space and cannot originate in any one body. It takes a decidedly impersonal vantage to generate the impression that Annie and Sam's union has transformed the entire continental United States into a place where love can flourish. Since the silent era, movies have underscored the incorporeal nature of this vantage point by insisting on the limitations of embodied vision within the frame. Because the lovers' points of view are limited to the spaces they inhabit, they have difficulty seeing one another, let alone the myriad dangers that confront them. As an attribute of Hollywood form, the agent responsible for narrating love must be an abstract presence hovering before, outside, and after the manipulation of the visual field. In concrete historical practice, however, its production apparently invited, then came to require, the participation of an expansive hierarchy of experts—from gaffers and continuity clerks to directors, screenwriters, and producers. True, the narrative agent implied by feature film form has lived a rich and varied rhetorical existence as "the director," "the camera," and even "the spectator." Viewers may or may not be fully conscious of its dependence on corporate production. The fact remains that multitudes apparently found it both plausible and desirable to be addressed by narration that pictured, arranged, and transformed spaces in a way no embodied person could. In effect if not in awareness, to recognize oneself in this address, to desire and debate the machinery that posed safety and happiness as various problems of sightlines limited in space, was to assent to a particular model of authority. When movies made the proper arrangement of space depend on the ability to represent it according to particular rules, they effectively implied that such arrangement would require a complex technical apparatus controlled by a hierarchy of expert professionals.

The Hollywood love story posed a question of authority and answered it. This, I contend, was its contribution to the shift that occurred, roughly speaking, between 1880 and 1930, when the America of industrial capital and "island communities" gave way to a corporate America at once more tightly knit by mass media and more vocally subdivided into diverse groups. I am not suggesting that cinema alone asked who and what should represent and arrange American society. Nor do I maintain that the movies were unique in offering a managerial answer. I propose only that cinema made a decisive historical contribution by presenting such a question and offering such an answer. To the love story's spatial machinations we may credit the shift in national mediation associated with Hollywood's success. This narrative form provided a clear, reproducible, and readily adaptable means of demonstrating who belonged where. In the process, it demonstrated that national supervision and arrangement would require an expertise no one person could possess. Teams of information specialists would be necessary to demonstrate public security via the couple's private sightline and to distinguish the public from an alienating mass. In this way, movies fundamentally revised the traditional categories of American national culture and legitimated a rising professional managerial class.

SPACES, NOT SHOTS

No one disputes the prominence of the love story in American cinema, but few have looked to this narrative pattern to define Hollywood's historical contribution. In fact, generations of film historians have encouraged us to accept at face value the observation that Hollywood borrowed its favorite narrative from prior forms, especially the novel. Filmmakers, we are invited to assume, simply put old wine in new bottles. Given this dubious assumption, it has made sense to look for the new and distinctly cinematic features of motion pictures in such production techniques as editing, camerawork, and mise-en-scène. The shot has been the privileged unit of analysis. Through investigation of shots and their articulation, film theorists and historians have distinguished the Hollywood feature from other types of films and chronicled the relationship between its formal development and the organization of its production. In the process, however, they have largely abandoned the content of the love story to an associated field of study, the history of culture, in which thematic comparisons among films and contemporary texts chart continuities and changes in such matters as American sexual mores, gender roles, and racism. To this body of work we owe our sense that the rise of Hollywood had everything to do with changes in national culture after the turn of the century. A great many studies rely on both sorts of arguments.[8] Indeed, some kind of collaboration between the two must occur to avoid producing an entirely schizoid account of Hollywood cinema. Yet this very scission makes it difficult, if not impossible, to explain why the world's leading capitalist nation wanted particular stories of love and romance in the form of the feature film.

When Hollywood form is defined as a matter of production technique, its historical contribution tends to disappear into one or another very broad trend. In the great outpouring of film theory and criticism during the 1970s, it became commonplace to describe the feature film as continuing a twofold realism. Strategies of framing and editing were said to reproduce the perspectival arrangements of quattrocento painting, while Hollywood's narrative patterns reprised the ideology of "the classical realist text"—prototypically the nineteenth-century European novel. By describing paintings, novels, and films as realist, diverse theorists implied that these media all interpellated the same sort of individual, whom they identified as a modern, capitalist subject.[9] In 1985, David Bordwell, Kristen Thompson, and Janet Staiger succeeded in making this kind of account look vague, if not ahistorical. Dispensing with "realism" as an ideological problem, the authors of *The Classical Hollywood Cinema* chart the concrete connections between Hollywood's evolving "style" and its corporate mode of production. To define that style, however, Bordwell resorts to a "classicism" more venerable than realism ever was. Its telltale features of "decorum, proportion, formal harmony, respect for tradition, mimesis, self-effacing craftsmanship, and cool control of the perceiver's response" ultimately derive from seventeenth-century French models, if not from Aristotle.[10] Miriam Hansen did not displace this emphasis on classical form when she reintroduced the problem of Hollywood's sociohistorical function in 1991. Rather, her *Babel and Babylon* depicts "the elaboration of a mode of narration that makes it possible to anticipate a viewer through particular textual strategies, and thus to standardize empirically diverse and to some extent unpredictable acts of reception."[11] More emphatically than any prior approach, Hansen establishes that movies called a national mass audience into being when they addressed viewers in a uniform manner. Yet insofar as this address remains a technical matter, cinema's effect on a national public becomes difficult to separate from the standardizing force of commodification in general. A change is far easier to discern, for instance, when Hansen looks to fan magazines and reviews to argue that movies provided an alternative public sphere for women. Doubtless, movies are commodities, just as they plainly have classical attributes and bear some relation to the realist novel and perspectival painting. But their commodity character will not suffice to explain why audiences and filmmakers wanted the movies to repeat a specific kind of visual story at a particular moment in time. Nor will arguments over whether movies are primarily "realist," "classical," or "melodramatic" in nature explain what the Hollywood love story contributed to any of these traditions.[12] Nor, finally, will emphasis on realism, classicism, or commodification explain why this type of movie is perceived to be American. When Hollywood form is collapsed into European tradition, its nationalism can only seem a matter of content that could exist quite independently from it.

A related complaint holds for those approaches that place Hollywood films in historical context by means of thematic comparison with other texts. In 1975, Robert Sklar used just this method to provide the first major social history of American cinema. His *Movie-Made America* takes full advantage of the scandalized rhetoric moralists employed in describing the nickelodeon's boisterous working-class and immigrant audiences and defines the medium accordingly as a populist endeavor hemmed in by traditionalist forces. Ultimately, the industry's quest for social legitimacy requires a reassertion of "elite," "Victorian," middle-class ideals. Despite an abiding undercurrent of populist sexiness, normative sexuality is confined once more to the private home and nuclear family. Thus, the movies serve primarily to update bourgeois romance by making court-ship and marriage appear more erotic and fun.[13] This thesis has proven extremely productive. Study after study explains what Hollywood has to do with American culture by pointing to writing that disputes or de-fends cinema's depiction of sexuality (broadly defined). Through its pro-liferation, however, this approach has undermined almost every plank of Sklar's initial argument. Lary May corrects Sklar's hypostasized an-timony of "popular" and "elite" when he shows how Hollywood's up-dated version of Victorian values is better understood as the emerging ethos of a new middle class.[14] Examination of the industry's internal documents has revealed a sustained collaboration between supposedly old-fashioned, elite moral guardians and nominally populist, up-and-coming businessmen.[15] New data on theater locations has sparked dis-pute over whether early audiences really comprised the working-class viewership various writers identified as the target of reform.[16] Those who have focused on writing by and about working women and men have found evidence of a contradictory and contentious relationship with prevailing feature film content.[17] Focus on sex, class, and gender has been amended, though not displaced, by consideration of how the industry and its critics discussed crime, religion, race, and ethnicity.[18] Far from being an essentially populist medium coopted by an enduring elite culture, it now seems clear that the movies promoted a wide range of discourses through which various groups and institutions aimed to regulate all manner of behavior during the first third of the twentieth century. Yet this line of historical argument does not limit itself to the claim that motion pictures were of a piece with contemporary discourse about them. Rather, it draws strength from the contention that cinema had a special prominence and distinct function. In one way or another, most social histories of U.S. filmmaking repeat Sklar's contention that the movies made America what it is. Given the productivity of corporate filmmakers, I suspect that every discourse contemporary to the silent feature has a counterpart in it. Such is certainly the case for discourse about national identity itself. But thematic connections will not explain what was specific about the movies and thus cannot really demonstrate what it meant for American culture to appear in cinematic form.

To move beyond this impasse, we ought to relinquish the proposi-tion that something called "the love story" flows from epoch to epoch and form to form and instead take up an investigation of the distinctive patterns through which Hollywood tells that most familiar of narratives. I have described those patterns as spatial in character and proposed that the opposition, transformation, and reconciliation of different kinds of spaces brings about the famous Hollywood happy ending or dramatically fails to do so. This process depends on those techniques that typically characterize Hollywood production, but it is by no means reducible to them. Continuity editing, three-point lighting, framing conventions such as the medium-long shot ("plan Américain") and close-up, "realistic" acting, and mise-en-scène—all these and more collaborate to distinguish and articulate spaces. A single shot may show more than one space, as when the villain looms in the window behind the unsuspecting heroine. Likewise, more than one shot may be required to depict a space, as in those final sequences that establish the security of the lovers by first showing their shared gaze as a connection across framelines and then showing them united in the frame. It is through that shared gaze, and not shot-reverse-shot editing per se, that we recognize resolution. Indeed, this type of sequence may be filmed in a wide range of ways, so long as it seems to restore the lovers' mutual stare within a clean, well-lighted space. The visual love story progresses not through shots and their articulation, but by means of spatial differences.

Here it bears remembering that the shot has been a controversial entity even among its biggest promoters. Consider André Bazin's famous argument against Sergei Eisenstein. The dispute between the two may readily be described as one in which Bazin promotes the realism of the deep focus, long take "sequence shot" against the principle of montage Eisenstein had earlier celebrated. While accurate, this summation overlooks each theorist's suspicion of the shot itself as an analytic unit. Eisenstein declares: "The shot is by no means an element of montage. The shot is a montage cell (or molecule)."[19] Against the idea that shots are the "building blocks" of film, he insists that the contents of the frame provide their own principles of division, conflict, and articulation. Bazin therefore attacks a straw man when he counters Eisenstein's "montage" by finding "at the very heart of silent film . . . a language the semantic and syntactic unit of which is in no sense the Shot."[20] If Bazin and Eisenstein agree on nothing else, one might even go so far as to say, they agree on the shot's inadequacy for their respective critiques. A similar point might be made about Laura Mulvey's foundational essay,

"Visual Pleasure and Narrative Cinema." Like its predecessors in arguments by Christian Metz and Jean-Louis Baudry, the essay relies on the category of the shot to make an analogy between the "look" of the camera and that of the spectator at the screen. Mulvey gives this analogic structure a gender by reintroducing content: specifically, the look of the male protagonist at the woman within the film. Devices such as the close-up work to define the woman as the object of a threefold masculine gaze. But not just any close-up will do. In fact, Mulvey identifies a primarily spatial distinction. To define the woman as "to-be-looked-at-ness" requires images that take "the film into a no man's land outside its own time and space."[21] I believe this "no man's land" may be described far more precisely than Mulvey describes it. My point for now, however, is simply that Mulvey's argument, like Eisenstein's and Bazin's, calls attention to the disarticulation of technique and content that invariably results when shots define film form. The apparently concrete unit of the shot, so useful in breaking down the work of production, proves inadequate to the task of explaining how films actually make meaning for their viewers. This insight recurs, albeit ambivalently, throughout film theory.[22]

Many of the editing techniques typically used to mark the emergence of Hollywood narration make sense only as procedures for distinguishing and articulating spaces. In parallel editing, for instance, the alternation of shots signifies that spatially discrete lines of action occur simultaneously. As Noël Burch famously argues, this technique was not at all self-evident to the earliest filmmakers. Edwin S. Porter's 1903 film *Life of an American Fireman,* to pick the conventional example, steadfastly refuses to alternate between the inside of a burning building and the rescuers outside it. In its preference for showing the rescue "twice," from different points of view, Porter's film testifies to a mode of narration and address quite foreign to the institutional mode that prevailed just a few years later.[23] The work of D. W. Griffith has long exemplified that later mode. Significantly, however, the most extensive study of Griffith's early work available finds his contribution not in "parallel editing" per se, but in a particular adaptation of that technique. Tom Gunning reminds us that the alternation of two discreet lines of action was already conventional in the chase film when Griffith began directing in 1908. The decisive change came, he argues, when Griffith used such alternation to interrupt actions "at a point of intensity" and to imply a psychological connection between characters who could not see one another.[24] Through its power to establish such connections, the kind of narration we associate with Griffith distinguished itself from the cameraman's ability to record actions and the editor's ability to link one action to the next. Gunning takes his example from Griffith's early adaptation of Alfred Tennyson's "Enoch Arden," *After Many Years.* Here, in the instant the shipwrecked husband raises his wife's locket to his lips, we cut to an image of the wife, at home in England, extending her arms as if to embrace him. In the process of demonstrating that "devotion overcomes geography," Gunning observes, Griffith creates "an omniscient narrator, who unites on the screen what is separate in the space [sic] of the story."[25] Gunning's principal aim is to explain how Griffith developed a "narrator-system" that led to the feature film. But Virgina Wright Wexman draws another, logical implication from his observations. "For Griffith," she writes, "parallel montage is a way of constituting the couple.[26] Through juxtaposition, parallel editing implies the interdependence of two or more spaces and the figures they include. That interdependence animates the developing love story and defines the entity that will narrate the feature film. Although this spatial dynamic is implicit in most discussions of parallel editing, it has not been the primary focus of critical investigation.

Emphasis on "the diegesis" thwarts such a focus and may well be the main obstacle to understanding Hollywood form. It is this "fictional world of the film" that Gunning refers to as "the space of the story" and that allowed the theorists of the 1970s to associate realist perspective with realist narrative. "The diegesis" thus functioned as a key concept in the model of film spectatorship that preoccupied film theory for the last third of the twentieth century. In Christian Metz's famous account of the spectator's ideological identification with the cinematographic apparatus, the coherence of the diegesis promotes the fantasy that the viewer occupies a position of transcendental mastery with respect to the visual field.[27] Burch describes the historical production of that position through the particular structures of editing and framing that allowed movement and space to appear continuous from shot to shot.[28] Mulvey relies on "the diegesis" to distinguish masculine narrative from feminine spectacle. And more radically, Stephen Heath shows the stability of this perspectival space to be contingent upon "the narrative itself," in particular the narratively significant use of characters' looks across frame lines.[29] Interestingly enough, however, "the diegesis" also thrives in the formalism that opposes these arguments. In *Narration in the Fiction Film,* David Bordwell makes a sweeping critique of the notion of spectatorship as position. He resolutely opposes both analogies between the camera's vantage and the spectator's look and those between cinematic perspective and that of Renaissance painting. This argument comes remarkably close to dethroning the shot and the diegesis in favor of all manner of "cues" for construing spatial, temporal, and causal relationships. Yet Bordwell's approach to narrative ultimately extends their reign. He borrows from the Russian Formalists to distinguish "style"— "the film's systematic use of cinematic devices" ("mise-en-scène, cinematography, editing, and sound")—from plot *(syuzhet)*—the "formal patterns of withheld knowledge or abrupt revelation" on the basis of which viewers retroactively construe a story *(fabula)*. Accordingly, style is "wholly ingredient to the medium," while narrative remains a "dramaturgical" entity that may be abstracted from any medium in which it is told. Bordwell does point out that "Fabula events must be represented as occurring in a spatial frame of reference, however vague or abstract."[30] Nonetheless, his strict separation of "style" from "narrative" makes it impossible to consider that cinematic narrative might be an immanently spatial process. In his account, events occur "in" the space of a diegesis constituted by various cinematic devices, but narrative itself must be defined apart from space. Like its predecessors, then, Bordwell's model falls short when it fails to recognize that the love story does not happen *in* space so much as *to* space.[31] If a singular, unified space exists in the ordinary Hollywood feature film, it exists through the centripetal movement that collapses diverse spaces into a space two lovers share.

As a form based on articulated spatial differences, the love story does not merely provide a narrative template. It also structures content. In order to present the white man and woman as the socially reproducible couple, the rising feature film required distinctions among races and genders. Such distinctions help to define space. The space of resolution is not formed when two men come together, for example. Their mutual look typically indicates friendship or, when manipulated to mimic the lovers' gaze, a deviant state of desire. Similarly, when a black man stares unimpeded at a white woman this typically indicates an unwelcome advance. Each type of look introduces a complication and suggests that further spatial transformations will be necessary to make the normative romantic couple secure. Films set in place a differential system of eyeline matches, in other words, that distinguished reciprocal love from friendly admiration and lustful intrusion, and they employed that system to make qualitative spatial distinctions. Although logically arbitrary, the race and gender conventions of that differential system have clear historical determinations. They bear a striking debt, for instance, to the categories nineteenth-century fiction employed in representing the American family. But it would be a serious error to presuppose that those categories remained unchanged once expressed in cinematic form.

Hollywood made it appear self-evident that the future stability of the nation depended on the safety and happiness of a white man and woman. That state of safety frequently requires nonwhite persons to be banished from the frame. It almost always calls for the white woman to be represented as a desirable object and often demonstrates that she needs a man's protection. For these reasons, it has made sense to argue the movies conserve the traditional privilege of white men. That proposition, however, is complicated by the fact that definitions of race and gender were hotly contested during the period of cinema's emergence. Nativists and pluralists produced sharply divergent accounts of America's component populations, for instance, and scientists themselves could no longer agree on what race was or even that it existed. Similarly, the middle-class woman's power to influence the nation through the domestic sphere began to seem quaint as well as limiting; not only did she vote, but her sexual prerogatives were significantly dissociated from the institution of marriage. Such contests substantially revised the categories of race and gender. It is not uncommon to argue that movies played a crucial part in that revision, and I certainly believe that they did so. In chapters 1 and 4, I describe how visual love stories set the parameters of racial difference and then used the supplemental properties of sound to locate the emerging category of ethnicity within it. In chapters 1 and 3, I consider how Hollywood distinguished a woman's face from a man's and used it to pose the problem of how an alluring visual object might also be the source of a subjective look. Here and throughout, however, I want to insist on the difference spatial form makes to such categorization. No examination of how Hollywood classified and ordered populations can explain what movies meant for the historical privilege of white men until it accounts for the form's insistence on the limitations of all embodied points of view.

If, as I argue, the visual love story made the constitution of the couple depend on a narrative agent that could have no body and could not belong to the spaces represented, then movies cannot simply have maintained the preexisting authority of one particular population over others. Rather, they must have revised the character of the relationship between embodiment and supervision. Movies made classification by race and gender essential means of determining where various individuals belonged. At the same time, the authority to arrange them derived less self-evidently from bodily markers than it traditionally had. To order a social whole required a necessarily incorporeal vantage and the corporate hierarchies that produced it. As I will explain, this strained the logic of liberal democracy, producing new double binds and contradictions. For the moment, my point is simply this: the question of what movies did to and for racism and patriarchy can only really be answered within a consideration of their contribution to the more general problem of national governance. To understand that contribution requires an account of how movies departed from those forms of mediation through which class, race, and gender had previously defined the ability to represent the nation in both the semiotic and the political sense.

THE PROBLEM OF VISUAL MASS MEDIATION

Since the beginning of the nineteenth century, Raymond Williams explains, modern usage has made the "the masses" a chiasmus. On the one hand, the term describes "a many headed multitude or mob: low, ignorant, unstable." On the other hand, it designates "the same people but now seen as a positive or potentially subversive force"—as in the late-nineteenth-century antagonism between "the masses" and "the classes." Depending on one's point of view, then, "the masses" might have named a multitude desperately in need of regulation by a more reasonable few or a heterocephalous population capable of governing itself given the chance to do so. Williams notes that this relationship underwent a semantic shift in the twentieth century with the development of such new compounds as "mass society," "mass market," "mass media," and, presumably, "mass culture." Although these terms emphasize "the large numbers reached" and thus reprise the senses of "the many-headed multitude or the majority of the people," they also convey a new mode of reaching them. This mode itself may be defined as "manipulative or popular" and, accordingly, may be said to promote either "alienated and abstract" relationships or a more positive "new kind of social communication."[32] Whereas the nineteenth-century "masses" named a large number of people who might or might not be fit to govern themselves, the twentieth century revises the nature of that problem by using "mass" to associate a historical break with a type of mediation that arguably rendered the very question of self-governance obsolete.

Although the concept of "mass media" has become indispensable for understanding the movies, one must admit that it poses a vexing historical problem. I understand "mediation" to designate the process whereby various semiotic forms constitute social relationships. The concept is distinct from "communication," in the ordinary sense of that term, which involves the transmission and reception of information.[33] Like a language or sign system, a medium lives a life of its own apart from any particular message or message maker. "Mediation" describes not the sort of relationship that exists between one individual and another, but rather a process that defines numerous individuals as part of a group or larger social formation. This raises the question of whether the term "mediation" makes any sense at all without its partner "mass." The problem, Williams reminds us, is not primarily a quantitative one. Although the masses must be numerous, there is no particular number beyond which a group of people, novels, or movies becomes a mass phenomenon. Above all, the term makes a qualitative distinction. But to complicate matters further, the qualitative distinction it makes changed through the concept of mediation itself. That is, a shift in the meaning of the term "mass" apparently coincided with the insight that the circulation of information constituted groups (in either a "manipulative" or "popular" manner) rather than simply allowing their members to communicate among themselves (or thwarting their ability to do so).

To equate twentieth-century mass media with the problem of visual representation makes this semantic shift still more difficult to grasp. It is true that images proliferated during the final decades of the nineteenth century. The introduction of the halftone screen process alone has been described as "an iconographical revolution of the first order" in its ability to circulate pictures faster, farther, and more reliably than ever before.[34] Alongside it, one might set museums of art and natural history, world's fairs, department stores, and technologies ranging from chromolithography to glass and steel architecture. Already by the turn of the century it seems, members of urban-industrial societies were liable to experience the world as a series of prearranged views.[35] The coincidence of this image boom, on the one hand, and the developments in sociology, psychology, political economy, and semiology that ultimately lead to a critique of "mass society" on the other, may well account for the pervasive tendency to damn images and mass media in a single stroke. In any event, that particular condemnation recurs in remarkably consistent terms throughout the twentieth century: because people think and communicate with one another in words, we are told, the propagation of pictures necessarily mystifies social relationships.[36] Once upon a time, people read, wrote, and talked with one another. Now, images hold the masses in thrall. Understood thusly, the problem of visual mass mediation marks an exemplary instance of the tendency, critiqued by W. J. T. Mitchell, "to imagine the gulf between words and images to be as wide as the one between words and things, between (in the largest sense) culture and nature."[37] The visual character of "mass media" has come to seem both all important and not important at all. When images are opposed to supposedly more authentic verbal communication, arguments over their essential falsity trump concrete historical discussion of how they mediate. To have that discussion, images are typically subsumed under the general category of "text." By turns opposed to verbal communication and collapsed into textual mediation, the historical contribution of any particular visual medium becomes, once again, impossible to discern.

The movies have long served as a chief, if not the defining, instance of visual mass culture. If we are to understand, first, how they mediate the nation, and second, what they had to do with producing "mass mediation" as a critical problem, we can neither ignore their visual basis nor assume that it suffices to explain them. Rather, we require at least a provisional account of what it meant for the category of "the masses" to appear in cinematic form.

One might begin with the observation that the modern capitalist nation-state required print mediation to come into being. Although some will no doubt quibble with this assertion, I hope it will be granted that a wide range of arguments could be summoned in its favor. From Thomas Carlyle's assertion that "Printing . . . is equivalent to Democracy" to Benedict Anderson's discussion of how print capitalism generates imaginary national communities, the rise of print and the rise of the bourgeois nation go hand in hand.[38] Publication in print distinguished the private individual who thought, read, and wrote from "the author," a self-abstracting individual who addressed a large, anonymous readership. It also implied a necessary connection between the two. Print made it possible to imagine that reasonable persons, although unknown to one another, would be able to participate in a long-distance conversation about how to govern themselves as citizens. By a similar logic, a man's interests as a property holder were distinct from, although related to, his responsibilities as a citizen. Democracy was thought to reside in the open contention of private interests; ownership of property and participation in the democratic state were thus two sides of the same coin. Whereas the newspaper served as the form through which private citizens discussed public matters, the novel provided the means by which a rising middle class described its private life as private life in general.[39] Precisely because the novel seemed to provide apolitical information, it worked all the more effectively to naturalize the racial hierarchies and gendered division of labor characteristic of European and American nations. In their ability to distinguish and relate matters private and public, then, novels and newspapers joined diverse persons into a type of social formation that had not existed before. Despite ample evidence that white male property owners governed, the nation was held together by the proposition that all of its members might govern themselves insofar as they could communicate their private interests in a publicly intelligible manner. The ruling class began as a literate class. By the same token, reading and writing would allow the masses to rule themselves. In its basic structure, this contention survived even the mid-nineteenth century critiques of democracy's practical exclusions (Mill and Tocqueville) and its ideological character (Marx and Engels).

When movies gave the love stories of nineteenth-century fiction a visual form, they redefined the relationship between private reader and public nation. Hollywood's spatial story has no precise equivalent in the novel.[40] The difference resides not in "the image" per se, but in the habitual use of images that makes true love contingent on a perspective neither private and embodied nor public and disembodied. Once defined as a matter of sightlines limited in space, individual thoughts and feelings could hardly serve as a basis from which to address the national whole. Instead, movies established a qualitative distinction between (good) privacy and (bad) alienation. In the process, they made the difference between the public and the mass correspond to that distinction.

As I explain in chapter 2, *The Crowd* (1928) encapsulates this cinematic matrix by demonstrating the relationship between private and public to be essentially one of scale. Draw back from the private couple and one might see the public. Move closer to the masses and one will find an alienated man. With the proliferation of this type of visual relationship, the problem of how one's body was socially placed supplanted the question of the ownership of one's body, labor, or words as the basis of the private. Accordingly, publicity could no longer be conceived on the model of authorial self-abstraction extended by novels and newspapers. "The public," rather, was an entity addressed and made visible from a position of authority that never had an individual body to begin with. Only from this perspective could persons and space be arranged so as to lodge the private within the public and make the two categories confirm one another. When the visual love story established such a vantage as both possible and necessary, it effectively divorced the authority to represent the public from private reason. By definition, a "private" interest could not place itself within "the public." To establish that relation required an impersonal and purportedly neutral third party.

Movies addressed large numbers of persons. They brought bourgeois readers out of their homes, promoted commodified relationships, and promulgated new rules of behavior. But cinema's effect on the American public ultimately had less to do with any of these developments than it did with a structural change in the categories of private, public, and mass.

The imperative to search out the origin of mass culture and explain its power over us followed, in part, from this shift. When cinema revised the central categories of print democracy, it made publication itself seem the hallmark of a bygone era. It also required that print be described as a comparable form of mediation. Reading and writing were thus set at odds with speech. In other words, motion pictures did not massify print culture so much as they exposed the faulty logic of the print-as-conversation model. Such, in any case, is the lesson of Walter Lippmann and John Dewey's landmark 1920s debate over the public. Lippmann and Dewey draw upon the young fields of sociology, psychoanalysis, and semiology to attack the premises of liberal political philosophy. Despite their differences, each argues that semiotic behavior constitutes human individuals and communities as such. Thus, democracy ceases to be a problem of majority rule, the contention of private interests, or allowing silenced voices to be heard. It requires, rather, scientific representation and evaluation of those diverse voices and interests (Lippmann) or an all-inclusive program of radical education capable of revising semiotic practice (Dewey). To critique the public, that is, the debators embraced what may be regarded as the founding premises of cinematic culture: first, that to safeguard the lives and happiness of the members of a society will require the ability to represent the social whole, and second, that the social whole can only be adequately represented from an impersonal, collaboratively produced, point of view. This is not to say that either Lippmann or Dewey thought the movies would lead to a democracy worthy of the name. Rather, they developed a shared critique of the modern nation-state commensurate with the manner in which motion pictures represented it. That critique tends to be read as a symptom of or response to twentieth-century mass culture.[41] But it also constituted a state-of-the-art theory of mediation. Indeed, when they made such a theory indispensable for an account of democracy, Lippmann and Dewey laid the conceptual groundwork for many of the more familiar twentieth-century considerations of the public, including that of Jürgen Habermas in *Structural Transformation of the Public Sphere.* Whenever this work makes the difference between a public and a mass homologous to the difference between print and visual mediation, it urges us to overlook the critical turn that enabled that homology in the first place. In contrast, Lippmann and Dewey refuse any simple equation between visuality and massification. For this reason, they better enable an immanent critique of cinematic culture.

The most commonplace discussions of mass media do not, of course, feel compelled to decide if democracy remains possible. Liberalism survived in a rhetoric of "influence" that domesticated the critique of mass mediation and put it to professional use. As the silent feature film reached its apogee during the 1920s, the language of influence saturated discourse on propaganda, public relations, advertising, social survey research, and even civics. Work in these fields conceived the nation as a large group of individuals that existed prior to and apart from any particular form of address. Thus, its individual members could be persuaded. Precisely because efforts to persuade were pervasive, however, individual citizens, consumers, readers, and viewers had already, inevitably, succumbed to diverse influences in ways they themselves could not fully apprehend. No individual, then, could be relied on to know or represent his or her own self-interest. By sustaining a logic of this type, the notion of influence legitimated the work of professional public relations experts, marketers, social scientists, and critics who competed with one another to represent what the public really wanted and needed, and what, therefore, it could be persuaded to purchase or believe. It seems clear enough that the movies supported development of this professional model and thrived on it. In sources ranging from general-interest business magazines to censorship tracts, social scientific reform literature, and fan magazines, discussions of Hollywood's "powerful influence" established that films had a potentially positive effect on the public or a darkly mysterious power over the masses. In this way, movies repeatedly testified to the fact that the capacity to influence a national whole existed. Such testimonials, like movies themselves, ultimately conferred authority on the class of experts who represented the qualitative difference between mass and public, demonstrated how a relative state of personal security and happiness might be achieved, and made those two sorts of distinctions coincide with one another.

I propose, in sum, that the Hollywood feature film fundamentally altered the manner in which democratic governance could be understood and thus legitimated a new type of authority. This revision contributed to contemporary changes in discourses ranging from political philosophy to marketing—the very discourses typically called on to explain the "mass media" and to regulate them. In both ways, movies mooted the ideological equation of white male property holder to self-governing citizen that founded the nation. In its place, they promoted the authority of an administrative class that was primarily an information-manipulating class.

These proposals do not require a new periodization of American culture. Rather, they further clarify the shift first mapped out by Robert Wiebe in his 1967 history, *The Search for Order.* By 1880, Wiebe explains, America had outgrown its existing economic and political structures. Cities were booming, transcontinental expansion complete, and industry more productive than ever before. Yet, periods of depression in the 1870s, in the mid-1880s, and again after the panic of 1893 demonstrated a need for the regulation of cutthroat competition, better organized distribution networks, and new outlets for accumulated capital. The state provided little help. Not only were bureaucratic structures underdeveloped relative to those of European countries, but the traditional habits of American governance did not provide the necessary coordination and control. City neighborhoods and rural townships composed a nation of "loosely connected islands" within which interpersonal relationships, often informal and extralegal, held sway.[42] The challenges of a continent-spanning, urban-industrial nation required nothing short of a new America, quite unimaginable from the perspective of the one that preceded it. It took some forty years, from the end of the Reconstruction through the Progressive era, for this new order to emerge. In it, the corporate organization of industry dovetailed with "national centers of authority and information."[43] An emphasis on constant regulation to ensure a productive workforce gained ascendancy over violent outbursts against an unruly one. And the supervising authority of a "new middle class" of managers displaced that of the rugged industrialist, ward boss, and rural landowner.

Over the years, various historians have developed and complicated Wiebe's sweeping hypothesis.[44] No one has conjoined it with the problem of mass mediation more clearly and powerfully than Richard Ohmann. For Ohmann, monthly magazines of the 1890s such as *Munsey's* and *Ladies' Home Journal* provide the paradigmatic instance of national mass culture.[45] The short fiction, editorial advice, and, above all, pictorial brand-name advertising circulated by these magazines had two, closely related effects, he argues. First, they helped establish the type of consumerism that corporate capitalism counts on to solve its perpetual crises of overproduction. Second, they allowed the members of an emerging class of professional managers to recognize themselves as such nationwide and thus helped to constitute that class. The rise of this type of mass culture, then, amounts to a major event in the "search for order" described by Wiebe.

Even so, Ohmann's study cannot encompass the 1910s and 1920s, when the search came to a close and the process of extending and consolidating corporate America began in earnest. I take this to be the implication of Ohmann's concluding paragraph, which asks, "What has it meant that commercial practices honed on the PMC were then extrapolated to other audiences, other consumers?"[46] Although I agree that the question of how managerial culture turned into American culture is a crucial one, I do not think it can be posed in these terms. The forward march of consumerism will not suffice to explain how it came to seem a commonsense proposition for salaried professionals to supervise the day-to-day operations of the state, the corporation, and all manner of social organizations. Nor can a new order have arrived through an extrapolation of the address that interpellated readers as members of this class. In other words, the professional managerial class may have emerged within new forms of print mediation during the 1890s, but professional authority could not be taken for granted until movies altered what it would take to represent and order relationships among individuals, spaces, and groups.

THE RISE OF PROFESSIONAL AUTHORITY

Considered as the ability to regulate property and persons through the control of information, the history of professional authority arguably coincides with modernity itself. Contemporary disciplinary knowledge certainly has a predecessor in the work of the seventeenth- and eighteenth-century mapmakers, merchants, and scientists who made the modern state possible by abstracting and quantifying territories, economies, and types of individuals.[47] On a less grandiose scale, one might point to the market for the specialized skills and services that arose in mid-nineteenth-century American cities.[48] Then, the general merchant lost ground to distinct importers, exporters, and distributors, who might themselves concentrate on only one or two lines of goods. Insurance, shipping, and banking emerged as distinct enterprises.[49] The social distinction between manual and mental labor increased, as did the numbers, still relatively few, of clerks, bookkeepers, and salesmen.[50] The traditional professions changed. Aspiring midcentury ministers, for instance, began to talk about their "careers" rather than their "calling."[51] And the American Medical Association, one of the first American professional associations, was founded in 1847 (although the rudiments of a twentieth-century relationship between professional organization and university training may arguably be discerned in New England medicine as early as the 1820s).[52]

There are good reasons, however, to consider professional management a twentieth-century phenomenon. That was when specialized knowledge, produced by universities and regulated by semiautonomous professional associations, significantly displaced ownership, inheritance, and apprenticeship as the prerequisite for power.[53] The AMA, for instance, grew dramatically after its reorganization in 1901 to include some 60 percent of doctors by 1920.[54] One index of what it meant to enforce a national credential, standardize training, and limit it to approved medical schools may have been found in the campaign of newly specialized obstetricians to stamp out the midwife.[55] In business too, training was formalized as the distance between ownership and administration grew in increasingly large corporations. Unheard of in the 1870s, degrees in business prospered both at elite, single-sex, private schools and coed state universities by the mid-1920s.[56] Whereas the mid-nineteenth-century clerk had been a proprietor in training, young managers went to college. And it was there, rather than at the factory, that Fredrick Taylor's 1911 *Scientific Management* apparently found its most devoted audience.[57] Meanwhile, the rise of independent professional specialties transformed the university. The beginning of a sea change in academic inquiry may be marked by the founding of the Modern Language Association (1883) and the collapse of the American Social Science Association (1865–1909) into more academically oriented and highly specialized groups such as the American Historical Association (1884), American Economics Association (1885), American Political Science Association (1903), and American Sociological Society (1905).[58] The list of new professional specialties, subspecialties, organizations, and credentials goes on and on. Social work, distinguished from charity in the late nineteenth century, emerged as a full-blown profession in the early twentieth.[59] Certified public accountants became indispensable to government and business, precisely because they could claim professional autonomy.[60] Public relations and opinion polling emerged as professions distinct from advertising and social science.[61] And I would be remiss in failing to mention the film industry. Although the distinct models of guild apprenticeship, organized labor, and professional association apply to different occupations at different moments in the developing industry, there is no mistaking the modern ring of the American Society of Cinematographers (1919), Society of Motion Picture Engineers (1916), and Motion Picture Producers and Distributors Association (1922).[62] Unquestionably, the industrial structures that yoked "management" and "talent" relied on professional expertise. In background, industrial pioneers ranged from self-made men who had learned on the job in retail clothing (Carl Laemmle) and the fur trade (Adolf Zukor) to the college-educated son of a successful saloonkeeper-banker-politician (Joseph Kennedy). As managers, they recruited personnel from the nation's top universities and made themselves spokesmen for cutting-edge methods of organization.[63]

To be sure, professional training and credentials do not confer authority in and of themselves. Their power exists only within a division of labor and mode of discipline that allows behavior to be regulated through the manipulation of information. Despite precursors in eighteenth- and nineteenth-century disciplinary knowledge, it took some time for professionalism to establish and generalize its authority. Once this occurred, the day-to-day administration of economic, political, and social affairs became the prerogative of those who could lay claim to an institutionally ratified, discipline-specific expertise.

In a landmark 1979 essay, Barbara and John Ehrenreich argue that this emerging professional managerial class must be understood as a supplement to the two modern classes defined by Marxist political economy. On the one hand, management had an antagonistic relationship to the nineteenth-century working class. It began to regulate not only production but any aspect of social life that could be defined as in need of rationalization, reform, or commodified services—managers opposed the patronage system every bit as strongly as "the rule of thumb" on the shop floor. On the other hand, rising professionals were salaried employees who did not own the means of production and who found themselves in conflict with the capitalist class whenever their expertise produced imperatives and solutions at odds with established business methods. During the 1910s and 1920s the conflict was especially acute as college-educated engineers and scientific managers wrested control over day-to-day operations from traditional businessmen and their sons.[64] Because of its antagonistic relationship with both capitalists and workers, and because of its increasing importance in the social division of labor, the professional managerial class also differs from the old petite bourgeoisie of self-employed professionals and service workers— the doctors, barbers, lawyers, and shopkeepers of the eighteenth and nineteenth centuries. According to the Ehrenreichs, the rapid proliferation of management both substantially revised the relationship between workers and capitalists and changed the relation of each to the means of production. In their view, then, professional managers behave as a class in their own right and not as a fraction of the bourgeoisie. This has been a controversial proposition among political economists.[65] To my mind, the Ehrenreichs' articulation of it remains indispensable for the clarity with which it approaches the problem. They allow us to understand that the rapid rise of professional management must have supplemented the very structure of nineteenth-century capitalism.

The Ehrenreichs' explanation of that structural shift is not, however, an unqualified success. In fact, their definition of the professional managerial class seems to me to retreat from the dialectic that animates their argument. "We define the Professional-Managerial Class," they write, "as consisting of salaried mental workers who do not own the means of production and whose major function in the social division of labor may be described broadly as the reproduction of capitalist culture and capitalist class relations."[66] Here the Ehrenreichs aptly capture the position of professional managers as neither capital nor labor, but the definition does not encompass the notion that the rise of this class transformed capitalism itself. Indeed, the language of "reproduction" suggests that capitalist class relations remained more or less the same. The authors reinforce that suggestion later in the essay when they declare that "to the extent that the PMC established itself as a major class in twentieth-century American society, it did so on terms set by the capitalist class."[67] Thus, even as the Ehrenreichs point to the new importance of professional authority for twentieth-century capitalism, they also imply that the interest it serves is not really its own (but rather that of the big bourgeoisie) and that the kind of authority capitalists wielded was not much changed by professional management. They leave an opening for more orthodox Marxist critics to counter that the managers should not in fact be understood as a class but rather as an overgrown petite bourgeoisie. My own complaint differs; I think there is an unacknowledged tension in the Ehrenreichs' essay between two different models of authority. In one model, new institutions for producing and disseminating knowledge mark a transformation of the division of labor and provide the basis for management's power within it. In the other model, managerial authority is delegated from an unchanged capitalist class and ultimately derives from private property.

This second model of an abiding bourgeois authority makes less and less sense when examined in light of changes to the organization of capital. Historians of business and political economists alike emphasize the process whereby control of accumulation became separate from ownership. Business history defines the "modern business enterprise" by its organization into multiple operating units administered by a hierarchy of professional managers and owned by far-flung shareholders. While this kind of firm did not exist in the United States during the first half of the nineteenth century, most of the largest American firms had at least a rudimentary version of multidivisional organization in place by the end of

World War I. Still, family ownership and control of even large firms remained common in the 1910s and 1920s, and significant sectors of the economy had yet to be organized in corporate terms. By the middle of the twentieth century, enormous publicly owned enterprises dominated the U.S. economy, and management hierarchies could be found in relatively small local or regional U.S. businesses.[68] In the same period, state bureaucracy began to manage the economy in new ways. The Federal Reserve Act of 1913, for instance, removed U.S. monetary policy from the arena of political debate that characterized the "free silver" campaigns of the 1890s and entrusted it instead to a team of experts.[69] That same year the Sixteenth Amendment allowed for, and the Underwood Tariff Act established, a progressive federal income tax. Legislation in 1914 founded the Federal Trade Commission. As ownership of capital was separated from its direction by salaried managers, the state acquired qualitatively new and quantitatively increased involvement in economic matters. In these developments, and in the growing importance of financing relative to production, political economists discern a new phase of capitalism. Paul Baran and Paul Sweezy's *Monopoly Capital,* to pick the classic account, describes how the rise of management hierarchies enabled state-assisted coordination to prevail over cutthroat competition. Thus, the immortal corporation replaced the tycoon as "the capitalist," and the problem of absorbing surplus capital replaced the classic problem of the falling rate of profit.[70] In other words, the interests of the capitalist class, once served by the industrial enterprises it created, were subordinated to the interests of corporate institutions themselves. This simply had to entail a change in the status, if not the very definition, of the capitalist's authority.

In the posthumously edited third volume of *Capital,* Marx himself implies as much. He describes the rise of the "joint-stock company" run by mere managers as "a self-destructive contradiction": "It is private production unchecked by private ownership." The joint-stock company "provokes state intervention. It reproduces a new financial aristocracy, a new kind of parasite in the guise of company promoters, speculators and merely nominal directors; an entire system of swindling and cheating with respect to the promotion of companies, issues of shares and share dealings." As Marx would have it, separation of proprietorship from control amounts to a fatal contradiction. It is "the abolition of the capitalist mode of production within the capitalist mode of production itself."[71] We should be so lucky. Instead, public ownership—that is, private ownership by a large and far-flung group of persons and institutions with little day-to-day control over corporate decisions—came to be the essence of twentieth-century capitalism and its triumph. Along with Wiebe, then, Marx reminds us that incorporation was anything but a predictable or inevitable development. In fact, it was nearly unthinkable from the point of view of entrepreneurial capitalism. And this difficulty in conceptualizing the corporation has precisely to do with the difficulty of understanding managerial authority, which is not based on personal reputation or private wealth but serves the interest of capital accumulation nonetheless.

I know of no account of professional managerial authority that can explain how it was able to generalize itself so rapidly in the face of the self-destructive contradiction Marx identifies and the antagonisms the Ehrenreichs so aptly chronicle. Nor is it entirely clear how American capitalism in particular was able to succeed so very well precisely by displacing the authority of its traditional entrepreneurs. To be sure, business histories provide ample demonstrations of the greater efficiency of modern business enterprise and the system of monopoly capital it wrought. Along with work in social history and political economy, they detail many of the concrete economic and institutional battles through which groups of businessmen and various types of experts convinced their contemporaries to do business in a new and different manner. These accounts make the victory of management as plain as its antagonism toward nineteenth-century industrialists and laborers. But the story of how this new kind of authority was able to extend itself into every nook and cranny of American life has yet to be told. Certainly, it is not told by the social psychology of management—a tendency that begins in the 1950s with the work of C. Wright Mills, David Riesman, and William Whyte.[72] To describe managers as the most alienated of individuals, the most obsessed with the opinions of others, or the most afraid of falling behind their betters may partly explain why they continue to reproduce a system that does not ultimately benefit them the most. But this does not explain how they were able to impose themselves on an entire nation. Either a professional managerial class won substantial authority to run national culture or it did not. If it did, we may assume that its members have been as demoralized by their failures as they are proud of their successes.

The need for an account of how professional management became the commonplace administrative solution becomes even more urgent if we shift focus from the relationship between ownership and rule to the problem of who constituted the new administrative class. To authorize themselves, teams of professionals had to dissociate the ability to control information from any particular type of body far more emphatically than modern cultures had done before. The new emphasis on training and merit provided openings for women, racial minorities, and recent immigrants. Even the male members of America's oldest families had to win their credentials. Although it is tempting to say that white men "retained" power despite these changes, a careful look at early twentieth-century America reveals an extensive struggle to determine the limits that categories of identity would place on professional authority. That struggle gave rise to the phenomena of tokenization, segregated professions (black doctors for black people), and the feminized specialties (e.g., nursing and social work).[73] Even though such arrangements do resemble old-fashioned racism and sexism, they have little to do with the paradox that equated the white man with the human being and citizen at the nation's inception. Professionalization posed the problem not of deciding who could be considered fully human and thus self-governing, but of how membership in any particular group would affect one's claim of disciplinary objectivity. Given the history of purportedly disinterested disciplines, it is not at all surprising to find that professional neutrality reproduced white and masculine norms. But the institutional proliferation of these norms came to require a distinction between discipline and practitioner. This gave new form to the double bind traditionally faced by members of marked populations. Historian Nancy Cott points out, for instance, that as early as the 1880s a now familiar kind of argument had emerged among "lady lawyers" over whether they should constitute a separate feminine specialty within the law and risk marginalization, or speak with the voice of the masculine profession and risk reproducing sexism.[74] Similar but distinct dilemmas prevailed among the black doctors, lawyers, and sociologists of the talented tenth, and among the Jews who began to find their college admissions limited in the late 1910s.[75] A professional managerial class did not succeed simply by reprising earlier exclusions, in other words, but by means of a new logic that differentially empowered its internally diverse and often conflicting members.

In 1932, *Fortune* provided a stunningly precise formulation of the contradiction that results when one attempts to think of the new corporate order in nineteenth-century terms. "Whenever a motion picture becomes a work of art it is unquestionably due to men," declares the business magazine. "But the moving pictures have been born and bred not of men but of corporations." Here, as elsewhere, the movies point to a far more general and vexing problem: "Somehow, although our poets have not yet defined it for us, a corporation lives a life and finds a fate outside the lives and fates of its human constituents."[76]

We need not wait for a poet to explain the corporate age; the movies themselves have made sense of it. From the silent feature film to the contemporary blockbuster, American motion pictures have repeatedly demonstrated the capacity of corporations to order our world. They do so by showing what it will take for love to survive: endless obstacles must be cleared and a clean, well-arranged, and illuminated space produced. No embodied point of view, the movies insist, can or should possess the capacity to distinguish and arrange persons and spaces in this manner. Nor could disembodied language provide the means to do so. By practical implication, proper representation and arrangement of social space became the prerogative of a management hierarchy. Accordingly, once the American feature film had established itself, it became impossible to imagine the national public as a print readership. Even as the dream of universal suffrage finally became a reality in 1920, movies made clear that national governance would require feats of representation vastly exceeding an individual citizen's capacity to read, write, argue, and vote. A rhetoric of "influence" trumped earlier rhetorics of communication and persuasion as the way to explain the relationship between information and a national public.

Many who believe in cinema's influence have been tempted to find a cabal of ideologues behind it. An even more commonplace explanation depicts a group of alienated men who yearn to meet the public's approval. Since the 1920s, Americans have been taught to believe in a mythic Jewish movie mogul, whose ambition to assimilate produced on the screen a nation more hyperbolically WASPish than ever before. In fact, the great virtue of the mogul figure has been his capacity to embody the paradox of professional authority: his personal power derives from the subordination of private interest to public, institutional interest; he succeeds because he is Jewish and despite that fact. But we ought not mistake a consequence for a cause. Jewish alienation will not account for why corporate filmmaking developed when, where, and how it did. The more significant fact is that the authority to represent America can now be explained in this manner. Only after movies had disarticulated control of information from the individual body on a socially inescapable scale did a psychic struggle between "Jewishness" and "Americanness" describe Hollywood's rise and function. Although this and many other oft-repeated stories about Hollywood producers and directors try to find the poet within the corporation, they all in one way or another acknowledge the problem *Fortune* brings to the fore. The more labyrinthine the effort to make a handful of people responsible for cinematic culture, the more it goes without saying that large corporations produce it. These corporations did not precede the feature film, but arose through it. In the process, they did not "influence" a movie audience that somehow existed before the movies. Rather, they mediated diverse constituents of America and called a new national order into being.

Cinematic culture was, and is, professional culture. This book stems from my conviction that most viewers take such a connection for granted, even if it is not often explained.[77] I try to make the linkage clear by showing how Hollywood's most conventional content defines feature film form. On the basis of that demonstration, I pose the question of what cinema's rise meant for the categories of the public, private, and mass. I then consider the limits and virtues of "influence" as a description of what motion pictures did to and for their audiences. Finally, I investigate why it became important to attribute Hollywood's corporate filmmaking to the inspiration of Jewish immigrants. Throughout, I endeavor to show how a wide range of permutations of the visual love story ordered the nation. From the Civil War and Reconstruction *(The Birth of a Nation)* to World War I and its aftermath *(The Big Parade)*, from the windswept western desert *(The Wind)* to the big city sidewalk *(The Crowd)*, in sex comedies *(Why Change Your Wife?)* and early musicals *(The Jazz Singer)* alike, movies reminded viewers of the element of chance in their most intimate relationships with one another. Lovers came together across the most improbable distances. Complex and unpredictable spaces simultaneously thwarted their togetherness and made it seem more desirable than ever. Under these circumstances, to specify who the socially reproducible couple would be, and to order the world so that it might be secure, presupposed the ability to represent social space as if from a position outside of it. When it gave this form an institutional basis and all-but-inescapable distribution, Hollywood cinema made kismet require a management team.

1. The Visual Love Story

The movies became indispensable to American culture by giving new form to a well-established kind of story. In their landmark study of Hollywood filmmaking, David Bordwell, Janet Staiger, and Kristin Thompson estimate that 95 percent of all U.S. films released between 1915 and 1960 include a romance plot. Bordwell notes that this "is not startling news" and goes on to provide the customary reminder that such stories stem from "the chivalric romance, the bourgeois novel, and the American melodrama." He also suggests that American cinema may be distinguished from its antecedents by the degree to which it makes all subplots "causally related to the romantic action."[1] Given the pervasive character of the love story, one might expect it to be the pivotal term in this, or any other, account of Hollywood form. Yet following a precedent set by the Soviet filmmaker-theorists of the 1920s, *The Classical Hollywood Cinema* looks to production technique to define the movies' most cinematic features. The love story all but disappears in the ensuing chronicle of procedures for creating and articulating shots, and narrative is reduced to patterns of cause and effect that might exist in any medium. Thus, a defining trait of Hollywood movies seems not to be a distinguishing one. It is as if romance narrative were a legacy from prior forms to which movies themselves did not much contribute. Such an orientation inevitably leads to the classic idealist error. It requires us

31

to imagine that narratives, contents, and categories exist apart from the manner in which those narratives, contents, and categories ordinarily appear. In contrast, I argue that the visual conventions of the love story constitute the form commonly known as "the movies" and define its contribution to U.S. culture.

Everyone knows what love looks like on the screen. Those who have seen American movies will easily recall glowing images of lovers gazing deeply into each others' eyes before collapsing into an enthusiastic embrace. This series of images appears with increasing frequency after 1907 and became the rule in almost every American film genre during the 1910s and 1920s. Relatively early on, it seems, filmmakers expected such pictures to appeal to a kind of common sense about what love looked like. Even if sheer repetition has endowed them with a self-explanatory character, however, the ubiquity of such images does not tell us why love should be represented on the screen in this way and not some other. Movies might have represented love by letting us read the couple's correspondence, as novels often do. They might have offered metaphoric substitutes such as exploding fireworks and crashing waves or merged the man's face with the woman's through the technique of double exposure. Although films do sometimes represent love in such terms, these alternatives are clearly subsidiary or adjunct to the look lovers share both across and within the limits of the frame. In Hollywood cinema, the union of two eyelines defines love. Movies thereby pose a spatial problem.

A drama of separation precedes every picture of the luminous heroine reunited with the leading man. When the woman's glowing face at last returns the look of her male partner, this picture equals resolution because her longing look across the frameline called out for the absent hero in a prior series of images. The narrative function of their shared look, and its privilege, also depends on its difference from the numerous other exchanges with which it is compared. It depends, in other words, on a differential system of facial expressions and conjoined eyelines that serves to distinguish the lover's gaze from the friend's glancing admiration and the villain's intrusive stare. This differential system relates a lover's internal and external qualities. Especially meticulous attention to the heroine's face implies that beneath the glowing surface of her image, behind its large expressive eyes, lies a consciousness uniquely capable of ratifying the man's stare or rejecting it. Such pictures distinguish men from women. They also give visibility to racial difference and set the pa-

rameters that require us to identify Hollywood's conventional couple as
a white one. Thus, by proliferating seemingly endless manifestations of
the love story, American cinema made racial classification, heterosexual
desire, and spatial differentiation mutually dependent visual structures.
In the process, it provided a rapidly changing culture with a powerful
demonstration of who belonged where.

To ensure the proper placement of individuals required a narrative
agent capable of distinguishing, manipulating, and transforming the
spaces they inhabited. Such a narrator cannot be thought according to
the paradigm set by print. When the novel distinguishes author, narrator, and character, for instance, it also implies that each is a unique
source of words. It thus makes them comparable entities—a comparison to which we may also credit the notion that every reader is, potentially, a distinctive writer. Hollywood makes pictures of the heroine's
face every bit as expressive of her interior qualities as the words novels use to represent them, but movies insist that neither seeing nor having a face qualifies one to represent it. To be sure, the reciprocal look
of the Hollywood happy ending leaves the impression that the lovers
see one another independently from the film's mediation. But consider what it takes to achieve this mutual stare. Whether the couple survives the Great War *(The Big Parade)*, the French Revolution *(Orphans of
the Storm)*, shipwreck and past-life regression *(Male and Female)*, mere
divorce and remarriage *(Why Change Your Wife?)*, or the difference between heaven and hell *(Home, Sweet Home)*, visual narrative repeatedly
calls attention to the limited nature of the look that bonds it. A character's eyeline always emanates from a particular face in a particular location. Embedded in the space it inhabits, it helps to define that location.
A space may lack one of the partners, for instance, or be complete in its
inclusion of both. Similarly, separation is called for when an undesirable
pairing occurs. By logical necessity, to assemble limited sightlines into a
stable whole requires an agent capable of seeing and arranging space as
if from outside it. Hollywood narration propagated a noncorporeal perspective, one whose skill in representing relations among any number of
bodies and spaces depended on its ability to distinguish itself from all
embodied points of view.

This amounted to an implicit argument in favor of an emerging class
of largely anonymous managers. In the period of Hollywood's dramatic
rise, members of this class began to win the argument that professional

methods and credentials would be necessary to represent and secure the many individuals, groups, and corporations that make up the modern nation. Only the methodical oversight of a management team, within a strict hierarchical division of responsibilities, guided by large amounts of scientifically gathered, abstract information, could responsibly evaluate and regulate competing interests. The visual love story offered a kindred perspective. And indeed, the rise of the vertically integrated, multidivisional filmmaking corporation depended on that of the feature film. Well before the great wave of mergers, buyouts, and stock offerings that inaugurated the studio system in the late 1910s, cinematic romance had decisively separated the authority to narrate relations among spaces and persons from an embodied point of view. Once this leap had been made, narrative filmmaking could take full advantage of an increasingly complex hierarchy of producers, directors, writers, cinematographers, editors, set designers, continuity clerks, grips, gaffers, and technical experts of every stripe.

The success of America's corporate filmmaking, then, has little to do with its reprisal of realist, classical, or melodramatic themes and forms. It has still less to do with whether or not spectators identify with the camera or with particular characters. Instead, Hollywood's historic power derives from its specific manner of composing and arranging images to tell the story of love and to demonstrate what it needs to flourish. In the process, the movies redefined the modern nation's fundamental kinship unit and altered the nature of the authority to see, know, and order national culture.

LOVE

The lovers' shared look bonds them. It objectifies their emotional attachment, as if they were joined by the eyes. *The Big Parade* (MGM, 1925), for example, implies a connection so strong that it must be forced apart. Its hero and heroine find one another after a protracted search. At first, their gaze remains locked across the limits of separate frames, despite the fact that they appear to move in opposite directions. But finally the look that joins them is rent, leaving the heroine incomplete and alone. When it represents the strength of the couple's emotional bond in this way, *The Big Parade* dramatizes an all-important fact: both lovers must be in the same space if they are to share the gaze that signifies love.

The breakdown of the joined eyeline shows us that the distance or difference between the spaces the lovers occupy has become either too great or too important. A similar sequence of images may be found in almost every Hollywood love story.

The objectification of the lovers' look both emphasizes its limitation (its embeddedness in surrounding space) and indicates an enduring connection. Once this sentimental attachment is established as a shared eyeline, a certain kind of look out of frame will suffice to indicate a lover's longing. This solitary look suggests a deeply desired object somewhere beyond the lover's field of vision precisely because the look is not given an object in a spatially adjacent shot. The 1915 film *Enoch Arden* (Mutual), for example, takes full advantage of the distance separating its shipwrecked hero (Alfred Paget) from his wife Annie (Lillian Gish) and their English home. Steady, wide-eyed looks out of frame indicate that their attachment to one another endures despite separation and Enoch's presumed death. Such yearning looks out of frame prevent Annie from truly returning the persistent stare of Enoch's rival, Philip (Wallace

Renée Adoree and John Gilbert in *The Big Parade* (MGM, 1925). Frame enlargements courtesy of George Eastman House.

Reid), even after she marries him. Indeed, Enoch has only to be res-
cued to appear destined to share Annie's gaze once more. Surrounded
by sailors onboard the homeward bound ship, he looks up and out of
the right side of the frame. Then, Annie rushes to the window of her
English cottage and looks hopefully out of frame left. Framing, composition, and editing conspire to suggest that their eyeline might just re-
connect across the sea that divides them. Yet this potential connection,
like the one that established them as a couple in the first place, proves
fragile, impermanent. Annie's face falls as she lowers her eyes. Such images give love a transcendental quality even as they insist that the lovers
must occupy the same space if their relationship is to be secure. In this
way, the movies picture true love as togetherness thwarted by separation and set the stage for the reunion that distinguishes the conventional Hollywood ending.

In order for the couple to be reunited, however, a particular kind of
space has to be produced. The bittersweet ending of *Enoch Arden* exemplifies the triumph of this kind of space. Enoch lays on a white bed in
a small chamber with crude wooden walls. Shadow surrounds the bed,
but a bright light focuses attention on his face at the right side of the
frame. Still enraptured by Annie, he stares and gestures offscreen, as if
toward a point over the viewer's right shoulder. Exhausted by the effort,
his eyes close in death. The next sequence presents an evenly lit, middle-
class interior defined by pictures on the walls, well-upholstered furni-
ture, and a well-dressed family of five. Yet something is awry. Although
Annie is surrounded by her children, a lingering attachment draws her
look away from Philip toward an invisible point out of frame, the same
point at which Enoch stared. She still loves him, although she has no
idea where he is or that he has died. In the background, Philip looks
away from her dejectedly and turns to walk off screen. Then, Annie's
entire aspect changes. Visibly relieved, she straightens herself and turns
away from the point that represented Enoch's presence elsewhere. She
beckons Philip, who crosses the room to join her. With their brightly
lit heads and torsos filling the frame, wife and husband at last share the
look of love. When *Enoch Arden* finally shuts Enoch's eyes, then, it also
eliminates the space in which his look is embedded. Thus it removes
the threat he represents to Philip and Annie's marriage. Similarly, when
the film redirects Annie's look from an undefined part of the visual field
to a well-defined part of the space that includes Philip, it indicates that

Enoch is no longer "out there" in either spatial or emotional terms. The clean, evenly illuminated parlor supplants his death chamber and becomes in the process a space where Annie can at last return Philip's loving gaze. The compulsion to render this kind of well-lit, uncluttered space may be considered Hollywood's formal imperative.

Filmmakers adapted Alfred Tennyson's poem "Enoch Arden" (1864) no fewer than four times between 1908 and 1915, exactly the period during which the conventions of feature filmmaking coalesced.[2] According to historian Tom Gunning, D. W. Griffith's 1908 version pioneered the use of parallel editing to interrelate "spatial separation and emotional connection" when it alternated images of castaway Enoch and Annie at home.[3] This adaptation of an editing technique formerly reserved for chase scenes marks a crucial turning point in the development of Hollywood narrative, Gunning argues. It exemplifies cinema's emerging interest in narrating psychological states. It also indicates cinema's reworking of the conventions of stage melodrama, which tended to render comparable moments in static tableaux.[4] Three years later, Griffith directed a two-reel version of the story that won contemporary praise as an example of the longer format that would soon lead to the feature-length film.[5]

Something about Tennyson's story clearly enticed moviemakers, but their movies transform the poem's story in telling it. Although Tennyson does on occasion render Enoch and Annie's love as something that may be seen—"Philip look'd / And in their eyes and faces read his doom"—these legible eyes and faces neither structure his narrative nor provide its central figure. The poem does not alternate between Enoch's longing look and Annie's. It certainly does not end by envisioning her acceptance of Philip as a willingness to return his look. Rather, her acceptance occurs two-thirds of the way through the poem, when we read that Annie's "mysterious instinct wholly died" and the previously withheld chronicle of Enoch's fate begins. That chronicle, and the poem, concludes with Enoch's death and funeral: "So passed the strong heroic soul away. / And when they buried him the little port / Had seldom seen a costlier funeral." These final lines recall those that end the opening stanza: "And flying the white breaker, daily left / The little footprint daily wash'd away." Thus, the poem may be read as a eulogy for its eponymous sailor hero, whose final worth and stature far exceed, but are also defined by, his ephemeral "footprint" in the "little port" he called home. Although directors from D. W. Griffith (1908 and 1911 versions) to William Christy Cabanne (1915 version) peppered their films with intertitles drawn from Tennyson and reproduced the poem's principle episodes, their moving pictures tell a very different, visual story in which love triumphs by banishing uneven lighting, cluttered surroundings, and the unseen presence of others.

To be sure, not every film includes a love triangle as *Enoch Arden* does. Nor do films uniformly place their lovers within a middle-class, domestic interior. The setting may be far more humble *(Sunrise)* or extravagant *(Orphans of the Storm)*. The couple might be reunited at the seashore *(The Birth of a Nation)*, in a rowboat *(It)*, on a big city sidewalk *(The Cameraman)*, in the countryside *(The Big Parade)*, or even on a flying carpet *(Thief of Bagdad)*. But whatever the details of plot or setting, Hollywood's visual love story strives to transform disordered, poorly illuminated spaces into a simply arranged, well-lit, and apparently self-contained space in which nothing distracts the lovers from one another. In the process, American filmmaking made it appear as if this sort of spatial arrangement were necessary for the ideal couple to be constituted as such.

Films that do not deliver happy endings indicate as much by playing with this spatial logic. Serials may indicate there is more to see in the next installment by refusing stasis, enclosure, or full illumination in the final sequence. The *Exploits of Elaine* (1914–15) exemplifies this procedure in its depiction of the villainous "Clutching Hand." Each of the fourteen episodes first separates plucky Elaine Dodge (Pearl White) from scientific detective Craige Kennedy, then reunites her with him. But up until the last installment, the series contrives both to leave the precise nature of their relationship unresolved and to intensify the mystery of the villain's true identity. Some sign of the Clutching Hand always intrudes upon their shared look. In at least two episodes, such a sign manifests itself just as Elaine regains consciousness with Kennedy at her side: an unknown hand slides the villain's calling card under Elaine's door in the second installment ("The Twilight Sleep") and a blow dart launched from the opposite roof pins the villain's note to the heroine's bedroom wall in episode five ("The Poisoned Room"). Similarly, episodes four ("The Frozen Safe") and six ("The Vampire") interrupt Kennedy and Elaine's reunion to show the villain making his getaway. As if the viewer could possibly miss the import of such images, each reel except the last concludes with a visual signature: a black-gloved hand contracts into a claw before a question mark slowly fills the frame. Viewers could expect another episode so long as this contorted figure remained at large and likely to intrude upon the couple at any moment.

Other films manipulate the expectation of a tidy, self-contained space to produce a tragic ending. The last few shots of *La Bohème* (MGM, 1926), for instance, reveal Rudolphe (John Gilbert) staring at Mimi (Lillian Gish) from the shadows surrounding her deathbed. Her immobile face gleams, the single bright spot in this spare, darkened space. The film dissolves from a close-up of Rudolphe kissing her limp hand to a flashback of the lovers gazing happily at one another within a sunlit forest glade—an image of what might have been.[6] By contrast, the return to a gloomy long shot of the dusky room indicates that, although the lovers are together at last and despite reduction of the visual field to the space around them, the right kind of space has not been established. The sense of tragedy depends on this comparison to the space of the happy ending, which the flashback evokes only to withhold. Where the serial's ending provokes another episode by generating new problems of spatial difference at the last minute, the tearjerker's resolution refrains from offering the viewer a clean, well-lighted space in order to indicate that happiness has been finally denied the protagonists.

The happy ending requires a particular kind of space, but this space cannot be established simply by inserting the couple into some previously idealized location. The couple's shared look does not merely inhabit, but helps to define the mise-en-scène of resolution. A reprisal of the look that established their attachment to one another indicates that love survives. During the silent period, the lovers smile with partially open mouths and often extend their chins in the partner's direction; the neck thus makes a line that points to the lovers' gaze. A steady look is everything, since wavering eyes indicate either shyness or coquetry. As they look into one another's eyes, the similarity of the lovers' well-illuminated faces makes their differences all the more striking. The man is often shown in profile, poised higher in the frame where he can look down on the woman. Yet despite the literal superiority of his figure, the woman's face has far greater symbolic value. Numerous devices imply something special to be seen in her visage. The camera lingers on it and shows it more frequently from a frontal angle. Her face is brighter, yet makeup and lighting contrive to distinguish it from the background and to highlight the eyes and mouth, its expressive features. These techniques combine with casting and performance conventions to make her by far the more demonstrative partner—her large eyes may close dramatically, for instance, so they may then be opened wide.[7] Thus, although the space of resolution requires the man's face as well, the woman's countenance apparently provides its more decisive feature. Within this system of conventions, *La Bohème* could not hope to render a comparable tragedy by substituting Rudolphe's closed eyes for Mimi's.

The privilege accorded the heroine's face could hardly escape critical notice. It only makes sense that a major trend of late-twentieth-century criticism would found itself on the proposition that the ideology of Hollywood form can be understood in terms of this particular content. Indeed, in retrospect it seems remarkable that film theory had to wait as long as it did for Laura Mulvey's reminder that Hollywood's exemplary pictures are pictures of women. Her paradigm-founding description of Hollywood cinema famously characterizes certain images of women as "flat" and "iconic" and sets the nonspace of feminine spectacle in opposition to the perspectival, diegetic space of masculine narrative. The "visual presence" of "woman," she writes, "tends to work against the development of a story line, to freeze the flow of action in moments of erotic contemplation."[8] By setting spectacle and narrative at odds in this manner, Mulvey made the Hollywood heroine equal "to-be-looked-at-ness" and established a series of homologies between the stare of the male protagonist on screen, the organizing perspective of the filmmaking apparatus, and the look of the spectator in the theater. She thus established the centrality of sexual difference to the account of spectatorship theorists such as Christian Metz had earlier supplied. On this model, the iconic woman provides a fetishistic solution to the anxiety that must necessarily accompany the presumptively male spectator's (unconscious) awareness of his inadequacy with respect to either of the other two terms with which he is identified. Neither Mulvey's account of "the gaze" nor her implication that Hollywood denies women visual pleasure survived the century, as subsequent work successfully challenged the equation of the viewer's look with that of the cinematic apparatus and his or her identification with the male protagonist.[9] Yet few of Mulvey's critics would dispute the notion that women are filmed differently from men and that this difference has everything to do with the organization of Hollywood narrative.

Correct as Mulvey is to see the woman's image as a defining feature of Hollywood form, her characterization of that image as flat and capable of arresting narrative mistakes its semiotic function. American film-makers painstakingly separate the heroine's head from the background through lighting, camerawork, and mise-en-scène in order to present it as a three-dimensional object, as both part of a space and the site of a soulful interior. Moreover, the scale and relative stasis of such images endow even the slightest movement with a great deal of significance by rendering minute changes visible. The close-up reveals the softening of the heroine's gaze as she falls in love: the muscles around her eyes and mouth appear to relax, her chin extends in the direction of her partner as if compelled by an invisible force focused behind the eyes. Alternately, the close-up uses a contraposto of eyes and face to show her flirting: her face moves but her eyes to do not as she tucks in her chin to peek out from under thick lashes—or her face remains relatively still while her eyes move, momentarily breaking the eyeline. When she recoils in terror, the heroine's facial muscles tense to the point of trembling and force her eyes wide open. An elaborate choreography of eyes, mouth, neck, and head thus conveys love or danger, flirtation or lust, restraint or immodesty. Even when the face looks blankly and directly at the camera (e.g., in the famous case of Garbo), the slightest tilt of the head, motion of the eyes, or opening of the mouth is loaded with psychological information.[10] Far from halting the flow of the narrative, this kind of image tells the story of love.

Once the narrative importance of this picture is acknowledged, we cannot simply equate "to-be-looked-at-ness" with objectification. The woman's face must have the properties of a subject if her look is to testify to reciprocal emotion. In fact, a number of replies to Mulvey's argument have made clear that the allure of the woman's visage depends on its power to signify an invisible source of desire. Mary Ann Doane observes that the face, "usually the mark of individuality, becomes tantamount to a theorem in its generalizability."[11] Since every face implies a subject, and since the woman's face is so manifestly the privileged face in Hollywood film, filmmakers must go to extraordinary lengths to render it the entirely objectified erotic object Mulvey describes. By deliberately obscuring it with a gauzy veil, for instance, they may partly block the viewer's look and thus incite desire to see the surface of the face as such, rather than, as is more usually the case, urging us to read the face as sign of interiority.[12] Linda Williams makes a similar point about the film genre one might consider least likely to worry about the woman's qualities of mind, namely, hard-core pornography. Yet here too the face turns out to be an especially crucial term. Hard core, Williams explains, requires that this image testify to the woman's otherwise invisible pleasure. Whereas the Hollywood feature takes pains to make the woman return the man's loving look, however, hard core more frequently endeavors to pair her ecstatic visage with the ejaculating male member. Such pictures provide a ready distinction between "true love" and merely carnal desire.[13] Yet they also reveal these to be intimately related terms, insofar as the distinction derives from visual conventions both genres share. By calling attention to two uses of the woman's face that pointedly fail to render an intersubjective relation, both Doane and Williams expose the sexual asymmetry implicit in its more conventional function. Movies represent the woman's face in ways that set in place a gendered epistemological and erotic relation. This relation presupposes a masculine (though not necessarily male) knower and desirer. In it, the feminine object becomes especially desirable because it cannot be fully known. It cannot be fully known because the surface that represents it indicates subjective depth. Read in combination with one another and in light of the visual love story, then, the arguments of Doane and Williams make it impossible to consider "woman," "object," and "image" synonymous terms. Rather, it would be more apt to say that the woman's face encapsulates the paradox of picturing, and thus objectifying, a human subject.[14]

Hollywood cinema hardly invented this visual paradox, but it did significantly revise preexisting conventions when it pictured a woman's face so as to imply a desirable, because desiring, consciousness behind it. The movies bear a clear debt, for instance, to what Stephen Kern terms "the proposal composition." In this genre of late-nineteenth-century French and English painting, the arrangement of the figures, patterns of light and dark, and depiction of details make the woman's eyes the center of attention. The man is typically rendered in profile and stares at the woman, whereas the woman faces front and looks "down with the required modesty, up for heavenly inspiration, or out into the world with a variety of intriguing expressions — playful or serious, fearful or adventurous, hesitant or resolute." Whatever their manner, "Her eyes convey an impending answer to the question *Will she or won't she?*"[15] Because the proposal composition aims to inspire this hermeneutic, it tends neither to render a reciprocal look nor to foreclose its possibility.[16] Rather, such paintings make the heroine's face express internal delibera- tion by propagating visual conventions that distinguish anxiety from re- solve, modesty from the appeal for inspiration. Cinema elaborated that system and set it in motion. In the process, it annexed the question of the lovers' placement in surrounding space to the question of whether the woman would return the man's look. Hollywood performed a simi- lar operation on the acting and staging codes of late-nineteenth-century theater. It appropriated a highly codified set of theatrical poses for show- ing love, modesty, and so on, while subordinating the actor's face and body to processes of spatial differentiation.[17] By repeatedly joining and then pulling apart the lovers' mutual stare, the movies made paramount the problem of what it takes to keep them together. Thus, they built the heroine's face into a system of visual distinctions among welcome and unwelcome relationships that also signified the proper placement of dif- ferent types of persons.

We have only to add the problem of racial classification to under- stand just how specific and productive this cinematic revision was. *Birth of a Nation* (Epoch, 1915) famously demonizes a black man for looking at a white woman. Given America's preoccupation with the sexual ra- pacity of such figures, the filmmakers doubtlessly assumed that viewers would recognize the supposed hazard of racial mixture in his stare. Yet in order to make that danger visible, the film establishes and manipu- lates quite specific, visual distinctions between love and menace, black and white, male and female. In this narrative form, the black man's look achieves the status of self-evident threat precisely because it mimics the exchange that here and elsewhere indicates the possibility of shared de- sire. Early on, Ben Cameron (Henry B. Walthall) and Elsie Stoneman (Lillian Gish) become a romantic couple as images imply the connec- tion of their eyeline. Ben looks intently down at Elsie's picture, and in the static close-up that follows Elsie appears to look back at him from that picture.[18] From this moment the characters appear destined to oc- cupy the same space, which indeed they do in the film's conclusion. Be- cause it reprises this ideal pattern, the eyeline match between mulatto governor Silas Lynch (George Siegmann) and radiantly white Elsie rep- resents an obvious danger. Before she recoils from Silas's gaze, we see the resemblance between his look and Ben's. The difference between love and horror thus appears to be a function primarily of racial difference.

Racial distinctions have been crucial to American filmmaking, but to fully appreciate how they function, it is important to note that other differences are also in play. In *Birth of a Nation,* for instance, the looks of dark-skinned characters are not the only unwelcome ones. In one brief exchange, Elsie encounters the stare of a scraggly white Union soldier and flees. Moreover, affectionate eyeline matches between white faces do not necessarily equal romantic love. They may communicate sibling affection, for example, as when Ben and his dying sister look into one another's eyes. Rather than being sustained, then broken, according to romantic convention, this shared eyeline quickly dissolves into individual looks out of frame: one that registers Little Sister's death and another that reveals Ben's determination to avenge it. Similarly, the loving glances of old, immature, nonwhite, or same-sex couples typically appear as asexual, imperfect, or comic versions of the romantic ideal. In *Way Down East* (United Artists, 1920), for instance, elderly village lush Seth Holcomb and spinster gossip Martha Perkins exchange flirtations glances to comic effect.[19] And although the *Orphans of the Storm* (United Artists, 1921) causes one of its sisters go blind so as to magically restore her ability to see the other in conclusion, it takes pains to make that reunion contingent upon each sister's relationship with a romantic male partner according to the conventional pattern. Together, these Griffith films reveal how conventions of acting, casting, lighting, framing, and editing collaborate to distinguish unwelcome desire, admiration without desire, paternal love, and fraternal love from passionate romantic love. Those very conventions reserve the privileged eyeline for young, adult, white women and men. Just as the threatening look is marked by its difference from the lovers' gaze, so too does this gaze acquire its special status by virtue of its difference from many other kinds of shared looks.

Precisely because it is a set of conventions, this system of looks can be manipulated to render deviant combinations. If Lynch's illicit stare transgresses a racial boundary, *Birth* makes a black woman's infatuation with a white man provide the very image of depravity. Stoneman's mulatta housekeeper (Mary Alden) fixes her wide-eyed stare on her employer's off-screen presence and suggestively licks the back of her hand in grotesque exaggeration of a male villain's lustful demeanor. When Stoneman (Ralph Lewis) joins her in the frame moments later, however, she adopts the posture of the wronged woman and lowers her eyes to

evade his gaze. Her feminine modesty is as insincere as her approximation of masculine lust is brazen. In contrast to the black man's obviously
unwelcome advances toward the white woman, this couple's relationship
appears not merely illicit but aberrant, unnatural. Deviance need not inspire teratology, however. When the World War I flyer hero of *Wings*
(Paramount, 1927) leans over his dying comrade and looks deeply into
his eyes, it is difficult to resist the implication that a homoerotic attachment unites the two—despite the fact that each has a girl back home.[20]
Whereas Griffith's lustful mulatta can only be denounced for its racism,
the fly-boy "lovers" have inspired hope that such a look might claim
conventional status. Yet each deviation ultimately confirms the same system of looks, one in which a particular arrangement of eyelines will suffice to make the relationship of any two faces intelligible as an erotic relationship that is more or less concordant with the norm.

Because Hollywood's racial categories depend on such a system, its
racism cannot really be grasped under the rubric of an age-old Manichaean logic. Stark through the racial threat seems in *Birth of a Nation*,
the type of filmmaking it exemplifies does not resuscitate an antique opposition between black evil and white goodness. Rather, it reinvents
the modern process of classifying particular bodies within the ranges
of variation thought to delimit races.[21] Before cinema, different sorts
of pictures had been used to illustrate the features typical of any given
category. Line drawings accompany Linneaus's *Anthropomorpha* (1760),
for instance.[22] But photographic representation provides cinema's most
immediate antecedent. Thanks to Allan Sekula's pioneering work on
the subject, the distinct late-nineteenth-century approaches of French
criminologist Alphonse Bertillon and English eugenicist Francis Galton have come to exemplify what was required to identify individuals
and types through this medium. Bertillon found he could rely on police photographs to identify any particular body only when he combined them with more easily indexed and statistically manipulable data
such as physical measurements. Galton represented criminal and racial
types by means of composite photography, a method of superimposi-
tion he thought could emphasize typical traits while eliminating atypical
ones according to the logic of the bell curve. Each, in other words, con-
structed a differential system apart from the individual photograph. In
order for any one photograph to signify a racial type or designate a particular individual within that type, the photograph had to be combined

with other images and statistical descriptors that would allow it to be categorized and indexed—in short, archived. According to Sekula, "Bertillon sought to embed the photograph in the archive. Galton sought to embed the archive in the photograph."[23] In either case, the celebrated realism of the photograph derives not from the properties of light, optics, and chemistry, but from the ability to standardize a particular set of codes and conventions.

Like the photographic methods of Bertillon and Galton, the movies establish a differential system of bodies that testifies to the apparent naturalness of both racial type and individual racial identity. Through casting, makeup, and lighting, *Birth of a Nation* distinguishes a range of black characters from a range of white ones. Moreover, within the category "black" the film differentiates a range of mulatto characters. No particular image serves as an average or aggregate of any racial type (the equivalent of Galton's composite) in this classification system. Instead, a large number of images of each particular body establish a range, the limits of which equal race. The skin color of individual characters varies, sometimes widely, from shot to shot. Set side by side, certain images of Elsie and Lynch might appear equally "black" or "white," but Griffith never allows such juxtaposition to occur. Elsie's face is placed in proximity to Lynch's only to differentiate their bodies and to demonstrate the lack of any reciprocal emotion. Thus, we see different individual bodies as different kinds of bodies. It is as if the filmmakers merely threw different levels of light on, and put different kinds of makeup on, already black or white individuals. The effect of categorical difference is achieved, however, precisely through the deliberate use of such techniques. In this way, Hollywood cinema produces the equivalent of Sekula's archive: it creates the illusion that its particular racial classification system exists prior to filming and makes it appear that that system was self-evident on the bodies of those filmed. The observation that the principle actors in *Birth* are "really" white people made-up to look black does not alter this semiotic operation, which is designed to convince viewers that visible differences of skin, hair, and facial features similar to those depicted in the film set the parameters of whiteness as well as blackness.

The power and scope of this classifying scheme is especially evident in films that aimed to combat the racism of such films as *The Birth of a Nation*. Oscar Micheaux's *Within Our Gates* (Micheaux Book and Film

Co./Quality Amusement Corp., 1919), to pick a famous example, uses similar conventions to valorize African American characters. It makes its romantic couples paler than other black characters in the film and makes the female partner brighter than the male. Indeed, taken out of context, some of the close-ups of Sylvia Landry (Evelyn Preer) might be seen to represent a white woman. The film itself, however, carefully distinguishes even the palest black faces from white ones; it offers a range of images of Sylvia's face, so that she looks both darker than white women and lighter than black men. In one sequence, for instance, she lies on a hospital bed and seems quite dark against the sheets, much darker than the philanthropist who visits her bedside. In very next sequence, however, she seems only slightly darker than this same woman when they meet in her parlor. Paired with her lover in conclusion, she seems several shades paler than he. By providing an African American version of the bright, pale woman's face, *Within Our Gates* demonstrates its paradigmatic, sentimental power. In contrast, most early Hollywood features try to make brightness seem identical with whiteness.

When movies made racial categories depend on the illumination, makeup, casting, and juxtaposition of bodies in spaces, they participated in a much broader revision. Histories of race in early-twentieth-century United States describe changes not only to what the categories were but also to the status of the concept itself. Both a new theory of culture, associated with the anthropology of Franz Boas, and a new model of heredity, associated with the emergence of modern Mendelian genetics, called into question the very idea of biologically distinct racial groups. Measurement and tabulation of headform lost credibility as scientific indicators of racial difference.[24] "Miscegenation" became an increasingly vexed problem as case law began to challenge the state's role in maintaining racial distinctions.[25] Sociology began to describe as "ethnic" groups (e.g., Irish and Italians) that would have been understood as racial at the turn of the century. Similarly, it became imperative to distinguish racial categories from national ones.[26] These changes hardly abolished race or racism. Opposition to nineteenth-century law and science notwithstanding, any number of commentators presupposed that race could and would be seen. They sought to provide a superior account of what it was—whether in defense of eugenicist projects or to establish that race was a "cultural" or "ideological" system that a properly scientific view would debunk.[27] This was not the death of race, then, so much as the beginning of a new type of argument about it. That argument assumed that most Americans could and would spontaneously distinguish white persons from a handful of nonwhite populations even if the ability to discriminate among them had a purely habitual basis.

One might begin to understand the role of movies in this shift by comparing Micheaux's tactic in *Within Our Gates* to a similar procedure used by W. E. B. Du Bois decades earlier. When Du Bois compiled the images for *Types of American Negroes, Georgia, U.S.A.* in 1900, he borrowed from Galton a visual form that became familiar as the "mug shot": the photographs show their subjects' heads both in profile and from a frontal angle. As one might expect, Du Bois employs this form to very different ends than the English eugenicist. Rather than typify the American Negro, he directs the authority of pictures against the prevailing classificatory scheme. As literary historian Shawn Michele Smith observes, Du Bois provides a pictorial representation of "the variations of 'color, hair and bone' that were legally encompassed by 'one drop' of blood laws at the turn of the century." Accordingly, "blond and blue-eyed 'Negroes' take their place beside brunette and brown-eyed 'Negroes'." This produces the inverse of Galton's composite: "Instead of blending individual portraits or likenesses into a single abstract 'type,' Du Bois's albums dismantle the notion of a unifying image."[28] Micheaux adopts a similar strategy, but his film cannot be said to challenge the idea of a single Negro type. Instead, his film, like *Birth of a Nation,* presupposes blackness to be a heterogeneous category. Under no circumstances would it be susceptible to representation in a single image. Accordingly, the film critiques neither the contradiction a visual classification scheme presents to the "one drop rule" nor racial biology per se. Rather, Micheaux targets the structure that places the romantic heroine outside the visual range defining blackness.[29] *Within Our Gates* makes plain that the images of variously made-up and illuminated actors' bodies through which the mainstream feature distinguishes races are one and the same as the images of the various eyeline matches through which filmmakers specify the socially reproducible couple. The very pictures that indicate that Elsie does not care for Lynch also indicate she is white, and he, black. The repetition of such images made a particular scheme of racial categorization immanent in the Hollywood romance. In the process, it also established race itself as an intractable visual fact.

Early feature filmmaking not only disseminated images that distinguish white from black, it also provided clear-cut visual differences among the Indian, the Mexican, and the Oriental. Griffith's oeuvre alone demonstrates as much. Many of the tropes of imperiled white woman-hood that distinguish *Birth of a Nation* were first worked out in such films about Indians as *The Massacre* (Biograph, 1912) and *Battle at Elder-bush Gulch* (Biograph, 1913), and an even earlier series of films had demonstrated the impossibility of reciprocal love between white men and Indian maidens.[30] Griffith envisioned the Mexican's difference from whites (and from a Chinese waiter) in *The Greaser's Gauntlet* (Biograph, 1908), where the white heroine's rescue of the Mexican protagonist raises a possibility of love ultimately foreclosed by his subsequent kidnapping of her.[31] It is *Broken Blossoms* (United Artists, 1919), however, that undoubtedly provides Griffith's most extensive, and vexed, elaboration of the problem of interracial romance. The persistent stare of a character named The Yellow Man (Richard Barthelmess) seems menacing in one sequence as his enlarged face approaches that of beautified ragamuffin Lucy (Lillian Gish). She shrinks from his look, yet it seems to offer the only hope of love in an otherwise bleak mise-en-scène. The Yellow Man's immediate withdrawal stands in respectful contrast, for instance, to the relentless pursuit of Lucy's brutish father, whose "rescue" of Lucy from The Yellow Man sends her face into spasms of horror. Interracial romance is tragically impossible in this world. But Griffith's film also hints that, were it possible to produce a space in which the white woman could return the romantic look of a dark-skinned man, their reciprocal look would mark the end of racism. This filmmaking tactic achieved some prominence later in the century.[32] As a tactic, it testifies to the persistent self-evidence of the conventions such early features as *Broken Blossoms* established.

Silent Hollywood racialized the face of love so that normative desire appeared to require whiteness. This equation had precedents, but, I must insist, we misunderstand it so long as we ignore the mechanics of spatial differentiation that drive feature film narrative. Richard Dyer provides the most systematic consideration to date of how particular techniques of lighting, photochemistry, and makeup conspire to distinguish and privilege a white woman.[33] Hollywood's gleaming heroine, he observes, often appears to be a source of spiritual illumination, because, quite simply, she glows. Yet when it comes time to provide a history of this figure, Dyer posits a misleading continuity between American movies and the Christian iconography of nineteenth-century Europe. In his account, paintings, watercolors, and photographs in which the woman's translucency verges on transparency perfectly exemplify the vexed relationship between flesh and spirit that a commitment to racial whiteness as divine illumination produces. The less visible the glowing woman is, the more spiritual and virtuous she becomes; the very quality that makes her body desirable defies possession in bodily terms. The glow of Hollywood's heroine differs dramatically. Even when her light appears to come from within, the good woman must be three-dimensional. In just this manner, *Sunrise* (Fox, 1927) distinguishes the suffering virtue of its country wife (Janet Gaynor) from the calculating temptation of the city woman (Margaret Livingston). Whereas we see both faces brightly illuminated, the wife's face always indicates an interior volume. The mise-en-scène sets it apart from the background so that its liquid eyes appear to open on unplumbed depths. In stark contrast, the City Woman's pale face seems a flat, luminous plane when shown in profile against the night sky. And her figure becomes literally transparent when it is superimposed in double-exposure over the husband (George O'Brien) whose conscience she troubles. True love can never take this pictorial form. Whatever she owes to Christian pictorial tradition, cinema's white heroine must be a worldly woman, part of a particular space. When she becomes too manifestly a translucent picture, her image likely suggests not an angelic presence, but the good woman's duplicitous counterpart, the seductress.

Obsessive concern with sentimentalized heterosexual monogamy places U.S. cinema squarely within traditions of European and American theater, fiction, painting, and photography. Movies borrow from plays, novels, paintings, and poems any number of techniques for representing the bond of love and making it seem a universally human emotion. Nonetheless, Hollywood won the authority to designate such emotions by showing them in a very specific manner. As a distinct form for telling the story of romantic love, American movies also structure the categories that allow love to be seen. By the end of the first decade of the twentieth century, they had just begun to establish a set of conventions for distinguishing types of persons, establishing emotional connections among them, and relating types and emotions to placement in social space. By the end of the century's second decade, the heroine's pale face provided a reliable indication that a spatial transformation had occurred. In the most conventional rendering, love begins as a continuous eyeline, endures despite spatial difference, and either returns or dramatically fails to do so in the film's resolution. If it is to be a happy one, resolution requires a particular kind of mise-en-scène—a well-lighted space, clear of any obstruction to the lovers' shared eyeline. The eyeline match restored in this space is not quite the same as the one that is first pulled apart, however. Where the initial shared look established the transcendental properties of love precisely by being rent, this final look indicates enduring romance by bringing an end to the division of the visual field, as if the problem of spatial difference itself has been abolished. It takes nothing less than a transformation of the visual field to ensure the stability of the romantic couple.

DANGER

Repeated images of a young woman's terrified face indicate that the very possibility of love is in jeopardy. Near the end of *The Birth of a Nation* a leering Silas Lynch advances on Elsie. She retreats into a chair as Lynch, his eyes fixed upon hers, kneels to grasp the hem of her long blouse. Wide-eyed with horror, she recoils from his gaze. As parts of a single motion, her head draws back to the very edge of the frame while Lynch gently raises the blouse to his lips. She leaps up. Glowing and with tousled hair, she throws her hands in the air, rushes to the door, and, pressing herself against it, beats it with both hands. Lynch's eyes never leave her as he sits on another chair in the foreground.

Near the end of *Within Our Gates,* this pattern repeats itself. There, it is a white man who intrudes upon a well-illuminated black woman and backs her into a corner. But this kind of sequence works just as well when both parties are white. In *Sunrise* the husband's face looms ominously over his wife. In close-up, his narrowed eyes peer from beneath

Lillian Gish and George Siegmann in *The Birth of a Nation* (Epoch, 1915). Frame enlargements courtesy of Brown University Film Archives.

a furrowed brow. The reverse close-up registers her reaction. Her eyes widen as she looks upward out of frame and shifts her weight down against the bow of the small rowboat that contains them. Next, the film reduces scale to frame both in a single image. Standing in the boat, the husband advances with grasping hands as the wife retreats over the gunnel until her head almost touches the water and her clasped hands are raised in supplication. Self-consciously reprising decades of such scenes, *King Kong* (RKO, 1933) stages one well before it introduces its eponymous ape. On board the outbound ship, the coaching of showman-adventurer Carl Denham (Robert Armstrong) prompts Ann Darrow (Fay Wray) to produce a reaction every bit as legible as the one Kong appears to inspire spontaneously later in the film. She looks out of frame left; eyes widen; muscles contact; hands are raised to frame her face; and the mouth releases its famous scream. Denham's movie camera, one senses, may be as big a threat as the monster himself.

As much as resolution depends on the face of a pale young woman to signify love and safety, so too does her horrified look indicate a danger out of frame. On this alternation between horror and love the outcomes of Hollywood's visual narratives often hinge. Not that such films refuse to show men in jeopardy—they do. But throughout the 1910s and 1920s at least, U.S. motion pictures tend to use a woman's image to dramatize a threat to the formation of the couple and the kind of space it requires. Like the space lovers share, dangerous space has many different locations—from Silas Lynch's office to Kong's hairy palm. We recognize it as dangerous not because of the particular setting but because of the familiar spatial dynamic that generates it. Where love begins as an unwelcome separation, in these cases danger promises the collapse of spaces that should be kept separate.

In *Birth of a Nation*, Little Sister Flora (Mae Marsh) skips along one side of the fence while Gus (Walter Long) follows her on the other. The fence divides the background of the image from the foreground and makes the relationship between the figures who inhabit these two spaces absolutely plain. Crouching in shadow in front of the fence, Gus can see Flora, but he cannot be seen by her as she blithely traverses the well-illuminated background. The relationship of black man to white girl established by this picture gains intensity in the subsequent sequence and, in retrospect, seems to govern the visual narrative of the film as a whole. Gus follows Little Sister and stares at her through boundaries in the mise-en-scène. Looking fixedly off right, he creeps forward in a dark frame crowded with dead, overhanging branches. She sits on a log in a well-illuminated clearing and also looks off right. Unconcerned, she smiles and swings her legs back and forth. Tight, iris-masked close-ups of a squirrel on a tree branch at once visualize the object of her look and the limitations of her vision, which cannot penetrate the surrounding woods from which Gus looks at her with impunity. Her little patch of bucolic innocence is doomed.

When Gus enters Little Sister's frame at last, the resulting chase ends in her famous leap to her death. His pursuit thus implies an assault, and critic after critic has described Gus as "a rapist."[34] It bears remembering, however, that little physical contact occurs between Gus and Flora—far less, for example, than in Lynch's pursuit of Elsie later on. True, a title indicates Gus's wish to "marry" Flora. But the mere fact of this proposition cannot account for the special menace of the encounter. Lynch too proposes marriage without being labeled a rapist. The sense that Gus wants to violate Flora derives neither from physical contact nor from textual euphemism. Rather, Griffith employs codes and conventions specific to filmmaking in order to invoke the myth of the predatory black man. It is not simply "a black man's look" from which Little Sister flees, but a look painstakingly made threatening through well-established procedures for defining villainy. With slight changes, Gus's marriage proposal could easily be made to appear pathetically misguided, tragic, even comical. Only imagine the difference it would make to give Little Sister the aspect of the towering country husband from *Sunrise* by lowering the camera, reducing the light on her face, and narrowing her eyes to slits. Gus's menace becomes parody in this imaginary scenario as his wide, tremulous eyes look up and out of frame.

In the actual film, Gus's look penetrates spatial barriers. In thus intruding, it implicitly contaminates. By means of lighting and careful arrangement of mise-en-scène, the film represents the sides of the fence, like the deceptively well-illuminated clearing and the darkened woods surrounding it, as incompatible kinds of spaces. When Gus finally enters the frame with Little Sister, he transgresses a boundary that seemed necessary and proper, if insufficient. This results in a debased version of the space only lovers should share. Gus and Flora look at one another in corresponding close-ups of fascination and fear—the antithesis of true love. Although their exchange resembles Lynch's later approach to Elsie in many respects, Little Sister's encounter differs in repeatedly staging and collapsing a proper spatial difference. The subsequent chase promises to establish a stable separation of the two only to show Gus's relentlessness in overcoming the distance.[35] As fences, shrubs, trees, and mountains fail to contain him, the sense that Gus wants to penetrate Flora herself becomes more and more pronounced.

To assume that the gaze of a black man conveys violence apart from such visual narratives comes dangerously close to according that look an inherent menace—as if it had a natural, rather than cultural basis. True enough, other forms besides cinema had proclaimed the black man's threat to the white woman and encouraged Americans to suspect his look in her direction.[36] But when cinema rendered the danger in spatial terms, it both gave new specificity to the threat and changed what it would take to "solve" the problem. As part of a spatial story told largely through the orchestration of eyelines, Gus's penetrating stare sets in motion a struggle between seemingly antithetical spaces. It thus implies that no white woman can be safe unless a rigid boundary is established. Earlier films had equated the collapse of spatial distinctions with violence to a white woman without racializing the threat, as when bandits intrude upon cringing heroines in *The Lonely Villa* (Biograph, 1909) and *An Unseen Enemy* (Biograph, 1912). Similarly, in *Orphans of the Storm* predatory aristocrats encircle Lillian Gish's character and control her movement. Images of her horrified face are intercut with a series of extreme close-ups of leering, seemingly disembodied eyes as she is thrown from man to man. In this kind of story, resolution requires not simply the elimination of the villain or villains, but a transformation of the visual field. Only such a thoroughgoing revision can abolish the hazards entailed by the very process of spatial differentiation that animates the story.

The entire plot of *Birth of a Nation* may be understood in these terms. The sequence in which Gus chases Little Sister provides a prolepsis of the film's twin final rescues. Before this pivotal moment, the film represents the incursion of black bodies into spaces formerly occupied primarily by white ones; afterward, it represents the increasing domination of the white-robed Ku Klux Klan over all spaces. The rise of the "black South" appears as an increasing differentiation of the visual field—an expansion of the number of white interiors a black body politic necessarily threatens. The rise of the "white South," on the other hand, appears as a series of reunions. Differences are abolished and families reunited. A new order of distinctions takes over, indicating a stable zone of safety around the white couples. Thus, the film's final images of reunited lovers are predicated upon its images of black bodies held at bay on one side of the frame by a line of mounted Klansmen on the other. The latter images mark a crucial difference between the film's resolution and the conclusion of its first part, which depicts the Civil War. There, we see that the war produces a Union that is not one: North and South, like the "black South" and "white South," remain distinct kinds of spaces inherently hostile to one another. By contrast, the ride of the Klan appears to bring about a series of transformations that produce a stable, unified, national space in which these differences can be managed. Within the terms of the film's allegory of national birth, sequences of peril and rescue imply that a stable America rests on the formation of a secure space in which love can endure. To be secure, the national whole must plainly distinguish spaces occupied by whites from those occupied by blacks and subordinate the latter to the former.

Such racism has established *The Birth of a Nation* as a quintessentially American text. Criticism habitually associates all of American filmmaking with its brand of nationalism by noting that the film also marks an important moment in the development of feature film form.[37] But if the film's racism is its most salient American feature, it remains unclear wherein lies the Americanness of the hundreds of Hollywood films that offer neither so blatant a racial threat nor so clear a national allegory. Moreover, cinema's contribution to the history of U.S. racial categories is obscured by the presupposition that *Birth*'s particular brand of racism derives wholly from a precinematic American culture. In contrast, I argue that the film exemplifies and extends a distinctly cinematic system for articulating racial difference with spatial difference. This system made the shared look of a white man and woman the index of love and came to life through countless early films, most of which do not display the explicit racism and nationalism of *Birth*. Although one need not look far to find Negroes, Mexicans, Indians, and Orientals represented as a threat to the all-American couple during the silent era, Hollywood's persistent identification of this couple as a white one is more insidiously racist. While particular villains could substitute for one another, Hollywood made the notion that this particular couple defined safe space appear to be a universal proposition. Through seemingly endless permutations, American movies promised to make the whole world safe for lovers—providing, of course, viewers accepted its version of how love looked. The nationalist project of American filmmaking thus goes far beyond what an allegory like *Birth* can suggest.

With its emphasis on the lovers' shared look, Hollywood's favorite narrative made the problem of recognition paramount to the formation of a secure social space. Although silent features made clear that true love could only occur within whiteness, the threat of racial contamination was hardly the only obstacle it had to overcome. In *The Wind* (MGM, 1928), heroine Letty (Lillian Gish) faces lethal consequences when she fails to recognize the right man. Here especially, the opacity of the mise-en-scène constitutes part of the threat. Desert exteriors are defined by a cloud of wind-blown sand that threatens to drive Letty mad. In the climactic final sequence, the ferocious wind traps her in a cabin. A series of images depict the world outside as a dark cloud of dust that rips apart buildings and fences. Bursting through the walls and windows of the cabin, the wind seems to invade through any available aperture. Increasingly dazed and horrified, Letty raises trembling arms above her head and looks wide-eyed about the room—a conventional image of the endangered woman, here without a menacing male figure. The film thus differentiates the cabin's interior from the exterior atmosphere of dark gray sand in order to suggest the permeability of that boundary and to establish Letty's inability to know when to let the outside in.

The villain's arrival is presented as an extension of the atmospheric invasion. Outside, a man's hand knocks on the door, while, inside, Letty's face turns toward the door in close-up. As if from Letty's point of view, we see the door vibrate with each knock. In a series of shots, Letty opens the door and is blown back across frame onto the floor as the villain enters and closes the door behind him. He lifts her from the floor in a tight embrace; pinned beneath him in the frame, she revives and discovers to her horror that she has admitted the masher, Wirt Roddy (Montagu Love). Once again, endangerment becomes a problem less of bodily violation than of the collapse of spatial boundaries. We see Wirt assault Letty (he unbuckles his belt and forces her into the bedroom), and we see Letty shoot, kill, and bury him. But his death does not put an end to the threat. Indeed, close-ups reveal Letty's horrified face through the cabin window as intercut images show the wind exposing Wirt's face and hands in the ground where she has buried him.

The sequence ends with a lengthy close-up of Letty's face contorted by a scream as the sand blows unceasingly against the cabin.

The hero's arrival reenacts the villain's entry. The door strains against a shovel Letty has used to wedge it shut. A hand emerges through the gap between the door and jamb and discovers the shovel. Shots later, we find Letty collapsed in the corner, the back of her head—a tangled mass of wind-blown hair—turned toward the camera. Mysterious hands enter the frame from screen right and force her over to reveal her horror-stricken, alabaster face. Letty's cowboy husband, Liege (Lars Hanson), looks down at her in bewilderment. Wearing the same blank look, she is pulled up into a close two-shot. Liege props her up, but she backs away. Soon, however, her horror gives way to recognition. An exterior shot establishes that Wirt is indeed dead and buried. Suddenly illuminated, the two gaze lovingly into one other's eyes and then out the open doorway at the world outside, now free of danger.[38]

Throughout the silent period, U.S. features told many different versions of this story in which the heroine is imperiled by her inability to distinguish the right man from the wrong one. Indeed, the slightest suggestion of an affair will suffice to put her in jeopardy. In *The One She Loved* (Biograph, 1912), to pick but one early example, the wife (Mary Pickford) enters the back of her husband's office to see him embracing his stenographer. Our vantage on this scene makes plain that the husband rejects the stenographer's advances. The wife sees otherwise, however, and staggers home in despair, setting in motion a series of events that nearly result in her death. The consequences need not be so dire. In *It* (Paramount, 1927) a similar misapprehension on the part of the hero (Antonio Moreno) causes him to break with the heroine (Clara Bow), but she need only fall overboard for him to come to his senses, abandon her competitor, and swim to her rescue. The seduction of the hero by the wrong woman makes for a more serious problem. Yet, as is the case in *Sunrise,* his failure to see through her machinations usually seems more threatening to the heroine herself than to the hero or her seductive competitor. For example, although *Blood and Sand* (Paramount, 1922) encourages the viewer to take pleasure in the seductive woman's torment of its matador hero (Rudolph Valentino), the question of the wife's suffering and forgiveness plainly organizes the drama's final act. She cannot bring herself to return his look and leaves him nothing to live for. When the bull gores him, however, her anguish appears greater than his own.

Lillian Gish and Lars Hanson in *The Wind* (MGM, 1928). Frame enlargements courtesy of Brown University Film Archives.

(The seductress, of course, does not bat an eye.) Absolution occurs on his deathbed as he casts off the duplicitous woman's serpent ring and at last looks up into his wife's eyes. Thus, plots with a man's distraction at their center only reinforce our sense that the outcome of the visual love story depends on a pale young woman's willingness and ability to return his look.

Each scenario of misrecognition sets up more or less the same kind of spatial problem: discontinuities, obstacles, or opacities in the mise-en-scène both prevent the lovers from recognizing one another and promise the viewer that, under the right circumstances, such recognition can occur. This problematic structures films as different in mood and setting as Joseph Von Sternberg's gritty drama *The Docks of New York* (Paramount, 1928) and Cecil B. DeMille's costume spectacular *Male and Female* (Famous Players–Lasky, 1919). In the former, a nighttime milieu of docks and dives makes it difficult for the heroine (Betty Compson) to distinguish stoker Bill's romantic attentions from sexual opportunism. Bill (George Bancroft) thwarts her attempt to drown herself and even marries her, but poor illumination, barroom crowds, and his apparent desire for her unconscious body inhibit a steady look between the partners and raise the question of his sincerity. Similarly, in *Male and Female* an English Lady (Gloria Swanson) hardly looks at her butler (Thomas Meighan) at home in the manor, but when shipwrecked on a desert island, she swoons for the commanding figure he presents. The solution to such problems of recognition always entails a qualitative change in space that allows the lovers to see each other for what they really are. In *Male and Female,* a flashback to antiquity provides the governing metaphor for their relationship. As a Babylonian King, Meighan tries to compel Swanson's surrender by threatening her with death. The screen crackles with erotic energy whenever their eyes meet, but she will not be mastered and prefers the lion's pit. When she marches resolutely to her doom, Meighan's face registers an internal torment that one can well believe would survive the centuries. Once it is shown to derive so explicitly from a struggle for dominance, this couple's attraction cannot provide the basis for a lasting union. *Male and Female* returns the would-be lovers to civilization and separates them once more. For its part, *Docks of New York* ends by at last uniting the couple in broad daylight. Though circumstances require that Bill be led off to jail, the steady gaze he and his wife share leaves no doubt that his wandering days are over.

Where the obstruction or limitation of a lover's enframed vision can make for thrilling melodramas of predatory passion, betrayal, and redemption, another kind of story uses a similar emphasis to an entirely different end. By making the hero's incapacity to see and move through space the primary difficulty, the comedy feature may dispense with the villain's threatening look altogether. In *Safety Last* (Pathé, 1923) spatial complications conspire to force The Boy (Harold Lloyd) to scale a tall building. On the inside of the building The Boy's friend Bill (Bill Strother), a competent climber who would substitute for him, cannot make the switch because he is being chased by a policeman. Meanwhile, outside the building, The Boy's struggles to overcome a number of unexpected obstacles drive him to ever more dangerous heights. On the second floor, seeds dumped on The Boy's head from out of the top of frame inspire a pigeon attack. Between the second and third floors, he reaches for a handhold and grabs an entangling net. Nearing the top and hanging desperately from one of the hands of the building's clock, he reaches for a rope Bill has offered. Straining and stretching, he grabs it at last—and plummets out of frame. In order to prepare these gags and give them their punch, the film shows us what The Boy cannot see. An interior shot of a sporting goods store and exterior shot of a man dropping a tennis net partly out the window prepare the net gag, for example. And intercut interior shots show us, first, that the rope is not attached to anything and, then, that Bill has managed to evade the cop long enough to dive for the rope just before it disappears out the window. Sequences like this one generate humor as well as suspense by revealing the visual field to be defined by obstacles to enframed vision and movement. It is the trouble we see moments before the comedian does that gets the laugh.

Always caught unaware, the male comedian has something in common with the imperiled heroine. *Exploits of Elaine,* for instance, reaches its climax in the final reel when, as a title puts it, "Fear and fury at Kennedy's nearness turns Bennett, polished lawyer and lover of Elaine, into the insane criminal who many times has endeavored to do away with her." As she waits in the office of her upright fiancé, Kennedy's rival, she could not possibly anticipate his transformation into the contorted villain who enters behind her.

When the great male comedians encounter the unexpected, however, their faces present a marked contrast to the terror of the imperiled heroine so meticulously rendered in close-up. In long or medium shot, we see The Boy's mild surprise as he hangs from the clock, the perplexed expression of Charlie Chaplin's tramp as he is devoured by an enormous machine *(Modern Times),* and Buster Keaton's stonefaced visage as the

The Clutching Hand intrudes upon Elaine (Pearl White) in *The Exploits of Elaine* (1914). Frame enlargement courtesy of George Eastman House.

facade of the house crashes down around him *(One Week; Steamboat Bill, Jr.)*. Such images provide the comic inversion of the heroine's frantic, wide-eyed horror. Yet, even as they parody the melodramatic race to the rescue by putting a white male face at the center of suspenseful action, these comedies cannot do without a love story and the dynamic of separation, threat, and reunion it requires. In *Safety Last,* as The Boy nears the top of the building, we cut away to a shot of his fiancée, who looks up in horror. At the end, swinging from a rope attached to his ankle, The Boy miraculously lands on the top of the building in a bright medium two-shot with The Girl (Mildred Davis).

The Hollywood love story comprises a sequence of spatial oppositions, transformations, and reconciliations that strive to picture as homogenous, stable, and therefore "safe" the space that includes a white man and woman in love. When American motion pictures popularized this particular way of narrating romance, they redefined the categorical relationships earlier forms had set in place. They made particular images of the heroine's face necessary to signify the romantic couple. They made racial classification inhere in the relationship between any two given faces. And they pictured relationships among persons as relationships among different kinds of spaces. Within this narrative form, the view of any character is limited to the space that character occupies. When a character's look temporarily exceeds those limits, as when Gus peers through the bushes at Flora, it threatens (or promises) to alter the relationship between the two spaces involved. To transform one kind of space into another—to reveal the threat to love and then to secure the couple—therefore requires a narrative agent adept at seeing and arranging spaces and setting proper limits for character looks within them.

EXPERTISE

Such expertise exists in contradistinction to embodied vision. It is a commonplace of film criticism that cinema's allure derives from the superior view it grants the spectator. And indeed, in order to show that the bond between the lovers endures despite their separation, images are juxtaposed as no single person could see them: Enoch onboard his ship, Annie at her window; the hero at the front, the heroine in her village. Such images also indicate the potential limitlessness of the visual field. Each reframing can offer an extension or subdivision of a film's spaces. It is not only the juxtaposition of distinct locations, that is, but the potential multiplication and elaboration of spatial distinctions in general that drives cinematic narrative. The obstacles and hazards generated through this dynamic of spatial differentiation are not of the sort that can be removed by the couple's shared look alone. Rescue does not result from any one character's ability to see. Indeed, the limitations of character eyelines typically help to define the threat. Rather, resolution requires a thoroughgoing shift in the relationship among competing types of spaces. A particular kind of space must be established, or its failure demonstrated. The visual field must be transformed. No matter how privileged the audience's vantage on this transformation, their seeing it does not offer the possibility of controlling it. It must be imaged for them. By definition, then, the audience's view of this series of transformations is also partial and limited.

The sense that Hollywood's narrative vantage is a transcendent one derives not from optical powers inherent to the camera, but rather from the conventional manner of organizing content on screen. The best theorized histories of feature film form acknowledge as much, but too often fail to press the point to its logical conclusion. So long as techniques for producing and articulating shots define Hollywood form, "the camera" remains an all-too-handy term for its narrative address. On the basis of this misleading metaphor, Hollywood is often said to offer viewers the fantasy that they themselves might see from the camera's ideal point of view. Such an identification may readily be shown to mystify the actual production process. If, however, we eschew the formalism of technique in favor of the form of visual content, a history of mediation can finally supplant a history of mystification, and the relationship between the feature film's narrative address and Hollywood's corporate institutions can be made plain.

Production-oriented arguments have established the set of procedures known as continuity editing as the primary historical maker of feature film form. Since the days of Eisenstein at least, the technique of crosscutting in particular has organized arguments over the rise of the American feature. A single early film has come to exemplify the difference this technique makes to cinematic storytelling and viewership: Edwin S. Porter's 1903 *Life of an American Fireman.* In his classic 1939 history, Lewis Jacobs celebrates the ending of Porter's short film for intercutting interior and exterior shots to depict a fireman's rescue of a woman and child. By pointing to this apparently early instance of what would become a convention, Jacobs both proclaims Porter's genius and announces the telos of American filmmaking toward the feature.[39] In the 1970s, however, researchers established that the film had originally circulated in a far different version and was modified sometime during the 1930s according to the norms of this later period.[40] Rather than indicating the logical progression depicted by Jacobs's history, the two versions of the film established a historical break separating two entirely different modes of representation.

The original version of Porter's film presents interior and exterior shots in series. First, in the smoke-filled interior, the imperiled heroine rushes away from the camera to a window at screen left, then, overcome by smoke, she turns to collapse on a bed in the foreground. The heroic fireman enters from the right, crosses the frame to break the window, collects the limp woman and carries her out through the bright aperture. Returning through the window after a brief pause, he retrieves an infant amid thick smoke before exiting the window once more. In the subsequent exterior shot, the second-story window briefly frames the woman's frantic face. Below, the heroic fireman breaks through the front door while other firemen place a ladder under the window and still others spray the house with water. Our hero carries the woman down the ladder; she revives and emphatically gestures that her child is in the room. The fireman mounts the ladder and returns with the child. All three are grouped together near the center of the frame.

The difference between this 1903 version and the altered one, Noël Burch famously argues, is not that one tells a story and the other does not, but that each assumes a different sort of viewer.[41] The original version, he contends, expects audiences to do most of the work required to understand discontinuous actions as aspects of a single event. Because each shot appears to stand on its own, because the significant action is distributed across the frame rather than being pinpointed for the viewer, and because distanced framing does not communicate the psychological complexity close-ups can, Porter's film may be considered a typical example of early filmmaking and presupposes a viewer "external" to the world of its story. By Jacobs's day, crosscutting had become so commonplace a technique that the original arrangement of images could only seem to be an unfinished or poorly assembled work. In contrast to the "external" vantage point of Porter's films, Burch explains, Hollywood cinema effaces the narrative agent as it identifies the spectator's point of view with that of the camera, thereby moving the viewer "inside" a singular diegetic space. He thus provides the spectator described by such theorists as Christian Metz and Jean-Louis Baudry with a concrete history in filmmaking practice.[42] He also refutes the historical model of a swift and logical aesthetic evolution such historians as Jacobs provided. In his account, neither the mere technology of the motion picture camera nor the commercial imperative of the movie business can have set the course of American filmmaking. While Burch does see an overarching kinship between capitalism and realist representation, he makes clear that this connection alone cannot have decided the particular form filmmaking would take. The same determinations produced, in early cinema, a very different narrative form. Rather than seeking a monocausal account of cinema's development, Burch in effect proposes, we should acknowledge it to have been a complexly overdetermined process and set our sights on identifying the discontinuities and breaks that distinguish one mode of filmmaking from the next.[43]

Powerful as Burch's revision is, it leaves a central premise of Jacob's narrative in place. Indeed, it gives new import to the old contention that the advent of continuity editing heralds the feature film. Subsequent work continues to reproduce this contention, despite challenges to Burch's account of the spectator and revisions of his periodization. Accordingly, scholars with such different approaches to spectatorship and history as Eileen Bowser, Miriam Hansen, and Bordwell, Thompson, and Stagier reproduce both Burch's description of Porter's original and his assertion that editing procedure distinguishes it from later forms of filmmaking.[44]

Life of an American Fireman does exemplify a formal alternative to the feature film, but Burch's emphasis on editing obscures as much as illuminates the difference. Burch describes the original version as showing the rescue of the woman twice, but from different camera positions. In so doing, he argues, it departs not only from the conventions of a later kind of filmmaking but also from those of written narrative. Those who modified the film "clearly sensed," he explains, that it does provide "a very early anaphore of camera ubiquity," that is, it evinces an impulse to convey simultaneous action in discreet locations. This impulse, Burch continues, "corresponded so easily and naturally to the most commonplace novelistic procedure—'Quickly the fireman climbed the ladder, *semi-colon,* inside the room he saw the inanimate woman on the bed'— *that it could be formulated on paper when it could not be on film.*"[45] While partisans of the novel may well contest its reduction to the mechanics of syntax, this description presents a far greater difficulty for those interested in the history of film narrative. On one hand, Burch implies that narrative can be defined apart from expressive form—that "the story" told by *Life of an American Fireman* is one that could be told on paper. On the other hand, he invites us to imagine that the expressive form of the novel set the paradigm for what cinema would become. Burch is not the only one to employ such paradoxical logic. Most approaches that reproduce his description of Porter's "repeated action" use this observation to estrange early film from a narrative model assumed both to follow it and to precede it by a century or more. One might almost get the impression that film proper enjoyed a brief efflorescence around the turn of the century only to become indistinguishable from novelistic storytelling. Although more recent, more concrete comparisons between cinema and a whole range of nineteenth-century forms have made such an account look reductive, the proliferation of comparisons has yet to displace the paradoxical conceptualization of narrative form at the core of Burch's account.[46]

In point of fact, the vast majority of the fireman's actions are not repeated. He completes entirely different sets of movements in each shot. Moreover, the order of the shots matters a great deal and could not be reversed without changing the story. One might imagine yet a third version of the film in which the well-illuminated exterior shot that reunites mother and child gives way to the smoke-filled interior of the firemen heroically battling the blaze. Such a finale could only undo the modest closure achieved by the preceding shot: do the firemen succeed or remain trapped inside? Is this a story of rescue or a dramatic testament to the hazardous life of firemen, one that cries out, perhaps in a sequel, for their safe return to the station house? The instant critical attention shifts away from the placement of the camera to the spaces represented by the mise-en-scène, it becomes clear that the shots figure a complementary relationship between inside and outside in order to stage a competition between the two. The shots each depict two distinct spaces and at the same time insist on a permeable barrier between them. The window serves in the interior shot to indicate the space from which rescue may come and in the exterior shot to indicate a still dangerous space inside. Once staged in this manner, we plainly see that in order for rescue to occur the outside must win.

Understood in these terms, the difference re-editing makes to Porter's film seems much less significant than the difference either version presents to the far more complex dramas of inside and out told a decade later. As in *Life of an American Fireman,* the finale of D. W. Griffith's 1913 *Battle at Elderbush Gulch* places its heroine (Lillian Gish) in a smoke-filled room. Here, however, no simple triumph of outside over inside will suffice to rescue her and her child. Rather, a wholesale transformation of relationships among a diverse set of spaces must occur. Indeed, *Battle at Elderbush Gulch* provides no clear-cut distinction between interior peril and exterior safety. Outside, Indians ring the cabin, set it on fire, and threaten to penetrate its protective enclosure—crosscutting and mise-en-scène collaborate to make interior hazard appear the extension of this exterior threat. Counterposed to the pending invasion of the cabin by hostile outsiders, moreover, is a competing "outside" from which rescue will come. *Battle at Elderbush Gulch* establishes another exterior space, further removed from the cabin, from which the cavalry is summoned. And there is still another crucial exterior location, one occupied by the young husband tragically separated from our heroine by the Indian onslaught in a prior scene. Moving en masse in its ride to the rescue, the cavalry sweeps up the husband, clears the screen of the ring of Indian attackers, and deposits him on the cabin's doorstep. In this manner, its arrival promises not simply rescue but "restoration" of an original whole signified, in typical fashion, by the couple's reunion. Yet even this emphatic removal of the natives will not suffice to bring the family together. *Battle at Elderbush Gulch* introduces a further complication that can only be resolved once the smoke clears. Nestled within the besieged cabin, a large trunk hides the couples' infant child and the adolescent sisters who safeguard it. As the trunk's lid pops open to reveal its precious, miraculously preserved contents, the final obstacle to reunion is removed.[47] To generate a picture of a stable and secure spatial whole, then, requires not simply that the exterior supplant that interior, or vice versa, but the transformation of relationships among a large number of spaces. It is not the presence or absence of parallel editing as such that distinguishes Griffith's film from its predecessor but the content and complexity of the spatial story that such editing helps to tell.

The two different sorts of spatial stories presuppose very different kinds of storytellers.[48] Porter's narrative shifts its vantage from outside to inside and back again to show that the outside triumphs. Only one boundary is at issue, and the window delimits movement across it. This crucial aperture demonstrates that exterior and interior are continuous and leaves no doubt about what it means to pass from one side to the other. Accordingly, to tell this story requires a limited power to see across a single boundary and the ability to show that the protagonists wind up on the right side of it. The ability to repeat what appears to be the same period of time indicates that the entity telling this story has powers its characters and viewers do not. Yet in relationship to the organization of the visual field, this narrative power seems to be of the same order as embodied vision. It shows more or less what characters see. The narrator's power supplements that of an embodied look, then, but does not entirely displace its authority. This straightforward story of inside and out, typical of early cinema, makes it appear as though the camera can substitute for the human eye and defines the narrator as the agent who controls that camera.

Whereas *Life of an American Fireman* bifurcates the visual field to show that one side is dangerous and the other safe, *Battle at Elderbush Gulch* represents an endlessly reversible relationship of spaces within spaces. When the elder sister braves flaming arrows, gunfire, and tomahawks to retrieve the infant from certain death outside the cabin, she finds the interior of the house relatively unsafe as well—if she can sneak through the doggy door to accomplish the rescue, surely the Indians will be able to get in. Thus she seeks refuge in yet another interior within the dangerous house, namely, the trunk where she hides with the infant. Far from establishing once and for all a stable boundary between inside and out, this minor rescue makes the overall peril even more acute, emphasizing as it does the nearness of the attackers to the cabin, the permeability of its walls, and that yet another obstacle exists between mother and child. Unlike *Life of an American Fireman,* but like films ranging from *Enoch Arden* to *Safety Last,* when *Battle at Elderbush Gulch* sets any two given spaces in competition it inevitably shows their interdependence and thus insists that a qualitative change in each will be necessary if we are to have narrative closure. Precisely because of its ability to bring about such changes, Griffith's film seems more resolved than Porter's; at the end, no loose ends remain. All spaces, interior and exterior, have been made safe—as if the entire space of "the West" has been secured for the white, nuclear family. This resolution depends on an agent that pictures and arranges multiple spaces to demonstrate complex relations of interdependence among them. No embodied human could accomplish as much, whether equipped with a camera or not.

This is so neither because of the mobility of the camera nor because of its difficult location both above and within the action, but rather because the film's discordant assortment of spaces makes plain that no vantage that remains within any one space could possibly manage all of the spaces it brings into play. To be sure, Hollywood's favorite editing strategies lend themselves to this narrative elaboration of space. Not only do they encourage the juxtaposition of one space with another, they also make the heroine's face readily intelligible as an enlarged picture of the space in which she is located. As these examples suggest, however, editing acquires narrative power only in relationship to the mise-en-scène.

Moreover, deliberate arrangement of the mise-en-scène can drive spatial narrative without cutting. When the Clutching Hand slithers through the doorway behind an unseeing Elaine, for instance, the evident transgression of boundaries cries out for intervention and rushes the story forward. To restore the possibility of love in such cases requires an accumulation of vantage points, a noncorporeal organization that works to frame, arrange, and assemble the complex spatial world of the film. As Tom Gunning argues, most accounts of Hollywood narration founder on this point and attempt to turn the narrator back into an anthropomorphic entity. Thus, acknowledgment that "the narrator" cannot be human compels Bordwell to contend that Hollywood narration needs no narrator whatsoever, Metz to impute narrative power to the spectator's identification with the camera, and partisans of the auteur to confuse the narrator with the author-function it historically helped to create.[49] Through their various disavowals, these arguments implicitly acknowledge that Hollywood's narrating agent can be neither the director, nor the camera, nor a disembodied "gaze," but must be something that never had a body in the first place.

The movies offer viewers less a fantasy of transcendence than a vision of order. They do not extend the ability to see so much as subordinate that ability to the arrangement of space. Indeed, the ordering of the visual field is far more important to American cinema than how much of it audiences see. Its favorite narrative aims precisely to reduce the significant portion of the visual field to the space surrounding the socially reproducible couple. To succeed, it must inspire the viewer's desire not for more and more visual information, but for proper arrangement, stability, the mastery of dangerous differentiation by an agency that cannot inhabit the space where he or she sits. Accordingly, the idea that seeing space will suffice to arrange it can only seem a quaint notion. This explains why critical models that turn the camera into a disembodied pseudo-eye inevitably end up positing a naive or deluded spectator. It also explains why efforts to understand film ideology in terms of a camera-eye analogy end up reproducing the paradox this analogy entails: the cinematographic apparatus offers a superior view insofar as the camera is analogous to the human eye, but this perspective can only be considered superior because the apparatus is not even remotely human.[50] Acknowledgment of this paradox leads Metz, for one, to found his influential model of spectatorship on the figure of disavowal: the spectator "knows very well" that he watches an image assembled by others "but all the same" mistakes his vision for that of the apparatus and the image for the object it purports to represent. No doubt, the removal of obstacles to knowledge, desire, and vision in the Hollywood happy ending encourages the fantasy that the camera's vantage, the character's look, and the spectator's view may somehow coincide. But we will not understand the structure of this fantasy under the sign of an idealized technical apparatus. What makes it so manifestly fantastic is not the phenomenological similarity between images and purportedly unmediated vision, but the fact that Hollywood's visual narratives themselves insist on the limitations of embodied vision.

When it makes true love depend on a story of spatial transformation, U.S. cinema at once defines a need and satisfies it. It implies that any social problem can be understood as one of eyelines limited in space and thus be solved by an agent expert at representing and ordering spatial differences. Through ever-increasing iterations, Hollywood narrative generates an infinitely expandable social map. It produces and reproduces readily intelligible iconographies of city and country, Occident and Orient, American regions (the West, the South, New England), and a wide range of historical locations (the aristocratic manor on the eve of the French Revolution, the trenches of World War I, the prehistoric jungle, etc.). More importantly, it establishes conventions for transforming any space whatsoever into a space of safety. When love appears as a mutual stare that endures despite separation, a bright, evenly illuminated, simply arranged space will suffice to guarantee it, provided one can be sure that no distracting outside forces remain. The work of Hollywood narrative is to conjure and master this antagonistic outside. To do so, it relies on a differential system of eyeline matches that distinguishes true love from mere admiration, appropriate from inappropriate looks, and socially sanctioned desire from its hazardous and/or naughty counterparts. In the process, it demonstrates who belongs where. It makes particular definitions of race and gender appear to precede filmmaking and bear a self-evident relationship to questions of love and safety. When the white woman returns the loving look of the white man, this seems an inherently desirable arrangement. No matter how self-sufficient and satisfying this look may be, however, the act of seeing cannot possibly produce it. Because the process of spatial division that defines the look of love in the first place also limits that look in space, it takes a spatial transformation to envision resolution. This transformation cannot entirely abolish the differentiation of the visual field; if it did, we would not be able to see the couple safely ensconced in a particular location. Spatial differences can, however, be more or less expertly managed to remove any significant obstruction to the lovers' movement or shared eyeline.

In practice, to tell this story of love required an increasingly complex division of labor. In the period before 1907 or so, skilled individual craftsmen such as Porter can be said to have made American films. They were responsible not only for selecting the subject matter but also for staging, direction, photography, and editing. Between 1907 and 1909, the director acquired a supervisory role apart from that of the cameraman, yet typically continued to stage, script, and edit the films he supervised. Between 1909 and 1917, these separate functions became the province of specialized personnel within a structured hierarchy of departments. Around 1914, the producer emerged as the central supervisor and with him the continuity script. As Janet Staiger points out, this detailed document was designed specifically to facilitate the complex coordination of personnel, equipment, locations, and narrative action required by the feature film. It provided an efficient means by which a producer could oversee planning, shooting, and final assembly as distinct phases of the production process, and it encouraged separation of the functions (if not always the persons) of director and script writer.[51] Increasingly, these jobs, like those of the art director, cinematographer, and editor, were defined as distinct professions. This division of labor eventually proved recognizable to finance capital. Both the feature film and basic division of labor characteristic of the "studio system" were already the norm in 1919 when the investment banking firm of Kuhn, Loeb, and Co. backed a $10 million stock offering for Famous Players–Lasky. With this capital, the studio acquired a chain of theaters and centralized control over the production, distribution, and exhibition of its films, becoming the prototype for the fully integrated corporate studio.[52] Although significant changes to industrial organization have occurred since, on the whole they have modified and developed, rather than fundamentally altered, the functional division of labor developed in the 1910s.[53]

In its essential features, the visual love story precedes the giant filmmaking corporation. Does this mean that it inspired changes in the organization of its production, or did an evolving division of labor ultimately cause films to develop in the way they did? I must side with those who answer such either/or questions about base and superstructure with a confounding "yes." It is possible for a small group of dedicated amateurs to produce a passable approximation of the Hollywood feature, given the time and money to do so. Similarly, ample funding and complex production processes can result in very different forms of cinema. As a matter simply of logical speculation, neither suffices to decide the other. Among film historians, however, the fact that Hollywood's success required the feature film is no more in dispute than the fact that it required a particular division of labor—as an institution, "Hollywood cinema" denotes both. Once we understand that the love story presupposes a noncorporeal narrator, the relationship of mutual implication between narrative form and production hierarchy becomes clear. Because it dissociates the narrative agent from any single point of view, the visual love story must have made it easier to imagine a production process that distributes decisions across a filmmaking team. By the same token, the specialized expertise and hierarchical coordination of this team uniquely qualify it to render the level of spatial complexity this type of story demands. Far from self-evident in the early 1900s, both this form and the division of labor that produces it began to seem inevitable by the mid-1910s, the moment at which U.S. filmmaking may unquestionably be said to have won a national mass viewership.

To understand what widespread moviegoing meant for the nation requires steadfast commitment to the insight that Hollywood's narrative form and its corporate organization entail one another. Although most histories written in the wake of *The Classical Hollywood Cinema* in one way or another acknowledge the relationship, they often tempt us to divorce the two by attributing Hollywood's institutional organization to contemporary business models, just as they attribute its narrative content to antecedent forms and its cinematic qualities to filmmaking technique.[54] To be sure, Hollywood's division of labor participates in the broad shift that separated ownership from control within a multidivisional corporate structure. But this shift occurred neither overnight nor independently from techniques for representing spaces, populations, economies, and institutions. Indeed, professional managerial authority is based on such techniques. This class, we must remember, includes not only businessmen but accountants and engineers, social workers and public relations experts, Ph.D.s and advertising executives. If they share nothing else, this interdisciplinary cast of experts shares the claim to administer on the basis of the training and specialized study—and not on the basis of private wealth, personal political interest, or individual genius. With increasing vigor after the turn of the century, diverse sorts of experts competed and collaborated with one another to provide information that could be judged disinterested and of superior accuracy and to develop organizational models adequate both to large-scale institutions and to the minute supervision of populations. Not all of the forms of representation employed by a rising professional managerial class were new. But all types of managerial endeavor derived authority by claiming a special, and relatively scarce, ability to produce and interpret information.[55] At a sufficiently high level of abstraction, then, cinema ranks alongside the accounting methods, time-motion studies, social research surveys, museums, national advertising campaigns, and opinion polls that allowed teams of professionals to present particular social arrangements as self-evidently desirable and, in the process, to authorize themselves to do the arranging.

Hollywood cinema differs concretely from other sorts of professional representation, however. It appropriates the narrative content through which a property-owning class had defined and generalized its categories of kinship, standards of sexual behavior, and mode of social organization. For more than a century, the Anglo-American novel had represented reciprocal love as the cornerstone of a nuclear family and the nuclear family as a fundamental unit of the modern democratic nation-state.[56] Because it is so clearly heir to this tradition, the visual love story simply cannot be confused with the time-motion study, the museum display, or the magazine ad—although the movies bear some relation to each. When cinema made true love reliant on an agent who represented and manipulated spatial relationships while appearing to remain outside them, it did not simply update standards of sexual propriety and make race, romance, and spatial differences mutually dependent visual structures. It also revised the very nature of the authority to represent the myriad problems of love and lust, honor and duplicity, sincere sensibility and craven calculation that preoccupied state-of-the-art novelistic narrative from Samuel Richardson's epistolary tomes through the abstraction, formal play, and elaborate scrutiny of consciousness in Henry James and Virginia Woolf. In the form of the novel, description of interior states cannot help but raise the possibility that one possessed of such an interior might describe it—even when the ultimate aim is to frustrate that expectation. The movies make the representation of interior qualities every bit as important, dwelling as they do on the most minute alterations of facial expression and posture. Nonetheless, the thoughts and feelings movies represent require an impersonal picturing agent to represent them. Inasmuch as cinema participated in the broad process through which the administrative habits of a rising professional managerial class became the regnant habits, then, it also helped to authorize that class by winning for it the right to define the individual, couple, and family unit through which national culture customarily reproduced itself.

Hollywood made an agent capable of supervising, arranging, and transforming spaces seem the commonsense requirement for securing an America where love could flourish. Whenever we forget the privileged content of its images, we turn a historically new form of mediation back into a mere technology of production or collection of themes. This form opposed the limitations of human vision not to limitlessness or transcendence but to order and expertise. It implied an expansive and complex visual field that no single human could, or should, adequately see, and demonstrated that it could be ordered by a team of largely anonymous experts. Thus, inasmuch as filmmaking institutions took advantage of the legal and economic developments that abetted the corporation, their products provided a profound justification for the extension of professional management into every nook and cranny of American life. To understand just how profoundly cinema's rise altered the authority to represent and order national culture, we need only examine what happened to the category of the public once that category referred to a movie audience.

2. The Public

In modern national cultures, "public" names the realm in which private individuals govern themselves as citizens. To function properly, it must be separate from the state as well as from private business interests and domestic life. At its inception, it required print to mediate its discussions; the circulation of novels and newspapers was prerequisite for the development of a modern public sphere. Numerous accounts of modern publicity have disagreed over the importance of reading relative to spoken debate, just as they have disagreed over the extent to which a public sphere ever served to capture a general social interest. Yet it seems clear that eighteenth- and nineteenth-century bourgeois nation-states made publication in print a hallmark of what it meant to be public and reading an emblem of private contemplation. In this they differed from earlier European cultures in which "public" designated not a social sphere but rather the authority represented by the feudal lord.

The public so conceived is widely felt to have suffered at the hands of American cinema. The movies have had ample detractors, but Jürgen Habermas's 1962 *The Structural Transformation of the Public Sphere* unquestionably defines the argument against the type of public they promote. One of the strengths of this volume is surely its opening observation that "publicity continues to be an organizational principle of our political order" and is "apparently more and other than a mere scrap of liberal ideology that a social democracy could discard without harm."[1] Even so, Habermas tells a narrative of rise and fall. If the public rises with the newspaper-reading disputants of the eighteenth-century English coffee house, it falls when "the public sphere in the world of letters was replaced by the pseudo-public or sham-private world of culture consumption." In the twentieth century, we are told, the culture industry, corporate capital, and a budding social-welfare state maintain the illusions of a public sphere and the privacy on which it depends. At the same time, they dismantle the conditions of possibility for the kind of rational-critical debate supposed to counterbalance government power. "The characteristic relationship of a privacy oriented toward an audience was," Habermas insists, "no longer present when people went to the movies together."[2]

Given this antagonism between cinema audiences and the nation of readers, it should come as no surprise that attempts to reclaim "the public" for twentieth-century criticism tend either to disassociate publicity from print mediation or to demonstrate that new media function in a print-like manner. After *Structural Transformation,* Habermas's own work abandons "the public" in favor of a transhistorical "communicative reason," which favors speech over writing.[3] Others have revised the term "public" to include spheres of experience ignored, marginalized, or designated nonpolitical by national media and thus unable to claim publicity in the bourgeois fashion. The resulting recovery of "alternative" or "counter" public spheres from the eighteenth, nineteenth, and twentieth centuries makes Habermas's historical account look reductive; but it also strengthens its appeal as a description of the dominant trajectory, against which the alternatives are measured.[4] Those who strive to establish a continuity between print's categories and those of visual mass mediation often tell a similar story. Michael Warner, for one, notes a similarity between the bourgeois author's "disincorporated" address to a readership and television's "noncorporeal" address to a viewership. But insofar as print remains the founding model for the public qua public, visual mass media ultimately suffer by the comparison—in Warner's account, they expose contradictions they can no longer mediate effectively and betoken a "refeudalization" of the public sphere.[5] Thus, late-twentieth-century scholarship leaves us with better reason than ever to believe that the once-dominant public sphere has been faked, "degraded," "sanitized," or simply fractured, in the age of mass produced and circulated visual narrative.

By argument and implication, Hollywood's efficacy in subverting the world of print is firmly established by these accounts. Yet its plan of attack remains ambiguous. Even if we accept the proposition that visual mass culture produced an ersatz copy of the eighteenth-century public or reversed the course of history through a refeudalization of the public sphere, this still leaves open the question of why twentieth-century capitalism, and particularly its American manifestation, required such a development. Ever-increasing commodification and bureaucratization do not, in and of themselves, explain why such a radical transformation of the public would be necessary. As Habermas observes and such scholars as Benedict Anderson further demonstrate, the "print capitalism" of eighteenth-century nations was commodified from the outset.[6] Likewise, a specifically bourgeois public sphere had everything to do with the establishment of governmental structures in which bureaucracy could thrive. Indeed, until its final chapters Habermas's narrative of structural transformation aims to describe shifts in the status and function of the public sphere as bureaucracies develop and increasingly commercial newspapers expand their circulation. Finally, narratives of the decline or disappearance of "the public" have difficulty explaining why so many late-twentieth-century commentators continue to feel that "a qualified but steadfast commitment to the concept" is something that "any supporter of democracy *must* share."[7] An explanation of why the public persists as more than "mere ideology" after the demise of its classic, eighteenth-century version requires a positive account of how the twentieth century reinvented the private-public distinction.

The rise of the feature film made it possible to conceive the spectator as an entity akin to the reader. Indeed, the very concept of a "spectator" may be attributed to the type of address the visual love story entails. The term itself began to describe moviegoers around 1910. Before this moment, a film "audience" designated a group that might be further characterized by occupation, gender, or social status. After it, the audience comprised a film's diverse individual addressees.[8] Shown in venues ranging from commercial theaters to museums, churches, and traveling tent shows, early motion pictures were elements of locally variable, heterogeneous presentations. Exhibitors selected and sometimes reedited short films, supplied the music and lecture that accompanied them, and decided their placement in programs that typically included other kinds of entertainment. These showmen continued to shape film presentation during the nickelodeon period (1905–1909), and the exhibitor retained an important role throughout the silent feature film era.[9] But longer and more complex film narratives began to stand alone in their address to viewers, even when part of a program that included other attractions.[10] The movie theater, which might be owned and managed by the same corporation that produced the film, became the standard exhibition venue.[11] Whereas the precise class, gender, and racial makeup of audiences for film before 1910 was (and is) a matter of some dispute, by the mid-1910s "the movies" plainly appealed to a heterogeneous mass audience.[12] National newspapers and magazines began to address readers as if they were moviegoers. And writers ranging from gossip columnists to sociologists frequently defined cinema in contrast to verbal language as a "universal language" that, paradoxically, was also supremely American.[13] In sum, these developments established the motion-picture spectator as a universalizable abstraction, one that referred both to a large number of different individuals and to their common participation in a national audience.

Had cinema merely replicated print's functional capacity to mediate a citizenry, we might take claims that it degraded that public at face value. But cinema also redefined the categories through which the public could be understood. When movies appropriated the stories of love and romance that novels had told, they made privacy visible in the reciprocal stare of their lovers. As a matter of sightlines necessarily limited to a particular sort of space, privacy needed an impersonal expertise outside of the frame to know and safeguard it. The private individual so depicted could not hope to address the public as a disembodied consciousness after the fashion of bourgeois fiction. In place of private verbal expression oriented toward a reading public, the movies established a qualitative visual difference between the public and the mass; the difference between (good) privacy and (bad) alienation was shown to correspond to this difference. To establish that correspondence required the ability to represent social space as if from outside it. By making such a vantage seem both possible and necessary, then, Hollywood promoted a kind of authority that did not need to declare its self-interest in order to seem reasonable. Indeed, to do so would jeopardize its claim to represent diverse private interests that, by definition, could not adequately represent themselves. When they redefined how the public looked and what it took to see it, the movies gave American democracy a professional shape.

Accordingly, cinema's rise encouraged a new kind of argument about the public. This argument proved exceptionally useful to the wide range of bureaucrats, sociologists, statisticians, public-relations experts, and market researchers, who claimed the authority to objectify the public, to distinguish it from the mass, and to "influence" it through information they produced and distributed. Its defining theoretical statement, however, is the 1920s debate between American intellectuals Walter Lippmann and John Dewey.[14] In stark contrast to similar work published as little as a decade before, Lippmann and Dewey demonstrated both that the public could not function as a community of private readers and that signs and symbols constitute it as such. With this two-fold contention, representation emerged as a principle actor in the performance of rule. Concern with how it might be controlled—and who might control it—displaced an earlier set of concerns with literacy, self-representation, and minority interests. Lippmann and Dewey embraced the view that expert control over representation would serve the public good, but unlike most of their contemporaries they took full cognizance of the degree to which this proposition vitiated the logic of eighteenth- and nineteenth-century liberalism. Each strove, albeit in different ways, to provide an account of how democracy might be possible under those circumstances. In the process, their debate raised the very issues that have preoccupied critics of modern democracy ever since. Like the cinema itself, then, the Lippmann-Dewey debate is less a symptom of the public sphere's collapse than a major event in that category's history. Partly in response to the rising feature film, the debate theorized the type of society it mediates. To understand this argument as a theory of an emerging professional public that was also a movie audience, however, we must first consider how the visual love story itself revised the category of "the public" and redefined what it meant to rule in its name.

THE CROWD

King Vidor's 1928 classic *The Crowd* offers a condensed visual representation of the relationship among public, private, and mass that Hollywood cinema establishes.[15] At first, the film seems preoccupied with the public's other, "the masses," which we see in scenes that set the individual at odds with his fellow man. In one of silent cinema's most famous sequences, the camera moves up the side of a skyscraper, through a window, and into a vast room filled with men bent over identical desks. The desks constitute an orderly grid, with the empty space around each demarcating a seemingly endless series of isolated workers engaged in identical, repetitive tasks. Positioned high above this grid, the camera moves diagonally across it, then slows and moves down toward the protagonist, John Sims (James Murray). Set against a backdrop of hunched regimentation, his figure violates the grid in every dimension. His torso rises through the plane of labor. An elbow juts into space. Eyes look out of frame toward an indeterminate space of contemplation and, moments later, turn to stare in anticipation at a clock that presides over the room. Even the ledger on his desk is askew. Although the vectors implied by John's gestures cut across the grid, its order and authority remain visible in the bent figures and downcast eyes of his coworkers in the background. The masses of men live by the right-angle. Our hero inhabits the diagonal.

By the time *The Crowd* arrives at its final scene, we are well prepared for a movement that rectifies this geometry of alienation. The camera draws away from John and his family in order to place them among a vast theater audience. Another grid is revealed. Each seat demarcates a subdivision of the larger space, an imaginary box within which each body moves. Unlike its dehumanized counterpart, this arrangement does not seem to require regimentation. Men, women, and children spill over grid lines in laughter. One leans back to slap his thigh, for example, and another holds her stomach and bends forward. The proximity of the seats also encourages a breaching of barriers, as when John befriends the man next to him. This spatial arrangement tolerates, even encourages, the sort of gestures that the office images present as distracted and insubordinate. Most importantly, this organization of space permits the exchange of looks. At work, uniform stares downward toward hundreds of desktop ledgers defined John's glances as a violation of workplace discipline. Here members of the audience turn to look at one another within and across the frame, and these shared looks indicate a beneficently undisciplined space.

Although they present a striking contrast to the well-disciplined office, images of the audience are not without their own principles of order. The camera moves directly up and away from the couple to reveal their position in the larger grid. No need for a diagonal movement to pinpoint the individual amid the mass—we are assured that were the camera to move in again toward any part of this image, it could locate a personal story similar to the one just told. The sequence suggests that John finally fits in, even as it places him in a different kind of crowd. Conversely, it also suggests that the mass audience is composed of a great many individuals who share the disappointments and aspirations that identify John as an ordinary guy. In this way, *The Crowd* annuls the opposition between individual and mass with which it began. By transforming the crowd into a voluntary gathering of private individuals, in a sphere of activity irreducible to government or paid labor, the film visualizes a public.

This demonstration requires a third kind of space in order to assure us that John is indeed a private man. *The Crowd* establishes a direct, visual relationship between the theater audience and a domestic interior. To begin the theater scene, an image of John with his wife and son in their home slowly dissolves into a similar image of the family amid the audience. Because the second image preserves the relative size and position of each figure, it appears that the family has been magically transported from one space to another and continues to exist as such, even after merging with the larger audience. It may seem self-evident that the home is a private space, and the theater, a public one. But the category of private space does not really exist for the film apart from the figures who inhabit it. Nor is it simply a matter of grouping mommy, daddy, and junior together in a single frame. It takes a particular arrangement of the lovers' eyes and faces both to let us know that they share an intense emotional bond and to define the space they share as an oasis of privacy. Before it withdraws, the camera lingers on the faces of John and Mary (Eleanor Boardman) as they look soulfully into each other's eyes. The good, public grid solves the problem presented by the bad, office grid precisely because the lovers' shared look has the power to designate the persistence of the private within the crowd.

The lovers' mutual gaze acquired its conventional quality through the decades of American filmmaking that precede Vidor's film. Even so, *The Crowd* is meticulous in its demonstration of what it takes to establish and secure this shared look. At first, the crowd that brings John and Mary together also inhibits their union. In long shot, a downtown office building disgorges a steady stream of women, while a line of men waits on the sidewalk opposite. One by one, the couples pair off and leave the frame. Viewed as an enlargement of this mechanical process, the images that render John and Mary's first meeting prefigure their destiny in a lingering look, which is nonetheless interrupted by the relentless movement of their companions. A later scene onboard the train that carries the newlyweds to their honeymoon spot further demonstrates that isolation will be necessary for a sustained, mutual gaze to occur. John lurches from one side of a curtained aisle to the other, disrupting unsuspecting strangers in his search for the compartment he shares with Mary. The repetition of identical bedroom units separated from the aisle and from each other by all-too-flimsy dividers makes privacy impossible. Even in his proper compartment, John remains an interloper. Luggage rains down upon him as he clambers into bed, and the film never allows his look to meet Mary's—it does not even let us see them together in the same frame. This sequence demonstrates that the couple cannot be truly together in this kind of space, which makes it impossible for them to be left alone and puts them in a comic state of peril.

Images of the couple against the backdrop of Niagara Falls tell a different story in the next scene. Unlike the cramped and confusing train, here nothing threatens to fall on their heads or accidentally to intrude upon them. A luminous close-up of the newlyweds together at last establishes this as the kind of space where love can flourish. Understood according to the visual conventions of American filmmaking, the crucial difference between the falls and the train is not really that between "nature" and "culture"—as it might be in another narrative form. The difference, rather, is a function of the illumination and arrangement of the mise-en-scène. Unlike the train compartment, this is a clean, bright, simply arranged space that includes the lovers' unimpeded gaze. Through such images, the film sets in place the features that will allow it to bring the space of privacy inside.

The scene at the falls relies on a conventional difference between the partners. John's repeated declarations of love (conveyed by intertitles) might seem to make him the more demonstrative one. But Mary's face decides the course of the scene and the film. A series of brightly illuminated close-ups invests her visage with a special value, and the sequence in which they are placed underscores the enhanced visuality of her face: it shows John photographing her. We watch Mary pose to become the conventionally beautiful image, while John's look in return is rendered metonymically as the camera's, seen in extreme close-up at the moment the shutter clicks. Having distinguished Mary's face from John's according to its photographability, *The Crowd* exploits the iconic status of this face by closing her eyes at the moment of rapture. The very conventions that make the woman's face legible as a locus of beauty and feeling encourage us to examine her face more closely and thereby imply more to see in her image than in his. In their difference from John's, Mary's closed eyes present a problem of knowledge and pleasure: the viewer is to assume that something profound and intriguing—something of great value—is being withheld.

The scene at the falls, then, makes the lovers' isolation in the frame equivalent to privacy in an emotional as well as a physical sense. It implies an emotional depth, a metaphysical connection that will endure despite separation and adversity. Accordingly, the couple's later troubles take the form of a series of ruptures and reconciliations of this look, as disputes of domestic life are measured against its idealized image. While these scenes repeatedly test Mary's devotion, the constancy of John's is never really placed in doubt. Tellingly, the penultimate scene hinges on Mary's love. Finally renouncing husband and home in a moment of frustration, she leaves the house only to reverse course on the front steps. The subsequent reconnection of their look indicates their reunion and allows the film to produce an image of the happy family, sitting together in their now stable home.

This home is a private space, yet the film insists that home and family neither guarantee privacy nor are its source in the manner of an eighteenth- or nineteenth-century domestic sphere. It takes repeated close-ups of the heroine's face to produce something equivalent to that earlier form of privacy. Through their scale, composition, and use of lighting, such images imply a precious and complex interior behind the heroine's bright eyes. This interior is the source of love, but not the source of language. In fact, by contrasting John's verbosity with Mary's look of bliss, the film demonstrates that love is deepest when it eludes verbal representation. In this manner, films recast the modern subject in visual terms.

Such a revision of privacy could hardly leave the category of the public entirely unchanged; the two are mutually defining. By locating privacy in the lovers' shared look, and transporting that look from Niagara Falls to the home and then to the theater, *The Crowd* indicates the persistence of private thoughts and feelings within the public audience. In the process, differences of kind become differences of scale. Just as a certain closeness reveals the private, so too is a certain distance required to see the public. The diagonal track down and in shows us an anomalous individual amid a homogeneous mass. The movement up and away places the couple amid similar but not identical individuals, in order to provide a picture of the public. "The private" retains its long association with domestic space, but, insofar as it is lodged in the faces of the lovers, it can be made visible anywhere the conditions for this look may be found. By the same token, "the public" retains its association with non-official and nondomestic spaces, but it must be seen in long shots that both recall and differ from those showing us the mass. Consequently, a rift opens between the public and its image, which now requires a vantage point outside and above it in order to reveal that the private abides within it. The image of the public requires an external vantage point to show us that it includes the private and thus is, in fact, a public and not a mass. This is not a public composed of individuals who are, even hypothetically, capable of representing themselves as such.

The Crowd indicates that a comparable gulf separates the film's viewers from its producers. To achieve visibility, the public must be seen from a particular vantage, according to certain principles of arrangement, and as a consequence of certain transformations of the visual field. Insofar as it takes a movie to provide this vantage point, "the public" as a category comes to depend on a complex apparatus that shows us the world in a way no embodied human could have seen it. No ordinary individual, or even a set of such individuals acting in concert, could resolve John and Mary's spatial dilemmas. It requires not merely an extensive technical apparatus (cameras, lighting, cranes, etc.), but also the labor of scores of writers, artists, technicians, and managers: a professional hierarchy.

By 1928, the myriad procedures of industrial filmmaking present a cipher to the nonspecialist viewer; that is, the procedures themselves are made obscure by the discourse that loudly proclaims their existence. Something of the author persists, of course, in legends of directors and stars. *The New York Times,* for instance, reports that director Vidor is making *The Crowd* "as a play is made."[16] Similarly, the paper casts the film's director of photography, Henry Sharp, as an author of sorts. It compares Sharp to Rembrandt, whose paintings in the Metropolitan Museum had apparently captivated him while on location in New York

City. Sharp's use of the "widest angle lens ever used in motion picture work" thus ranks alongside Rembrandt's use of "one positive light scale" as an artistic achievement.[17] Yet in making Sharp an artist, the *Times* also makes him an expert manager of technologies and men; we learn that "Sharp's contingent"—his camera crew—is engaged in tasks too technically complex to be readily explained. Such comparisons of author and filmmaker encouraged audiences to appreciate the contributions of individual members of the filmmaking team and to look for traces of their work in the finished product. At the same time, articles like these called attention to the difference between the individual's contribution and the narrative vantage point exemplified by the finished film. The juxtaposition of the pieces on Vidor and Sharp indicates a familiar reciprocity between filmmaking technology and the hierarchy of experts who manipulate it. The articles reveal the film to be the product of no one individual, but rather of an aggregate team effort bound together by an elusive technical expertise. In this way the *Times* confirms for its reader a fact readily apparent to the spectator: neither the camera alone nor any single person, no matter how gifted, can show the city and its inhabitants as *The Crowd* does.[18]

The Crowd both exemplifies and visually explains how the rise of the American feature film redefined an earlier category of the public. In a print culture, to be a citizen and author in the public sphere entailed an abstract individuality neither dissociable from the private person nor identical with that person. This abstract individuality enabled the author to speak to and on behalf of the many distant members of the public who were thought to enjoy a similar relationship between the public conversation and private contemplation. Cinema destroys the ideological reciprocity that joined reader and author, Man and Citizen. Having displaced the individual as the work's apparent origin, the movies can hardly mediate a relation akin to that of an author to a readership. As *The Crowd* clearly shows, participation in a public is a matter of an individual's relationship to a larger image. To "see oneself" as part of a viewership is, strictly speaking, a contradiction in terms: no individual can actually look at a visual field in which he or she happens to be embedded from a position outside and above it. The "private" person is identical with the "public" one. The image admits no possibility of an abstract self capable of speaking on the public's behalf in the manner of the bourgeois author. Instead, it posits two kinds of groups: the mass, from which John appears alienated, and the public, where he "fits in." These groups must be contrasted, but they pose no contradiction in visual terms. What might otherwise appear to be the mass, when seen correctly, turns out to be the public.

Hollywood accomplishes this transformation by redefining the private as that which eludes verbal representation and can only be seen in the reciprocal look shared by a man and woman in love. Images of privacy can then be manipulated to show that the mass has become a public. Thus, the authority to designate the difference between mass and public displaces the authority to address private readers as a public author. For a cinematic culture, then, questions of the relative health, safety, and happiness of the public take precedence over questions of who speaks for it. Experts speak about it. Expertise is not something they possess as individuals. It does not stand in the same relationship to privacy as the author's discourse. Nor does this expertise address viewers as if they were members of a public. The abstract entity it addresses is society in general, of which publicity is one state or condition. Where print encourages an imaginative relationship among a reader, an author, and many other readers, cinema asks its viewers to imagine their relation to the real in spatial terms, as embeddedness in a social space that they can neither see nor understand without expert assistance.

In picturing the new public, then, *The Crowd* helped to produce it. Released at the end of the silent era, it may be placed in a long line of films that distinguish the couple from the crowd precisely in order to redefine the larger group. True, most of these films do not end with images of the private family happily lodged within a public. Sometimes the placement of the couple amid the mass redefines it as a public but kills the couple—as it does in *The Scarlet Letter* (MGM, 1926). More often, movies redefine the crowd as nonthreatening and then situate the private couple elsewhere, as is the case in *The Birth of a Nation* (Epoch, 1915), *Orphans of the Storm* (United Artists, 1921), and *Sunrise* (Fox, 1927). And indeed, MGM distributed *The Crowd* with just such an alternative ending, which apparently showed the happy family grouped around a Christmas tree. Vidor claims of this ending that "I never heard of it being shown—it was so false, so ridiculous that I'm sure no exhibitor with an ounce of intelligence would ever run it."[19] The integrity of the film does reside in the explicitness with which it represents the mass as alienating and the public and private as contingent upon one another.

The similarity it draws between those two sorts of relationships, further-more, accounts for the observation that film's ending is an ambivalent one.[20] But the fundamentals of my argument would not be altered had the studio succeeded in promulgating its preferred conclusion. Cinema made it possible to see the difference between public and private as one of scale. Thus, it made each dependent on a kind of expertise that could designate their relation. The particular ending I have been describing is an exceptionally clear, but hardly unique, instance of this characteristic visual strategy. According to the terms Hollywood's images established, qualitative assessments of the public's security, disposition, and, in par-ticular, difference from the mass, displaced concern with its authority or capacity to rule. There could be no question of a public "delegating" its authority to the expertise required to objectify it in the first place.[21]

THE PROBLEM WITH PRINT

Once constituted as a cinema audience, the national public had to be described in new terms. Discussions of democracy began to abandon the presupposition that publicity could function on the model of an extend-ed conversation among a community of citizen-readers. No argument makes more plain the extent of the shift than the 1920s debate between Walter Lippmann and John Dewey. The debate began in 1922 with Lipp-mann's *Public Opinion,* which Dewey reviewed favorably but critical-ly in the *New Republic*.[22] It continued through Lippmann's *Phantom Public* in 1925, which Dewey reviewed somewhat less favorably (again in the *New Republic*).[23] And it wound up with Dewey's 1927 book-length rejoinder *The Public and Its Problems*.[24] Intellectual and social histori-ans typically place the debate in the context of American pragmatism and Progressivism and reveal that Lippmann and Dewey advocated ef-ficiency, scientific management, and expanded state authority.[25] Some cast both as "technocratic" supporters of a new corporate order (e.g., Lears), while others see the debate as an indictment of that order, and seek to declare a winner (e.g., West).[26] Still others (e.g., Aronowitz) at-tempt to subsume the debate to a tradition of American liberalism that runs back to Jefferson—a connection that Lippmann and Dewey were each at pains to refute.[27] While there are important differences between the two, Lippmann and Dewey both attack the concept of the public provided by eighteenth- and nineteenth-century political economy and philosophy. Each seeks to develop an alternative model for democratic rule more adequate to the complexities of "modern civilization." What animates the debate, however, and makes it a watershed in American letters, is the new way in which Lippmann and Dewey pose the problem of mediation.

The Lippmann-Dewey debate effectively displaced the set of concerns about print that had preoccupied nineteenth-century liberal critiques of democracy from Alexis de Tocqueville and John Stuart Mill through James Bryce and Graham Wallas. These commentators conceived the newspaper as an instrument for disseminating the information that citizens required to rule themselves. Accordingly, their criticisms focused on the accessibility of print, literacy, censorship, the degree to which publishers made their own interests plain, and the extent to which the press as a whole represented diverging interests, particularly those of political minorities. Concern with these problems kept pace with an ever-increasing volume of print during the nineteenth century. The well-read citizen faces a far greater challenge, for instance, in Wallas's 1915 *Great Society* than he does in Tocqueville's 1835 *Democracy in America*. With the Lippmann-Dewey debate, in contrast, the citizen-reader becomes an impossibility—and not only because the quantity of reading material finally overwhelms him. Lippmann and Dewey understood that mass-produced and circulated information has a constitutive function; it forms the very public the prior model supposed it to inform and persuade. With this insight, the newspaper becomes a technology for rule not by its readership, but by those with the authority to shape the information.

Walter Lippmann begins *Public Opinion* by making a distinction between the "world outside" and the "pictures in our heads." Initially, he explains the difference as a problem of spatial and temporal distance. Since we cannot know distant events immediately, but rather depend on the circulation of information about them, there is always a variance between our real "environment" and what we know of it (which Lippmann calls our "pseudo-environment"). This problem of distance turns out to be a manifestation of a more fundamental separation. Organized by powerful "codes," "symbols," and "stereotypes," the pseudo-environment determines our perceptions: "For the most part we do not first see, and then define, we define first and then see."[28] Without such organization, the world would be unintelligible; it is far too large and complex to be directly apprehended. Thus, the difference between environment and pseudo-environment is not the sort that can be overcome, even by direct encounters with events. While particular stereotypes (categories) may be changed, lose relevance, or even be newly created, stereotyping itself cannot be obliterated. When we act in the world, we always do so based on knowledge of a pseudo-environment. At best, one can hope to take the "degree of fidelity" of the pseudo-environment into account.[29]

This epistemology undermines the theory of the individual on which traditional accounts of the democratic state had been based. Perhaps most radically, it renders all opinion "public," by insisting that cultural processes determine individual thoughts and feelings. Whereas traditional democratic theory posited an individual whose more or less rational private meditations could be considered the basis of his public opinions, Lippmann redefines individual opinion as an effect of social circumstances and psychic history. He explains that members of an audience invariably give "stories" "their own character" and provides a long list of factors affecting the "character they give it": "sex and age, race and religion and social position" and "within these cruder classifications . . . the inherited and acquired constitution of the individual, his faculties, his career," and so on. Yet these determinations are largely invisible to the hypothetical audience member and leave unconscious residues he cannot readily apprehend:

> He does not take his personal problems as partial samples of the greater environment. He takes his stories of the greater environment as a mimic enlargement of his private life.
>
> *But not necessarily of that private life as he would describe it to himself.* For in his private life the choices are narrow, and much of himself is squeezed down and out of sight where it cannot directly govern his outward behavior.[30]

Just as he cannot know the world outside, the individual cannot know the impulses that determine, however indirectly, his thoughts and feelings. Only sociology and psychology can unravel the determinations that make an individual. In the absence of such science, the individual has no way of understanding his own constitution by the very field of information he would evaluate. And in the absence of such understanding, the most straightforward repetition of a prevailing stereotype can pass for his personal judgment on "the facts." Hence, public opinion is not "a moral judgment on a group of facts" but "a moralized and codified version of the facts."[31] Our opinions appear to be our own because self and opinion derive from the same signs. There simply is no private self apart from public representation, anterior to the stereotype, who might therefore contemplate and adjudicate it.

"Private opinion," then, merely designates those public (because socially determined) opinions an individual does not widely share because they are ruled out of bounds by certain kinds of discourse. In this respect, privacy may be considered a kind of censorship, and "private" a social category like any other.[32] On the other hand, "private" retains a psychological connotation. Beneath or behind our multiple conscious selves lurks an unknowable, though perhaps unifying, unconscious.[33] In neither sense, however, can the private be considered the basis of public opinion and the kind of state it is supposed to rule. "And so," Lippmann sums up, "while it is so true as to be mere tautology that 'self-interest' determines opinion, the statement is not illuminating, until we know which self out of many selects and directs the interest so conceived."[34] By insisting that the individual is culturally defined rather than defining, Lippmann effectively pulls the linchpin from accounts of the democratic state that credit the deliberations of private individuals with the formation of a common will.[35]

If all opinion is "public" because socially constituted, Lippmann needs another name for "those pictures which are acted upon by groups of people, or by individuals acting in the name of groups." He provides one by capitalizing "Public Opinion."[36] In contrast to those who would attribute this Opinion to a popular will, Lippmann explains its production through the skillful manipulation of representation. Political leaders use symbols to organize as many disparate beliefs as possible and thereby to secure the consent or approval of the governed. They do so only when and to the degree necessary for a particular task. In the process, they frame choices so as to exclude from discussion matters thought to be divisive, to present issues in terms of abstractions that capture the widest possible interest, and to admit only a "yes" or "no" response. The "will of the people" does not precede its representation and is not the basis of rule in America, but rather is itself a stereotype manufactured by political discourse.[37]

The stereotype of national will has been fundamental to American rule from the outset, Lippmann argues. He identifies Jefferson as the one who "first taught the American people to regard the Constitution as an instrument of democracy" and "stereotyped the images, the ideas, and even many of the phrases, in which Americans ever since have described politics to each other."[38] The Jeffersonian model requires us to imagine America as an "isolated rural township." Only in this way is it possible to maintain the fiction of an "omnicompetent citizen" who could know all he needed to know about himself, his neighbors, and his world and could elect his representatives accordingly. Even in Jefferson's day, however, this agrarian idealization depended on holding the real environment at bay; one had to wear "glasses that obliterated the slaves."[39] With Jackson and the rise of the party system, the party leadership relied on Jeffersonian stereotypes to give popular legitimacy to their decisions. They thereby ensured elite control despite a series of democratic reforms. Short terms of office, the extension of the franchise, party control over the electoral college, and the like may be regarded as progressive improvements to the mechanics of government, but insofar as reform fails take the control and circulation of information into account, it only further binds the expanded electorate to a specialized ruling class. Lippmann blames this failure on what he considers a general notion among eighteenth-century thinkers, namely, that "Men took in their facts as they took in their breath."[40] Thus, "democratic theory by failing to admit that self-centered opinions are not sufficient to procure good government, is involved in a perpetual conflict between theory and practice."[41] Knowingly or not, American government has from its inception mystified the actual process of rule in a twofold maneuver: it pretends that it has consulted an Opinion that it has largely manufactured, and it conceals, even from itself, the process whereby its own official opinions are generated.

Once he has described the mechanics of Public Opinion in this manner, Lippmann critiques—even mocks—the very notion that the press might allow the public to counterbalance, let alone direct, its representation. Through three chapters, he explains the social and economic reasons why the press tends to confirm preexisting stereotypes. For one, the newspaper reader has neither the time nor the resources to judge the accuracy of its information, even if so inclined (and, Lippmann observes, most of us are not). For another, the economic imperative to sell newspapers well below cost requires the support of advertisers, which in turn obliges editors to present news in ways amenable to their readership in order to guarantee a circulation. Lippmann's overarching critique, however, targets the expectation that the press will enlighten the public simply on the basis of unrestricted reporting. He poses Milton's question, "Who ever knew Truth put to the worse in a free and open encounter?" in order to reply, "Supposing that no one has ever seen it put to the worse, are we to believe then that truth is generated by the encounter, like fire by rubbing two sticks?"[42] Clearly not. The notion that unrestricted publication will necessarily enlighten Public Opinion, he explains, has been a key feature of the prevailing stereotype of democracy. Nonetheless, because newspapers discourage analysis of the dissemination, contingency, and control of information, their readers can neither be expected to know their own interest nor be said to govern themselves.

Accordingly, Lippmann sees hope for American democracy in an expertise capable of challenging and revising stereotypes. He envisions a network of "intelligence bureaus" charged with the collection and dissemination of information at every level of government—indeed, in every industry and social agency. Staffed by experts, these bureaus are to be as independent as possible from political and economic interests and thus serve public ones. Such independence is part of the definition of expertise, for "the power of the expert depends upon separating himself from those who make the decisions, upon not caring, in his expert self, what decision is made."[43] Once he becomes a partisan, the expert's facts can no longer be trusted. Although Lippmann occasionally writes as if scientific expertise could give us a world free from stereotypes, he does not mean by "science" a kind of discourse that would transparently render the "real environment" as a series of facts. Scientific information is not inherently stereotype free. The advantage of science is its process, its "perfectly self-conscious use of a schematic model."[44] Because the fictionalization of world is inevitable, science works to apprehend the efficacy and mutability of this fictionalization.[45]

The claim that democracy will be best served by the professional managerial class thus begs a question: what guarantees that "impartial" expertise will be in the public interest? According to Lippmann, "the practice of democracy" is already "ahead of its theory." He praises a number of government agencies (including the Bureau of Internal Revenue) for providing statistical representations of "persons, ideas, and objects" that would otherwise remain invisible to the government and the electorate. For example,

The Children's Bureau [est. 1912] is the spokesman of a whole complex of interests and functions not ordinarily visible to the voter, and, therefore, incapable of becoming spontaneously part of his public opinions. Thus the printing of comparative statistics of infant mortality is often followed by a reduction of the death rates of babies. Municipal officials and voters did not have, before publication, a place in their picture of the environment for those babies. The statistics made them visible, as visible as if the babies had elected an alderman to air their grievances.[46]

Here Lippmann uses the rhetoric of electoral representation to describe an altogether different technique of rule. The statistics confer upon those claiming to act on behalf of the babies an authority the babies themselves can never have. The choice of example is telling. It would be absurd to ask "the babies" what interest they might have in the matter. At the same time, the public interest seems clear. Who would dare describe infant mortality as a public good? The statistics thus appear to be a neutral field of information enabling officials to see and to make the proper choices; the mere printing of death rates precipitates their reduction. Had Lippmann made plain the authority of this information by mentioning the mechanisms of that reduction (regulations, educational campaigns, and so on) and their real targets (mothers) he might have strained the rhetoric of spokesmanship.[47] To propose unqualified rule by experts would be to invalidate the basis of that rule, namely, the claim to have impartially discovered the common good. Yet the common good so discovered is, by definition, not something the electorate itself can know or adjudicate in a deliberative fashion; to be known, it requires expertise. In effect, Lippmann conducts a critique of Public Opinion in order to redefine the public as something only experts may discover. The electorate cannot represent its own interest, but representative government will be served by an expertise that purports to do so.[48]

John Dewey's disagreement with Lippmann begins with a critique of the elitism this commitment to expertise implies. His review celebrates *Public Opinion* as "perhaps the most effective indictment of democracy as currently conceived ever penned" and particularly approves Lippmann's facility with philosophical and social-scientific argumentation.[49] Nonetheless, Dewey suggests that Lippmann wrongly casts government as the seat of all social regulation and for this reason leaves himself with no way to imagine the regulation of the state by the governed.

Thus, Lippmann has made a critique of democracy that overwhelms the reformist solution he offers. Dewey writes that Lippmann's "argument seems to me to exaggerate the importance of politics and political action, and also to evade the problem of how the latter is to be effectively directed by organized intelligence unless there is an accompanying direct enlightenment of popular opinion, as well as an ex post facto indirect instruction." While "the expert organization for which Mr. Lippmann calls is inherently desirable," it will not be adequate to the task without a "fundamental general education."[50] Where Lippmann calls for the professionalization of democracy, then, Dewey weighs in for the democratization of expertise.

Dewey elaborates this position in his 1927 book *The Public and Its Problems*. The volume acknowledges a debt to Lippmann "for ideas involved in my entire discussion even when it reaches conclusions diverging from his."[51] Nonetheless, without directly refuting him, Dewey accuses Lippmann of a fundamental conceptual error. It is incorrect, he insists, to collapse "the public" into "the social." He clearly agrees with Lippmann's critique of theories of "the public" that understand private opinion both as individual opinion and as the basis of public authority. Even more emphatically than Lippmann, he insists that shared "signs" and "symbols" constitute the public as such. But where this insight leads Lippmann to dismiss the private-public distinction altogether, it allows Dewey to describe private and public as different modes of "communication" and to proposes public communication of a sort that has yet to emerge as the mechanism for truly democratic regulation.

An examination of how Dewey makes this argument immediately corrects the impression left by some scholarship that he "defends" a preexisting democratic tradition. A practiced lecturer on political philosophy, Dewey develops his argument in contradistinction to the pre-social individual imagined by the social-contract theory of the eighteenth century and the nineteenth-century liberalism that amended it.[52] Ridiculing the opposition of "individuals" to "society" and the premise of natural or prepolitical rights, Dewey begins instead with the premise that humans are social creatures: "There is no sense in asking how individuals come to be associated. They exist and operate in association. If there is any mystery about the matter, it is the mystery that the universe is the kind of universe it is. Such a mystery could not be explained without going outside the universe."[53] Thus, the "problem of the relation of individuals to associations—sometimes posed as the relation of *the* individual to society—is a meaningless one."[54] There is no "why" to human association; it is. The only meaningful questions concern the kinds of associations that exists, and such questions cannot be separated from how the members of a group describe, or fail to describe, their relations with one another.

Accordingly, Dewey's account of the state does away with the problem of an abstract individual's relationship to the sovereign and the "common good." Rather than positing an original cause such as a "general will" or fictitious contract, Dewey insists that the many concrete decisions that already social persons make under historically contingent circumstances give the state its form. The development of a new state is a question not of "authorship," but of "authority." The "public" neither founds nor follows government, but emerges alongside it. To explain how, Dewey distinguishes "public" and "private" as ways of describing interpersonal "transactions" (a category of action that includes the exchange of signs). Transactions having consequences for only those involved in them are "private"; those affecting "others beyond those immediately concerned" are, in a loose sense, "public." This distinction merely gives "the germ of the distinction between the private and the public," however, because the public only recognizes itself as such once it begins to regulate the indirect consequences of its members' actions. To illustrate, Dewey rewrites the passage from the "state of war" to "civil society" celebrated by theorists of the social contract. Rather than individuals, warring families are the protagonists of his tale, in which a Hatfield-and-McCoy type of violence gives way to the recognition that both clans would be better off if the indirect consequences of their members' actions were regulated. Before this hypothetical moment, the public exists but is unformed. While the indirect consequences of some transaction between an ancestral Hatfield and an equally venerable McCoy are serious and durable, the feuding parties do not behave as though they all belong to the group of persons so affected. This changes once they begin to regulate their actions. The public becomes a public for itself once regulation shapes its activity. Thus, the same movement that establishes the coherence of the public inaugurates the state and its government.[55]

To properly theorize the state, Dewey insists, one must grasp the dialectic whereby a public in itself becomes a public for itself (a state) by establishing regulative functions (a government). This distinction provides

Dewey's answer to the problem of popular rule posed by Lippmann's critique.[56] He theorizes that all government is "representative" in the sense that its officials are members of the society who have been granted "special powers" to administer public affairs (the indirect consequences of transactions between persons). Of course, such officials may do their jobs poorly by acting on behalf of private interests. Here, as in Lippmann, such private interest could only be a factional social interest, since the individual does not precede the group.[57] But because Dewey has theorized the public as the shared interest that defines the state, he can give the term a positive value it lacks for Lippmann, who, in Dewey's terms, collapses the state into the government when he depicts the (lower case) public's domination by the elites who define Public Opinion. For Dewey, such a society remains "private," effectively stateless. To describe modern democratic nations in these terms, he follows Marx in emphasizing the kinship between the "natural" individual of bourgeois social theory and the "private property" and "economic laws" naturalized by bourgeois political economy (i.e., Adam Smith). By appearing to place the economic outside the social, individualism instituted a phobia about "state interference" in the economic realm. This fundamentally slanted the development of democratic government in favor of "the new class of business men," thwarting the development of a true public.[58] In the twentieth century, he writes, "The democratic public is still largely inchoate and unorganized."[59] Thus, where Lippmann renders the public interest unknowable by the public—and hence suspects the term—Dewey's account makes this interest merely unknown so long as the public remains a public in itself but not for itself.

Dewey sustains this argument only by strongly distinguishing actually existing democracy from its ideal. True, he claims to discern an overarching historical tendency toward representative government—the organization of governments to ensure the "dominance" of the "public weal."[60] Nonetheless, he insists that governments are not "democratic" by virtue of their institutions or procedures. "There is no sanctity in universal suffrage, frequent elections, majority rule, congressional and cabinet government." Rather, "the clear consciousness of a communal life, in all its implications, constitutes the idea of democracy."[61] "In all its implications" ultimately refers to the fundamental proposition that individual and society cannot be opposed. Hence, something has gone haywire where individuals seek "freedom" at the expense of the group or where the group seeks to oppose its good to that of its members. Either situation can be attributed to a competition between groups that have yet to acknowledge their relation. Thus, for Dewey, democracy would be nothing more or less than the conscious, political realization of what he takes to be overriding fact of human existence: association.

It may seem self-evident that the "clear consciousness of communal life" would require "*communication* as a prerequisite," but this is so for reasons far more fundamental than traditional democratic thinkers supposed. Dewey insists that any understanding of the social whatsoever requires that it be symbolized and that the symbolization determines how "society" is understood. "Only when there exist *signs* or *symbols* of activities and of their outcome can the flux [of social forces] be viewed as from without, be arrested for consideration and esteem, and be regulated."[62] "Communication," for Dewey, does not simply refer to an exchange of ideas, nor is it to be imagined as a debate in which the most reasonable or logical position would necessarily win. Rather, true "communication" generates categories of common understanding that simultaneously define participants as members of a group and as individual human beings:

> To learn to be human is to develop through the give-and-take of communication an effective sense of being an individually distinctive member of a community; one who understands and appreciates its beliefs, desires and methods, and who contributes to a further conversion of organic powers into human resources and values. But this translation is never finished.[63]

To stop talking about associated activity, to halt the "translation" from the "organic" or potentially human into the actually human is to destroy community and to imperil humanity.[64]

On the other hand, to arrive at a shared set of symbols is to generate "what, metaphorically, may be termed a general will."[65] By encouraging us to take this metaphor literally, the liberal theorists of democracy obscured the centrality of sign making to social definition. On this point, Dewey wholeheartedly agrees with Lippmann. Unlike Lippmann, however, Dewey strongly distinguishes between symbols that enable a community to think itself (true, public communication) and those that merely create social cohesion (and by implication serve private interests).[66]

When it comes time to explain how a public for itself might emerge,

Dewey finds no more help in the newspaper than Lippmann does. He locates the communication that might bring about a self-aware and thus self-governing community exclusively in face-to-face speech:

> The connections of the ear with vital and out-going thought and emotion are immensely closer and more varied than those of the eye. Vision is a spectator; hearing is a participator. Publication is partial and the public which results is partially informed and formed until the meanings it purveys pass from mouth to mouth.[67]

This is not to say that just any talking will do. In order to animate a public, a conversation requires the participation of all those whose actions might indirectly affect one another, would make use of the methods of social science, and would undergo continual revision as the parameters and self-understanding of the community change. In effect, Dewey asks us to imagine a vast conversation that obeys the logic of his own philosophy of "experimental education," a pedagogy built on the continual testing and revision of the categories, premises, and limits of thought.[68] Education, communication, and the democratic state require one another.

If Lippmann's account runs aground on the problem of elitism, Dewey meets his own dilemma here, with the problem of communication. How, after all, is this vast conversation to occur, if publication can only produce a partial public? Like Lippmann, Dewey understands the public in itself as, at least, "America" or, at most, a "Great Society" global in scope. But according to his model, the public for itself can only be a "local community," an association of persons whose understanding of their membership in the group (and hence of themselves) can be continually remade through conversation. "Unless local communal life can be restored," he urges, "the public cannot adequately resolve its most urgent problem; to find and identify itself."[69] This community is to be local yet not isolated, stable yet flexible—Dewey was perhaps the first to urge us to "think globally, act locally." But he leaves us with no account of how the global is to be thought on the basis of local communication, in the rigorous sense of experimental education.[70] No doubt this is why Dewey entitles his final chapter "The Problem of Method." It seems fair to say that the problem has yet to be solved. This is because it is *the* problem proponents of democracy face once print is no longer imagined to enable an extended conversation among citizens.

Lippmann, predictably, offers cinema's pictures as a metaphor for the operation of stereotypes themselves.[71] He also suggests that movies will increasingly supplant newspapers as organizers of stereotypes.[72] Dewey, on the other hand, tends to lump cinema together with other relatively new kinds of entertainment that distract people from properly political questions.[73] He makes a twofold objection to the medium. First, cinema is not language, "the medium of communication as well as thought." Second, motion pictures do not take public life as a content (whether by choice or necessity is unclear) and hence cannot provide symbols necessary for its organization. Considered in the abstract, however, these objections are precisely those leveled at the newspaper. Dewey clearly places reading under "vision," and thus pries "publication" away from "public," abolishing the link that made print an extension of, or substitute for, speech. Because print is "seen" not "heard," it cannot be true communication and hence cannot make community its content in a vibrant sense. Despite his greater suspicion of the cinema, then, Dewey has begun to imagine the newspaper on its model. Lippmann does so as well when he uses the movies to demote the newspaper from the organizer of opinions to something already organized by stereotypes. Each groups newspapers and cinema together as forces of social cohesion, in which publicity is either incipient (Dewey) or claimed in bad faith (Lippmann).[74] While it only makes sense that Lippmann and Dewey would focus their arguments on print, given its long-standing importance to discussions of the public, both presuppose that it has been displaced—if not as an organ for the dissemination of certain kinds of information, at least as the model of mass mediation.

The very notion that publication is a species of mass mediation rather than an extension of face-to-face conversation may be attributed to this shift. Published roughly a decade before, and focusing on English democracy, Wallas's *Great Society* provides much the same conception of society as do Lippmann and Dewey. All three refute the proposition that society is a collection of wholly autonomous individuals or an organism that may be regarded as the mystical sum of these parts (e.g., as a collective "mind" or "will"). Each, instead, describes society as "organized" in and through its members and institutions.[75] Each presents contemporary society as far more expansive and complex than its predecessors and calls for more comprehensive organization to ensure the common good. All agree that social science provides a necessary aid to this organization.

Wallas, however, assumes a distinction that Dewey and Lippmann explicitly attack when he distinguishes "Organised" from "Individual" thought. With "the invention of writing," he writes, it becomes possible for the "intercommunication of Thought to take place without bodily presence," thus:

> A thinker could then write in solitude arguments addressed to unknown readers, or read in solitude the arguments of others. In such a case Thought is "Individual" if the moment at which it takes place is alone considered, and "Organised" if the whole process from the original writing to the final reading is considered together.[76]

In contrast, Lippmann and Dewey eschew the proposition that individual thought becomes organized as it travels disembodied to its destination in another reader. That journey, they insist, happens only in and through stereotypes, signs, and symbols that are themselves organized through a process neither party may control.

Wallas's description of the individual reader has less in common with Lippmann and Dewey than with the account of public opinion provided by nineteenth-century liberalism, from which he differs in most other respects. For example, Lord James Bryce's 1888 *The American Commonwealth,* often cited by turn-of-the-century commentators, describes how "leaders of opinion" write accounts of distant events that circulate among "ordinary citizens" by means of the press. He imagines a solid, newspaper-reading bourgeois whose reactions to the news exert a reciprocal influence on the press, albeit in a roundabout fashion: "This mutual action and reaction of the makers of leaders of opinion upon the mass, and of the mass upon them, is the most curious part of the whole process by which opinion is produced."[77] Gradually, this process produces a majority view. In this particular contention, Bryce's account does not differ radically from Tocqueville's in 1835. For Tocqueville, the press

> causes political life to circulate through all parts of that vast territory [America]. Its eye is constantly open to detect the secret springs of political designs and to summon the leaders of all parties in turn to the bar of public opinion. It rallies the interest of the community round certain principles and draws up the creed of every party; for it affords a means of intercourse between those who hear and address each other without ever coming into immediate contact. When many organs of the press

adopt the same line of conduct, their influence in the long run becomes irresistible, and public opinion, perpetually assailed from the same side, eventually yields to the attack. In the United States each separate journal exercises but little authority; but the power of the periodical press is second only to that of the people.[78]

Though Bryce's language of "the mass" and "opinion leadership" foreshadows the twentieth century, he, like Tocqueville, imagines that the citizenry constitutes a public prior to its mediation by print and that this public is composed of individuals whose interests, ill-informed and malleable though they may be, exist prior to reading.

Democracy, in these accounts, hardly requires that the newspaper be a disinterested or scientific vehicle for the facts; quite the contrary, it is by either consenting or not to the interpretation presented by the news that the readership establishes "Public Opinion," the majority view that constitutes the very basis of democratic rule. Accordingly, the problems of democratic participation are largely formal. Provided with the necessary institutions and opportunities, a readership will govern itself. In just this vein, Wallas advocates more and better opportunities for reading (e.g., Reading Rooms) accompanied by the development of new opportunities for face-to-face dialogue (e.g., discussion groups for Parliamentarians as well as for working men and women). The danger in this model is not one of the manipulation of opinion by a minority elite or private interest as it is in the Lippmann-Dewey debate. Indeed, such manipulation is taken for granted. Rather, the problem is Tocqueville's infamous "tyranny of the majority." Only after the agency of representation itself is established does the interestedness of the press become an obstacle to the formation of a public interest.

With this conceptual development, calls for the reform of reading could be seen as part of the problem. Lippmann's sequel to *Public Opinion, The Phantom Public*, begins with a survey of civics textbooks and the impossible feats of reading they mandate. In the very earnestness with which they urge students to buckle down and be good citizen-readers, Lippmann argues, they do the work of sham democracy and make it all the easier for particular interests to pass themselves off as public ones. Just so, Dewey declares that "the belief that thought and its communication are now free simply because legal restrictions which once obtained have been done away with is absurd."[79] No mere reform of the newspaper or of the nation's reading habits will suffice to establish a democracy worthy of the name. Rather, the future of democracy depends on one form or another of expertise.

So long as the nation could be thought of as a readership, the classic liberal conception of publicity held sway against a multitude of late-nineteenth-century "mass" phenomena—the large-circulation, general-interest magazine, image-based advertising, and an ever-increasing volume of national brand-name commodities. Only after the movies prevailed did Lippmann and Dewey divorce "publicity" from "print." To be sure, Lippmann and Dewey participate in a broad, transatlantic philosophical tradition that called the autonomous subject into question and produced the present preoccupation with the effects of representation.[80] Dissatisfaction with "the public" and "the press" has a long career. The nineteenth century had established the twin problems of the crowd mind and the alienated individual. A critique was underway of the reasonable individual on which the eighteenth-century conception of the public depended. And Marx had famously identified the eighteenth- and nineteenth-century content of "the public" as ideological in its identification of the property holder with individual and citizen.[81] Yet these important arguments did not succeeded in transforming the public as a political category until after the rise of a form of representation that could no longer be imagined to have its source in private opinion. With that transformation, the form of mediation itself became the principle issue. Thus, Lippmann and Dewey banished the possibility that a nonideological publicity might emerge within existing forms. Along with it, they dismissed any notion that a group could govern itself absent self-conscious manipulation of the signs that define it. Whether ideological or not, whether in itself or for itself, whether with a capital "P" or a lowercase one, the public so conceived cannot be known spontaneously. It needs expertise to discern its true interests, to distinguish it from an inchoate "mass." This explains why Lippmann and Dewey have been seen both as advocates of a rising professional managerial class and as its critics. They inaugurated an argument over whether professionalism's job was to reform the liberal democratic state or to revise its structure in a more fundamental manner. Strikingly, however, neither suggests that the public was something that once existed and no longer does.

PROFESSIONAL DEMOCRACY

Cinema is not social science, but it propagated the need for an expertise akin to that Lippmann and Dewey advocated. It did so not by self-consciously defending the virtues of a particular scientific or educational method, but by making a decidedly impersonal agent seem necessary to maintain the family unit on which public welfare relied. Visible in the faces of a man and woman in love, privacy required a certain arrangement of space in order to survive. The home of nineteenth-century domesticity remained an ideally private space, but its properties could be reproduced virtually anywhere even illumination and tidy arrangement prevailed. While chaotic or overly regimented images of the masses certainly threatened the private couple, nothing about the group per se was inherently hostile to it. Indeed, the same crowd that pulls lovers apart can also bring them together, as it does when Mary and John meet amid a throng of office workers on a city sidewalk in Vidor's film. Once transformed into an orderly, but less regimented mise-en-scène, the crowd provides a suitable backdrop for true love. Through such images, the movies redefined the category of the "public" and constituted that public as a viewership. Privacy and publicity ceased to obey the logic of reading and writing as each term became dependent on its difference from an alienating mass. To establish this difference required a vantage, neither public nor private, that could reframe the faces of the lovers as part of the public. What it meant to "govern oneself" changed accordingly. It became a matter not of autonomous self-representation but of understanding how one fit into a larger picture.

The Lippmann-Dewey debate both promotes this change and presses its limits. As advocates for the range of experts who sought new roles in government and business, Lippmann and Dewey participated in the rise of a professional managerial class. They also pioneered a critique of the authority of this rising class, one that differs markedly from the customary critique of the authority of the bourgeois public. The traditional critique targeted the practical equation of the ideally universal "citizen" with a white, male property owner and the institutionalization of that equation in the very mechanisms thought to ameliorate its exclusions (e.g., extension of the franchise). Lippmann and Dewey accept that critique and move beyond it. They make the case for an expertise that cannot be identified with the earlier category of private man and reveal the related notion of "private opinion" to be tantamount to self-delusion. All interests are social interests. As such, they require an agent capable of evaluating and revising the signs that codify those interests and thus constitute the group. If, as Lippmann suggests, this job is entrusted to a special class of experts, they cannot do it as individual citizens. The expert's claim to represent a group interest rests on the capacity to stand aloof from that interest. Whence the contradiction Dewey finds in Lippmann: this new professional class acknowledges that representation has the power to constitute the group interest as such, yet it also claims to safeguard interests that precede representation and are thus not its own interests. It wins power over others through the scrupulously disinterested representation of what they want and need. In the process, it is liable to ignore its own immanent relation to the transactions it objectifies and regulates.

Two distinct approaches to "the public" emerged in the wake of the Lippmann-Dewey debate. Through them, a new kind of argument became inescapable. One tendency, which prevailed in civics instruction and in the emerging professions of public relations and social-survey research, makes "mass" and "public" competing descriptions of the same population, much as Vidor's film does. The other, developed in post–World War II American social psychology and significantly extended by Habermas, places "public" and "mass" on opposite sides of a historical dividing line. The first divorces the difference between mass and public from any particular form of representation and recovers the notion of a persuadable individual who precedes representation. The second writes the difference between mass and public into social history and makes it appear as though the shift from print to visual mass culture changed everything except the categories used to theorize that shift. Whenever either strand retreats from the account of the mediation the debaters supplied, it both deepens the contradiction Dewey identifies and mistakes cinema's role in founding that contradiction. Although the rise of public relations, market research, polling data, and sociology all clearly affected what it meant to represent "the public," these fields of information arguably would not be able to compete and collaborate in the ways they do had cinema not first established as common sense the proposition that private individuals are incapable of representing their relationship to a larger social whole.

For their part, liberal intellectuals moved quickly to rehabilitate the notion that political power ultimately resides in the private individuals who compose a public. In their 1930 *American Leviathan,* for instance, historians Charles A. and William Beard attempt to wipe away Lippmann's argument in broad strokes: "Powerful as it is . . . the political party is nevertheless sensitive to that elusive force known as public opinion. Since the rise of democracy, statesman and writers have paid tribute to this 'electric fluid'." Confident in this magical elixir, the authors scoff at Lippmann's description of the Public as a "phantom" and equate it with the assumption made by "two great dictators of the twentieth century, Lenin and Mussolini" that "the masses are incapable of ruling."[82] Nonetheless, it becomes clear that the Lippmann-Dewey debate has set the terms according to which the Beards argue. They are obliged to agree with Lippmann "when he says that there is no 'public' as such, no unified 'will of the people' but only special publics with reference to various problems and situations." When it comes time to explain how such publics guarantee a national democracy, however, combined acceptance of Lippmann's critique of a homogenous "public will" and resistance to his account of how stereotypes produce that will lead the Beards to sidestep the problem of mediation altogether. They recall neither Tocqueville's ever-vigilant newspaper nor Bryce's "leaders of opinion." Instead, they find that public opinion works "underground"; "creeping here, seeping there, it brings important ideas to fruition."[83] Somehow, behind the scenes of the political parties that so obviously control government, "the masses" have constituted themselves as groups that influence rule. The argument, then, depends entirely on rhetorical manipulation of the difference between "mass" and "public." As a mass, Americans cannot represent themselves—a status to which Lippmann, Mussolini, and Lenin purportedly consign them. Once described as public, however, the "ideas" of the masses become the basis of rule. By means of this brazen tautology alone, the Beards assure their readers that any "important idea" affecting government ultimately derives from "the public."

Even as they level a charge of authoritarianism against Lippmann, the Beards accommodate technocracy to America's political tradition. Revisions to Charles A. Beard's popular college textbook, *American Government and Politics,* indicate the change in conceptions of public service. Designed explicitly for the college-educated men and women destined to

swell the ranks of the professional managerial class, the text went through
six editions between 1911 and 1931. Whereas the first edition begins with
a historical account of the "forms" of American government developed
in the Revolution, the 1931 edition shifts focus to the question of government's "functions."[84] Incorporating material from *American Leviathan,*
this edition depicts not modest institutions for self-rule devised by the
property-owning protagonists of the early republic, but a government
so large and pervasive that it can be identified with no single group. Ap-
propriately, Beard added an epilogue to address the question, "How can
citizens play well their part in the development of American political
society?"[85] He frames the problem as one of scale: "Compared to the immense Leviathan, the State, how puny and inconsequential appears the
individual! Yet in some mysterious way, the destiny of the Leviathan is,
to some extent at least, shaped by the interests, activities, and ideals of
the individuals who compose the body politic."[86] Again, the rhetoric of
mystery is productive: it allows Beard to reproduce the liberal shibboleth
that individual citizens rule themselves, while acknowledging that they
do not control the state. It also allows him to define a new role for the
students his book addresses. The epilogue neither mentions voting nor
prompts the reader to study issues in print. Although Beard doubtlessly thinks these activities important, it has become impossible to imagine
that either could substantially affect "the immense Leviathan," a system
of governance too vast and complex to be revised via electioneering, letters to the editor, and so forth. Rather, he insists that institutions ranging from political parties to business, professional, labor, and civic organizations provide the conduits through which the people "influence"
rule and urges young graduates to participate in them. With this move
public service is redefined as a style of management, one that designates
the interests of various groups as public and advocates on their behalf
through discourses and institutions tailored to that purpose.[87] Beard re-
incarnates the Jeffersonian village as an interest group.

   In similar fashion, the new profession of public relations offered itself
as a necessary mediator between the public and all manner of corporate
and government clients. Public relations emerged in the United States
during the 1910s and, according to historian Stuart Ewen, reached maturity in the 1920s with a "marriage between theories of mass psychology
and schemes of corporate and political persuasion."[88] It developed, that
is, through engagement with many of the arguments that informed the

Lippmann-Dewey debate: scholarship on "crowd" psychology ranging from Gustave Le Bon (*The Crowd,* 1898) and Gabriel Tarde (*The Laws of Imitation,* 1903), to Wilfred Trotter (*Instincts of the Herd in Peace and War,* 1916), Everett Dean Martin (*The Behavior of Crowds: A Psychological Study,* 1919), and Lippmann's own *Public Opinion.*[89] In its use of these studies, public relations responded directly to business and government propaganda imperatives. Particularly formative was the work of the Committee on Public Information during World War I, which sought to "plead the justice of America's cause before the jury of Public Opinion."[90] With its emphasis on "pleading" a case, being both "student" and "educator" of public opinion, "interpreting" the client to the public and the public to the client, public relations distinguished itself from contemporary advertising and likened its work to that of the "research bureau" Lippmann and others advocated.[91] Like Lippmann's social science, public relations counted itself successful when it had both consulted a public whose mind it hoped to change and revised the client's practices to accommodate the public interest. Through a rhetoric of "interpretation" and "influence," it presented itself as a democratic instrument.[92]

The similarity between the version of the mass-public distinction provided by public relations and that of college civics textbooks is readily apparent in Edward Bernays's 1923 classic, *Crystallizing Public Opinion.* The most prominent spokesman for the new profession, Bernays both defends public relations against accusations of manipulation and introduces readers to its techniques. Like *American Leviathan,* he defines the public as a mysterious entity that nonetheless constitutes the very basis of the profession's expertise: "The public relations counsel is first of all a student. His field of study is the public mind." He gathers information from a wide variety of sources and "brings the talent of his intuitive understanding to the aid of his practical and psychological tests and surveys." Such "sensitiveness to the state of mind of the public is a difficult thing to maintain," Bernays confides.[93] Certainly the "public mind" could not interpret itself. In its raw state as a "crowd," "group," or "herd," the public is even less capable of rationally articulating its interests than are the individuals it comprises.[94] Bernays thus coopts and inverts Lippmann's critique: "Mr. Lippmann says propaganda is dependent upon censorship [i.e., stereotyping]. From my point of view the precise reverse is more nearly true. Propaganda is a purposeful, directed effort to overcome censorship—the censorship of the group mind and the herd reaction."[95] By setting public relations against "the mass-es," Bernays places propaganda on the side of "the public" and casts the experts who produce it as public advocates. In order to define influenc-ing the public and advocating its interests as commensurate activities, he proposes that public relations works by "crystallizing" certain preexist-ing opinions.

To be "influenced," public opinion must first be objectified in some manner. Various types of social surveys developed to fill this need, and the sort of national opinion polling that emerged in the 1930s has prov-en particularly effective. With roots in nineteenth-century statistics, the modern poll may be placed in the long line of attempts to distinguish between the putative facticity of numbers and the vicissitudes of inter-pretation.[96] It provides a field of data on which mass marketers, pub-lic relations personnel, and various political organizations may agree in order to disagree about its interpretation. From the late 1900s through the late 1920s, "individual or small groups of economists, sociologists, social workers, or other professionals working in state or local govern-ment agencies or in colleges" conducted thousands of specialized sur-veys. As historian Jean Converse notes, such "surveys provided not only facts for liberal reform politics but also basic statistical information for state and local units of government."[97] According to Converse, the par-ticular statistical fact we have learned to recognize as "national opin-ion" developed a bit later and required both the concept of "attitude" (as opposed to "idea" and "instinct") developed by social psychology and the particular techniques for probability sampling developed by mar-ket researchers. Although the early 1930s work of Henry C. Link and his Psychological Corporation moved significantly in this direction, it was the efforts of George Gallup, Elmo Roper, and Archibald Crossley, who forecast the reelection of Roosevelt in 1936, that established the national opinion poll as a democratic instrument. A prominent advocate for poll-ing, Gallup, like the Beards and Bernays, references Lippmann. But he finds Bryce's account more amenable to his contention that the opinion poll extends Jefferson's ideal of democratic participation.[98] Nonetheless, Gallup's promotion of polling as a neutral science situates him in a very different epoch than these eighteenth- and nineteenth-century sources. Here too we have a national mass of individuals who cannot speak for themselves, even with the assistance of the opinion leader. The nation be-comes a public through professional representation of its opinion; that representation is trustworthy to the extent it presents itself as a disinterested representation of the facts that precede it. As a method of objectifying opinion, therefore, the poll stands in contrast to the social science Lippmann advocated and is the antithesis of Dewey's experimental education. Rather than self-conscious attention to the difference between stereotype and environment or to generative acts of communication, the poll appears a democratic instrument only to the degree that the experts who write the questions succeed in making their work seem inconsequential to the result (hence the emphasis on its predictive powers).[99]

Although they advocate different ends, then, the Beards, Bernays, and Gallup describe similar projects of managing public opinion by manipulating the discourses supposed to represent it. Like Lippmann and Dewey, they depict a public that cannot be represented except through expertise. Yet where Lippmann had been centrally concerned with the difference between an inexpressible public opinion and Public Opinion writ large, and Dewey had worried over the relationship between a public in itself and a public for itself, these liberal intellectuals identified professional representation with "public opinion" itself. Simultaneously embracing expertise and suppressing its semiotic basis, they drove a rhetorical wedge between a public to be "influenced" and "interpreted" and a disorganized and malleable mass. To make the former appear a self-governing entity, they revived the "private man" and placed him at odds with "crowd psychology" and the "group mind"—a distinction filmgoers would have found perfectly familiar. In the process, they strove to institutionalize new professional practices for objectifying, interpreting, and influencing the public by claiming that such practices were the only means by which individual views might be represented. Despite the language of traditional democracy, however, each explicitly or implicitly acknowledged a new epoch of rule, one in which legitimate claims to administer rested on the ability to represent others in an disinterested manner. Various projects of "crystallizing" the "electric fluid" of public opinion appropriated the rhetoric of "we, the people" and competed with one another to wield it.

Before World War II, then, civics instruction, public relations, and opinion polling supplied a rhetoric of publicity adapted to an increasingly professionalized democracy. After the war, a vociferous critique of this tendency developed. In Habermas's exemplary account, such "social-psychological analysis of group processes" amount to the "liquidation" of the very concept of "public opinion."[100] Quite simply, he explains, they "do not fulfill the requirements of a public process of rational-critical debate according to the liberal model. As institutionally authorized opinions they are always privileged and achieve no mutual correspondence with the nonorganized mass of the 'public'."[101] In this manner, Habermas reproduces the very distinction between mass and public employed by the professions he critiques and uses it to condemn a contemporary "mass" society on behalf of a public held to have been socially regnant in the past and to remain the critical ideal.

As is well known, Habermas wrote his account of the public with and against the critique of capitalist society developed by Max Horkheimer and Theodor Adorno. Less often noted is Habermas's striking debt to American studies of social psychology published during the 1950s. C. Wright Mills gets nearly the last word in *Structural Transformation,* when Habermas reproduces a lengthy quotation from *The Power Elite* (1956) to summarize the difference between a "public" and a "mass." David Reisman's *The Lonely Crowd* (1950) and William Whyte's *The Organization Man* (1956) are similarly referenced. Indeed, it seems that Habermas's periodization of twentieth-century publicity derives in large part from these sources.[102] Whereas Horkheimer and Adorno cast mass culture as the victory of an instrumental reason that has roots in the Enlightenment, these American sociologists tend to criticize its difference from a prior, more authentic public, Enlightenment democracy. Riesman famously depicts print as crucial in the development of "inner-directed," nation-building entrepreneurs and sees the "mass media" as encouraging the "other-directed" social psychology of modern Americans, whose tendency to "over-conform" weakens the nation.[103] Inspired by Weber, Whyte draws a similar distinction between the nineteenth-century "Protestant Ethic" and a contemporary "Social Ethic."[104] Although Reisman sees the shift as incomplete even in the late 1940s, he and the others associate it with phenomena—rampant consumerism, the rise of visual mass media, the corporation, bureaucratization—that inevitably lead back to turn-of-the-century U.S. culture. Habermas resembles these writers far more than he does the Frankfurt school when he depicts the twentieth century as the era when the distinction between "private" and "public" collapsed (as opposed to the period when processes of commodification always implicit in that distinction finally triumphed).[105] The final chapters of Habermas's study not only focus on

the American case, then, but indicate an encounter with American intellectual history that informs the project as a whole.

If Mills left his mark on Habermas, Lippmann certainly left his mark
on Mills.[106] In his 1951 *White Collar,* Mills declares that "no one of liberal persuasion has refuted Lippmann's analysis."[107] Mills's 1960 anthology of sociological theory begins with the first chapter of *Public
Opinion.*[108] And the "mass society" section of *The Power Elite* on which
Habermas relies draws extensively from Lippmann.[109] Despite his praise
for Lippmann's achievement, however, Mills departs from his analysis in
two crucial respects. First, he finds no reason to be hopeful about the institutionalization of social science in government. By the 1950s, the kind
of expertise Lippmann advocated had become a bureaucratic practice to
be critiqued. Accordingly, Mills aligns "experts" with "the masses" and
opposes them to "the public."[110] Second, and more significantly, he represents the "liberal public sphere" as in fact functioning according to
the rules it sets for itself. Through this twofold maneuver, Mills writes
Lippmann's account into history not as a new theory of the public but
as a critique of a more authentic traditional concept; he then presents
this critique as itself symptomatic of a new age of mass media. Neglect
of the Dewey half of the debate only contributes to the impression that
Lippmann manages to demolish the traditional conception without promoting a new one. Whereas Lippmann and Dewey united in their criticism of the Jeffersonian model of the democratic village, for instance,
Mills seems to embrace something very like that notion when he con-
trasts a public formed through "discussion" with "mere *media markets*:
all those exposed to the contents of given mass media."[111] He conceives
of the public as "innumerable discussion circles . . . knit together by
mobile people who carry opinions from one to another . . . Out of these
little circles of people talking with one another, the larger forces of social
movements and political parties develop; and the discussion of opinion
is the important phase in a total act by which public affairs are conducted."[112] His nostalgia for nineteenth-century publicity notwithstanding,
Mills's "little circle" both obviates Tocqueville's powerful press and de-
motes Bryce's "opinion leader" to a mere transporter of opinion. It also
refuses Dewey's notion of communication as the process through which
signs define individuals as such. In fact, it best resembles the Beards's account of the "electric fluid," formed in many "continuously operating"
publics and exerting "pressure" on the political process. Whereas the Beards

make this a model for twentieth-century publicity, Mills uses it as a basis for criticizing the "society of masses" we have become.[113] Each, however, manages to overlook the fact that in describing an enduring ideal of "the public" he advocates not an eighteenth- but rather a twentieth-century conception: one in which "discussion" and "mass media" may be opposed.

In repeating this gesture, Habermas solidified the impression that visual mass culture could be understood as the negation of an earlier public sphere. Habermas restores print's role in mediating the modern public, but he inherits Mills' mistake of making the Lippmann-Dewey debate a symptom of "mass culture" rather than what it manifestly is: a highly productive effort to supply a new theory of the public adequate to the cinematic age. This explains why, as Craig Calhoun notes, Habermas "tends to judge the eighteenth century by Locke and Kant, the nineteenth century by Marx and Mill, and the twentieth century by a typical suburban television viewer."[114] At the very moment when it comes time to explain where his own mid-twentieth-century investment in the category of "the public" comes from, Habermas eschews the intellectual history of the category in favor of a history of the forms and institutions that mediate it. Until this moment, the book emphasizes the necessary connection between the two: the eighteenth-century category of "the public" could no more have existed apart from the forms that enable it (coffee houses, newspapers) than it could from the political philosophy that theorized it. In Habermas's account of the twentieth century, however, the "public" floats free from contemporary theorization. Apparently defined in the eighteenth century, it is falsified by twentieth-century forms. Only in this manner can Habermas lambaste the twentieth-century public for not working according to the eighteenth-century model after mounting a thoroughgoing critique of that model's ideological basis and function.

The position from which Habermas critiques eighteenth-, nineteenth-, and twentieth-century publicity is not in fact an eighteenth-century one. It reveals its twentieth-century basis in the way it describes the role of print. Although Habermas's emphasis on rational-critical debate retreats from Lippmann and Dewey's insight into the constitutive force of signs and symbols, he effectively reproduces their contention that democracy presents an essentially semiotic problem. Habermas repeats the traditional complaint that the abstract "citizen" is in fact a bourgeois man.

But he significantly amends that complaint when he theorizes, first, that this citizen required publication to exist, and second, that his invention amounts to the origin of ideology as such:

> Its origin would be the identification of "property owner" with "human being as such" in the role accruing to private people as members of the public in the political public sphere of the bourgeois constitutional state, *that is,* in the identification of the public sphere in the political realm with that in the world of letters; and also in public opinion itself, in which the interests of the class, via critical public debate, could assume the appearance of the general interest, that is, in the identification of domination with its dissolution into pure reason.[115]

When Habermas defines ideology as the conflation of "public opinion itself" with "the public sphere in the political realm" and the public "world of letters," he departs from the classic Marxist model. In *The German Ideology,* Marx and Engels famously attribute the birth of ideology to the development of a division between mental and material labor: "From this moment onwards consciousness *can* really flatter itself that it is something other than the consciousness of existing practice, that it *really* represents something without representing something real."[116] In contrast to this nineteenth-century conception of a difference between true and false consciousness, Habermas finds ideology in the rise of mediation that simultaneously extends and supplants face-to-face debate.[117] Because print does both, it founds an authentic public sphere and also leads to its dissolution. My point is simply this: insofar as Habermas's argument about the origin of a bourgeois public sphere presupposes a theory of mediation not present in his eighteenth- and nineteenth-century sources, it reveals more about the twentieth-century category than his critique of twentieth-century mass culture can.

The same conceptual shift that allows Habermas to distinguish public from mass on the basis of an opposition between debate and mediation has allowed others to distinguish alternative or oppositional publics from a dominant public sphere. The similarity becomes readily apparent when one takes the gender of the public into account. Proponents of the alienating mass culture thesis—from Reisman and Mills to Adorno and Horkheimer—famously identify massification with feminization.[118] This is not necessarily a bad development, several feminists point out. True, the implication that femininization of the public amounts to its dissolution as

such does reproduce the persistent equation of self-governance with masculinity. Yet the possibility of a feminine public also revises the traditional relationship between private and public, thus allowing for new arguments by and on behalf of women. Reasoning in this manner, Rita Felski
defines contemporary feminism itself as a counter-public sphere, and
Miriam Hansen characterizes moviegoing as an alternative public sphere
for women.[119] If we read the anxious male sociologists alongside their
more sanguine feminist counterparts, it becomes clear just how thoroughly the traditional contradiction of publicity has been revised. The former
depict feminized citizens who can no longer represent themselves. The latter depict women as a public group that cannot be represented as "the"
public. Each presupposes not the earlier common sense of an identification of "man" with "human being" and "citizen," but the subordination
of all individual citizens to an impersonal, yet masculine agent that claims
to represent "the public." With this shift, the paradox of the "woman citizen" gives way to the paradox of the "woman professional," whose representation of public interests requires a masculine rhetoric and whose
representation of "women" invites the charge of self-interested—that is,
unprofessional—conduct.[120]

Whenever twentieth-century thinkers misrecognize that transformation, they reproduce a telltale split between description of the public and its theory: the institutions and rhetoric of American democracy
appear in a Jeffersonian guise that (typically European) theory promises
to unmask or alter. In her "Contribution to the Critique of Actually Existing Democracy," for instance, political scientist Nancy Fraser works
with and against Habermas to outline several features that might characterize a "postbourgeois" public sphere. Among them are the notion that
"a multiplicity of publics is preferable to a single public sphere," the recognition that "a tenable conception of the public sphere must countenance not the exclusion, but the inclusion, of interests and issues that
bourgeois, masculinist ideology labels 'private' and treats as inadmis-
sible," and the acknowledgment that not all publics have the same relationship to the state at all times. Only by conceptualizing "the public"
along these lines, she argues, will we be able to work toward the egalitarian arrangements proponents of democracy advocate. Although she
writes as if this were a new model, versions of it have been in operation
for nearly a century. Lippmann and Dewey likewise critiqued the idea of
a single public, the notion of an opposition between private and public

(though *not* the gendering of that opposition), and the claim that public and state are, or should be, one and the same. And indeed, Fraser's argument founders on more or less the same point Dewey's does: it fails to account for how multiple local communities might govern de facto global relationships with one another. Moishe Postone makes this point when he notes that Fraser's argument in favor of a multiplicity of publics "conceptually embeds those multiple publics within a larger setting." Fraser "speaks of a single structural setting that advantages some people and disadvantages others in stratified societies, and of a comprehensive arena in egalitarian societies in which members of different publics talk across lines of cultural diversity." But she does not provide an account of "the structuring of, and historical conditions for, those two sorts of political metaspaces."[121] In this way, Postone both approves Fraser's argument and invites us to develop it by considering what it takes to produce the multiple and competing publics she describes.

In actually existing U.S. democracy at least, it takes a class of professional managers. It requires, that is, the entire array of pollsters, public-relations experts, civil servants, literary critics, editors, and so on that makes America intelligible as a hierarchy of competing group interests and that urges individuals to see themselves as part of one or more such groups (but never all of them). It is this class of experts that largely controls the mechanisms through which any group may claim national attention, that sets the terms in which competing interests are represented, and that thus defines the choices through which citizens are said to govern themselves. This does not mean that people uniformly act the way that professionals want them to, simply that deviation occurs within and further inspires professional administration. The distinction between mass and public, or among competing public interest groups, is the bread and butter of this class. Its members win authority by purporting to represent the interests of groups that cannot represent themselves.[122] This routinely involves the claims, first, that such interests precede representation, second, that they may be identified in a disinterested manner, and third, that to do so promotes the democratic process. Nonetheless, those who seriously consider the mechanics of these claims are in one way or another compelled to acknowledge that representations of "the public" are neither disinterested nor simply reflective of interests that precede them. That acknowledgment presents a characteristic dilemma. Today, one is still asked to side either with Lippmann—who accepts that "the Public" is a phantom, a technique of rule according to which different factions attempt to manage populations by giving definition to their interests—or with Dewey—who admits this critique, but holds fast to the possibility of generating new symbols of associated life, symbols more inclusive and equitable than those that presently define "the public." The intellectual project of the twenty-first century may well be to embrace both propositions and thus move beyond these two alternatives. The first step in this direction, I argue, is to admit the historical debt a new type of argument about "the public" owes to the rise of cinematic mediation.

I call professional any argument in which the difference between privacy and publicity dissolves into a distinction between a "public" and "mass," discussion and mediation, masculinization and feminization, or any other qualitative group difference requiring a purportedly disinterested agent to adjudicate it. Cinema did not invent professionalism, but it did make this kind of public an inescapable fact. Through repeated demonstration that the truths of the human heart and the proper arrangement of social space entail one another, Hollywood made the revelation of each dependent on a kind of expertise that could not be located in any single individual. Qualitative assessments of the public's health and safety displaced concern with its capacity to rule. Thus began a contest to explain how movies "manipulate" or "influence" viewers, as if the viewer qua viewer existed apart from cinema's address, either yielding to or resisting it. Just so, all manner of spokespersons proposed ways to safeguard America from the hazards of cinema's moral, aesthetic, and commercial depredations. When they distinguished a public persuaded from a mass betrayed, they promoted their own authority to tell the difference. In so doing, they simultaneously identified their professional power and denied the structures of mediation that sustain it.

3. The Influence Industry

No trope for describing how movies affect their audience has proved more durable than that of "influence." Such language reverberated through the magazines, daily newspapers, and social science journals of the 1920s and became indispensable to the two bodies of writing that typically organize histories of the motion picture industry in that period. Business writers called upon "influence" to explain what made movies a legitimate, profitable enterprise. Advocates of censorship and reform, meanwhile, used the term to dispute industrial control over motion picture content. The contest between these two camps took shape as an argument about how cinema's commercial appeal could be made compatible with positive moral or aesthetic values. While the sides disagreed over what this balancing act would entail, they agreed that it was not only possible but also imperative. Moreover, they did not differ over content as fundamentally as a superficial examination of their rhetoric might suggest. Censorship advocates raged against the depiction of sexuality on screen, for instance, but they united with producers in the contention that heterosexual love stories would prove profitable to filmmakers and beneficial to viewers. In this way and others, competing claims to improve America through the movies presupposed a national culture already mediated by their characteristic form.

The proliferation of "influence" as an explanatory term involved far more than the conviction that attitudes and behaviors represented on screen would be adopted by those who viewed films. It provided a social-psychological model in which subjects preceded the act of influencing them, but not as entities who might influence others. According to this model, the influencer succeeds through his (the position is proto-typically masculine) capacity to identify a preexisting desire in a very large number of individuals. He exercises a positive influence when he gives individual desire an expression that accords with the interests of society as a whole. When he turns it against the interests of individual subjects, however, he is guilty of manipulation. To distinguish a good influence from a bad one thus required an expertise capable of discerning unvoiced desires, articulating a social code, and tailoring information to suit the requirements of each.

Discussions of the movies naturalized this model in part by attributing the size and diversity of cinema's public to its pictorial qualities. Everyone agreed that the motion picture audience included children, women, and men from all walks of life. A great many credited its inclusiveness to the fact that movies spoke a universally intelligible and compelling language of images, "the most direct route alike to the emotions and the intelligence."[1] They thereby implied that cinema's vast audience could not possibly speak to and for itself. The members of this audience shared not the literal ability to speak a common tongue, but the ability to understand a pictorial idiom they themselves did not produce. To address them thus required an different sort of entity, one capable of self-consciously manipulating the highly influential language of pictures. Given the diversity of the movie audience, this image-manipulating entity would need to be especially judicious in order to find its common denominator. Such reasoning certainly underpinned the establishment of the Motion Picture Producers and Distributors' association, which in the early 1920s combined public relations and internal censorship functions by incorporating the advice of spokespersons from a long list of national organizations. Designed to encourage a consensus about what would be good for the public, the MPPDA's Committee on Public Relations in fact promoted a consensus about how to contest guardianship of it. Businessmen, censorship advocates, and all manner of reformers argued more vocally with one another in print than ever before. In so doing, they solidified a clear rhetorical means of explaining what diverse moviegoers had in common, why it was necessary for someone to protect those interests, and how protecting them might be balanced with the profit motive.[2]

First and foremost, they tacitly agreed to personify the public as a feminine consumer. To be sure, the consuming woman had nineteenth-century antecedents. But the project of influencing her through movies differed to the degree it was professionalized. The female moviegoer did not address others on the model of the antebellum novelist and woman of feeling.[3] Although businessmen and reformers counted on her femininity to connote vulnerability and virtue, they paid scant attention to her ability to shape the public habits of fathers and sons through her supervision of private sphere. Instead, they allegorized the public itself as a woman and vied to captivate, persuade, and educate her, or, conversely, to protect her from the seductive efforts of competitors. The woman-as-public was the object, rather than the subject, of social reproduction. At the same time, her subjective properties explained everything that was contingent about cinema's success. Her willfulness gave the public's "very changeable fancy" an imaginary source that preceded movies themselves.[4] It would thus take a good deal of skill, and some luck, to predict what she would desire and to tailor it to the national interest. Although this allegorical model invariably raised the prospect that movies would feminize men, those concerned with such an outcome proved far more likely to reserve purportedly masculine powers of deliberation for themselves than to propose how movies might cultivate those powers on a mass basis. By agreeing to describe cinema's public as feminine, in other words, professionals competed with one another to supply authoritative knowledge of what she really wanted and needed, and they more or less explicitly coded such knowledge as masculine. Women themselves could and did participate in this argument, it is crucial to remember, but only if they agreed to distinguish feminine intuition from knowledge of women, sensibility from science, their sex from the gender of their professional identity.

In the 1920s, then, a rich system of analogies organized a growing body of literature that described how movies influenced audiences: influence is to reason as femininity is to masculinity, as images are to words, as commerce is to morality. Inasmuch as such rhetoric appears to recycle nineteenth-century thinking, it elides the historical shift cinematic mediation brought about. To put it bluntly, movies did not "influence" anyone. Rather, they envisioned a culture in need of the constant regulation would-be influencers supplied. They did so by disseminating a heroine imperiled by forces she could not see and a nation-space made safe only when arranged so that she might return her lover's look of desire. In the process, they established that the American woman was both a repeatable picture and a unique individual—a paradox made possible by the definition of individuality as a variation on a standard image. Presented thusly, the exterior trappings of consumption posed little threat to the woman's interior. Indeed, the one confirmed the other: desirable as an image, the heroine was herself a source of desire. Arguments over the precise details of how a good woman should behave on screen, how a fashionable woman should appear on screen, and how she differed from her leading man only made it more important to repeat, extend, and update the formulaic relationship between desirable surface and desiring inside. Such arguments, in other words, subtend the movies themselves; they serve to reproduce and modulate the definition of "woman" cinema established as common sense. Contests over good and bad influence routinely denied this formative act of mediation. Censors, reformers, and businessmen vied for the authority to describe and address the audience created by cinematic convention by making the power of convention disappear. They claimed to speak to and for a public qua woman who preceded the movies. They idealized movies themselves as a universal pictorial language. In the process, they naturalized what appears within the cinematic frame and urged us to forget that the desiring woman of silent film belongs to a very different semiotic order than the desiring woman of nineteenth-century fiction.[5] In this way, they both misrecognized the agency of cinematic mediation and sought to appropriate it for themselves.

WHY CHANGE YOUR WIFE?

With a wink and a nudge to the audience, the final intertitle of *Why Change Your Wife?* (Famous Players–Lasky, 1920) explains the film's lesson: "And now you know what every husband knows, that a man would rather have his wife for his sweetheart than any other woman, but Ladies, if you would be your husband's sweetheart you simply *must* learn when to forget that you're his wife." The title invites viewers to interpret director Cecil B. DeMille's film as an object lesson, a demonstration to wives that efforts to improve a husband's manners inevitably doom marriage, while the alluring, fun-loving aspect of "sweetheart" will allow it to prosper. Given the wry tone of the text, and of the film that precedes it, the filmmakers doubtlessly assumed a viewer more likely to chortle at this lesson than to recoil from it. They may well have hoped *Why Change Your Wife?* would titillate and provoke, but they did not anticipate that audiences would perceive themselves to be in moral danger, even if individual viewers happened to resist the final message. In this way, the concluding title cannily preempts anyone who might denounce the film for having an immoral influence. It casts the denouncer as a humorless traditionalist, and suggests that a fun and even racy picture might influence lives for the better. Regardless of the success of this strategy, the very act of explaining the film as a marriage lesson calls attention to the possibility of other interpretations. One could laugh off the title's moral without dismissing the narrative that precedes it.

Even so, some of the more prominent social histories of U.S. cinema have read *Why Change Your Wife?* in just the way the final title suggests. Robert Sklar and Lary May each make DeMille's films of the late 1910s and early 1920s privileged examples for their arguments that Hollywood promotes a version of middle-class America in which eroticism both challenges and supports "Victorian" family values.[6] They interpret these films' demonstrations that marriage lacks sexual excitement as a critique of Victorian mores. Similarly, a new consumer culture may be seen in the erotic lures to which the couple succumbs: jazz, nightclubs, liquor, cigarettes, perfume, elaborate and revealing costumes—all of which the production team at Famous Players–Lasky contrives to render as youthful, decadent, primitive, Oriental, foreign, or some combination thereof. By incorporating some of these attributes into a restored marriage, writes Sklar, DeMille "was able to free the subject of marriage from the overstuffed [Victorian] parlors and infuse it with wit, style, vicarious pleasures, and above all, practical hints on contemporary ways to behave." This infusion was "one of manner, not matter," he contends: DeMille's "films suggested new attitudes," but "none challenged moral order."[7] May describes a more substantial change. For him, the films exemplify the demise of Victorian rules that restricted the middle-class woman's sexual behavior but also gave her moral and civic authority. In place of those rules, they promise the woman "mature sexuality" and entry into the public sphere, but they also resubordinate her to the patriarchal family in the new roles of sexual partner and consumer.[8] Sumiko Higashi calls attention to the major contribution of screenwriter Jeanie

Macpherson in making these films, and thus locates a woman behind the camera as well. Even so, she reproduces May's reasoning to describe the Macpherson–DeMille films as converting the "sentimental heroine" of Victorian convention into a "sexual playmate." Like May, she quotes the final intertitle of *Why Change Your Wife?* in support of this claim.[9] Thus, despite acknowledgment that "sweetheart" and "wife" are opposed only to be reconciled by the film, each author attributes that opposition to an older America in order to argue that cinema helped make America modern by urging wives to lighten up on their husbands, buy luxury goods, and enjoy sex.

This type of reading typically calls upon print discourse, especially the fan magazine, to support its contention that movies did in fact influence viewers in the manner they describe. Such evidence certainly exists for *Why Change Your Wife?* In *Photoplay*, for example, reviewer Burns Mantle enumerates in advance the "certain" stages of the film's reception.

> (1) Cecil B. DeMille's "Why Change Your Wife?" will prove one the sex [*sic*] best sellers of the month; (2) That somewhere out in the middle west, where the clean prairie winds blow across the brows of a native Anglo-Saxon multitude, a woman's club or two or four or six will meet, and in the course of the meeting, adopt resolutions condemning the present tendencies of the screen as they relate to the sensual and the fleshly feature; And (3) that later certain financial interests in conference assembled in richly paneled New York offices will give the resolutions a cursory glance, familiarly known as the once over, and proceed to a re-reading of the night letters received from the same locality relating the experience of Hiram Bezitz, the local exhibitor, who was forced to call out the fire department to help him shoo an overflow mob away from his theater after it had been packed to the rafters with those eager to see Cecil DeMille's, "Why Change Your Wife?"[10]

Mantle represents as entirely commonsensical the opposition of "clean prairie winds" to "richly paneled New York offices," of moral values to commercial mass appeal, and of a handful of ladies to the "mob" stuffing the theater of the hypothetical Hiram Bezitz. Since the "brows of the native Anglo-Saxon multitude" must be pointed at the screen, the reader might well find denunciations of the "fleshy feature" to be hypocritical.

A more direct assertion that movies transformed America by redefining wifely virtue comes from Mantel's more earnest counterpart, Adela

Rogers St. Johns. The interviewer provided *Photoplay* readers with DeMille's own answer to the question "What Does Marriage Mean?" Confessing herself to have been "spellbound" by the producer-director's "wholly unexpected statement of his purpose, his message," St. Johns avers that "I am quite, quite sure that because of the things he said to me that night [of the interview] I shall be a better wife." Conveyed by St. Johns, DeMille's "message" mimics the final title of *Why Change Your Wife?* minus the tongue-in-cheek. By denouncing wifely scolding in favor of frank attention to problems of sex appeal, DeMille declares, "I believe I can do more, that I am doing more to prevent divorce than any minister or anti-divorce league in the world."[11] In this journalism, Hollywood does indeed occupy center stage in a battle between Victorian ladies and a more modern sexuality. That sexuality was both more honest and more thoroughly commodified than its predecessor.

As a visual narrative, however, *Why Change Your Wife?* resolves the more fundamental question of how a commercially reproducible desire can be a more authentic one. True to form, it frames that question as a problem of eyelines limited in space. What critics conventionally interpret as an opposition between commerce and sentiment, sex and virtue, is a difference between two conventional sorts of images. One renders the woman's alluring surface and makes it the object of a man's desirous look. The other implies subjective depth by making her a source of sight. To produce a space in which the right man and the right woman can stare at one another unimpeded, the film demonstrates the mutual dependence of these two images. In so doing, the remarriage plot does not transform a purportedly repressed and uncommodified Victorian home into its sexy Jazz Age counterpart. Rather, it supplies merely the latest permutation of the visual structure that made twentieth-century America intelligible as a heterosexual couple secured by invisible experts.

The film begins by placing its couple in a well-lit contemporary bathroom. Robert (Thomas Meighan) suffers the interruptions of his wife Beth (Gloria Swanson) while shaving in front of an oval-mirrored medicine cabinet. Intent on his shave, he does not glance at her as she pushes past him to open the cabinet and withdraw a bottle of nail polish. He steps back automatically when she finds she has the wrong bottle and returns to exchange it. His concentration is interrupted only when she grabs his elbow to ask help in fastening her dress, which causes him to recoil from the safety razor on his cheek. After admonishing his wife's inattentive back, he puts down the razor and begins fastening. This apparently incidental task swiftly develops into a major undertaking. Beth vigorously shakes the bottle, pulling the dress from his fingers. He reaches over to still her arm. She begins to buff her nails instead, and a close-up reveals the fabric at the back of the dress separating and drawing together with the oscillating motion of her arms. Robert's fingers strive in vain to fasten the edges. When he stops her again, her sigh of impatience causes the dress to become further undone. He sits and draws her onto his lap to start all over. Beth glances over her shoulder, and they exchange perfunctory smiles. But a look of exasperation transforms his face as she turns away. A title and dissolve elide what is presumably a lengthy fastening procedure. Robert then returns to his shave only to be interrupted a final time as Beth pushes him aside, first, to inspect the back of her dress in the mirror, and then, to open the cabinet and replace the bottle. She delivers the coup de grâce as she exits, patting him rather strongly on the head and causing him to grimace at the razor under his nose. With nervous glances over his shoulder, he rushes back to the mirror to finish shaving. Through this meticulous choreography, *Why Change Your Wife?* presents intimacy as interference and places the husband in comic peril. Though they occupy a bright, well-lit, safely enclosed space, close quarters and a refusal to take notice of one another—especially the wife's refusal to take notice of her husband—define an asexual privacy.

Vexing though such sexless intimacy may be, it cannot be overcome simply through recourse to its opposite, as we begin to see two scenes later when Robert arrives at the dress shop Maison Chic in search of a solution to his marital woes. The presence of employees and other customers defines this as a public venue, but the fact that these others are all women, combined with the Orientalist exoticism of the shop's wares, clearly establish that Robert has entered foreign territory. The separation of the shop floor from the models' dressing room presents a particular hazard, one well codified by films featuring a predatory Vamp. Unseen by Robert, Sally Clark (Bebe Daniels) climbs onto her dressing table to peer out at him through an oval window. From the outside, mullions cut the opening into quarters, partly obscuring her face and contributing to the impression that this look is a furtive one. As she turns back toward the dressing room, she throws a look and a smile over her shoulder, clasps her hands at her chest, and glances heavenward in a mock swoon.

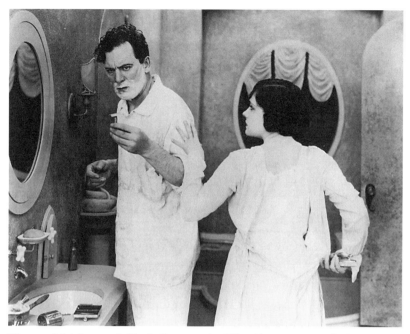

Thomas Meighan and Gloria Swanson in *Why Change Your Wife?* (Famous Players–Lasky, 1920). Still photograph courtesy of the Academy of Motion Picture Arts and Sciences.

Wife Beth has a competitor. Meanwhile, the object of Sally's gaze tries in vain not to look at his surroundings. In one shot, gauzy undergarments bracket Robert's seated figure; he turns in embarrassment from the one on the left only to get an eyeful of the one on the right. Penned in, he fidgets nervously with his hat. We may be sure that for a man to look at such garments in such a space is both arousing and forbidden and that Beth's rival has spied a target susceptible to this naughty lure. Thus the film sets the stage for the appearance of the costume that will thereafter organize the plot.

In the dressing room, Sally dons a long negligee in the style of Erté. Cut low in front and sleeveless, it nonetheless has gigantic fur cuffs that hang well below the knee. Strands of black beads link the cuffs to the dress and anchor an elaborate headdress to a large Oriental ornament centered on her chest. Backless, the negligee pulls yards of gauzy black train. As if this garment lacked sufficient allure right off the rack, Sally removes the slip to reveal a glimpse of stockinged calf under the filmy drapery. And on her way to the shop floor she further embellishes by applying a heart-shaped beauty mark to her shoulder and perfuming herself from a bottle labeled "Persian Night." When Sally strolls onto the shop floor, Robert stands with a stare of obvious appreciation. But he quickly glances away as Sally poses for him. He refuses to focus on her when she draws near and provokes him to notice the heart and perfume. Only when she walks away to reveal her naked back does an obvious indication of erotic interest finally occur. In the foreground, Robert stares toward her back in the depth of the image before turning away in embarrassment.

In stark contrast to the view from behind that inspired annoyance in the claustrophobic bathroom, this scene introduces a separation productive of desire. The framing and motion of the characters, the translucency of the fabric, and the costume's design all imply that some parts of the body within are specially hidden, may be revealed, and thus would be particularly desirable to see. Displayed thusly, the negligee presents a

Bebe Daniels and Thomas Meighan in *Why Change Your Wife?* Still photograph courtesy of the Academy of Motion Picture Arts and Sciences.

self-evident solution to the problem Robert and Beth face. Because the ability to mobilize desire appears to be a function of Sally's costume and demeanor, and not of any meaningful exchange of looks between the two, any woman who inhabits the negligee might be expected to provoke Robert's interest—including his wife. Precisely because the negligee effect is generalizable, however, the other woman can compete for Robert's attention. The garment promises an intimacy consistent with the imperatives of modern heterosexuality but threatens its monogamous expression.

Just so, the negligee's arrival menaces Robert and Beth's relationship as well as gives it an erotic charge. At Robert's request, Beth goes upstairs to try on his gift while he waits in the living room below. We watch her mortification grow as she sees herself in the dress. The camera lingers on her discovery of its backlessness and the missing slip. As she turns to face a tall mirror at frame right, her enlarged expression registers the shift from confusion and dismay to shock and horror. Wide-eyed and open-mouthed, her reflected image recoils as if from the look of the audience, while, on the left side of the frame, her unreflected profile draws back from the mirror. This is a metapicture.[12] It represents the process of subjection to an image. This process poses a threat to Beth insofar as the image, unlike the negligee qua negligee, presupposes the look of an other, a position here occupied simultaneously by the viewer offscreen and by Beth herself. It thereby raises the possibility that the visible surface will signify not the subject's "own" interior qualities but rather those qualities desired by the observer. These qualities stem from generalizable appearances (the negligee effect) and are thus independent from any individual woman. Semiotically speaking, then, the scandalized woman and her alluring outside arrive in a single stroke. By doubling Beth's visage, the film creates the impression that image on the left side of the frame is the horrified source of its reflection on the right side. She is scandalized by her objectification precisely because she sees herself in it. By means of this image, the film establishes Beth's interior difference from Sally even as it makes their exteriors interchangeable.

Although played for comedic effect, the remainder of the scene depends on the viewer's understanding of the threat of objectification this metapicture depicts. An impatient Robert knocks on the bedroom door, then bursts in with eager anticipation. His ebullient visage gives way to a furrowed brow when, in the reverse shot, he sees that Beth has withdrawn to the opposite side of the room and covered herself to the chin with the enormous fur cuffs. Striving for the same view Sally had provided, he tries to walk around her, but Beth turns to prevent him from seeing her back. Thus begins a competition between the two as he tries to uncover and embrace her while she covers herself and attempts retreat. In the end, Robert is left clutching the dangling end of a cuff, while Beth draws back to the opposite side of the frame. As he bends to kiss the fur, Sally appears between them in ghostly double exposure. His eyes seem to meet hers. But the translucency of Sally's face, in contrast with the solidity of Beth's, forces us to see this as a picture of Robert's desire for a superficial image, and not the sort of human interior that resisted him.

Through this series of scenes, the film construes the problem of asexual privacy as a problem of essence and appearance. Beth's very resistance to being seen as a repeatable image defines her as a source of authentic feeling. In contrast, Sally raises the specter of inauthentic emotion and with it the possibility that Robert desires not another person but merely a picture of one. Audiences could hardly have failed to understand what it would take to solve this problem. Somehow Beth's interior qualities had to be placed inside Sally's negligee so that this diaphanous garment might reveal not only a desirable body but a desiring interior, one capable of returning Robert's ardent stare. Only then could heterosexual monogamy provide a model of personal happiness and social stability.

The film achieves this combination though a series of coincidences so implausible as to foreground their contrivance by an agent out of frame. In the span of perhaps five minutes on screen, Beth misunderstands Robert's relationship with Sally and divorces him; Robert marries Sally; Beth undergoes a fashion conversion; and Sally persuades Robert to vacation at a resort hotel, where, by happenstance, Beth also stays. The pace of narration then slows to focus on the inevitable encounter. Poolside, Beth's bathing suit—an asymmetrical, floral-print wraparound that reveals one leg to the hip—attracts men of every description: an elderly gentleman with top hat and cane, a youth in a cap with a book in one hand, a golfer with clubs over his shoulder, a military officer in a white dress uniform, an aviator in leather, and so on. Cutaways reveal that she out-competes a potential rival who wears an equally outrageous suit (made from a large checkerboard print, it features a short skirt flared outward to the circumference of her wide-brimmed hat). Beth eventually fends off her admirers with the help of her parasol, but

The dilemma in *Why Change Your Wife?* Still photographs courtesy of the
Academy of Motion Picture Arts and Sciences.

this apparatus provides an additional layer of erotic intrigue moments later when Robert enters the scene. A close-up representing his point of view shows her legs emerging from beneath the parasol's screen, and the expression on his face in the reverse shot makes plain that his interest in them repeats the general male interest. As he walks around her for a better view, she maneuvers the parasol to block his look, just as she had with the other men. This barrier, however, only increases his desire to see the face attached to the body. When finally she pulls apart the threads of the parasol to peek out at him, surprised mutual recognition occurs. An exchange of gazes across framelines leaves no doubt that the ideal couple has finally arrived.

This established, the film need only rid Robert of Sally and restore Beth and Robert to their shared home. It does so with a banana peel. Each seeking to avoid the painful presence of the other, Beth and Robert leave the hotel separately only to find themselves seated next to one another on the train home. As they arrive at their destination a title informs us: "If this were fiction the train would be wrecked or they would have a terrible automobile accident on leaving the station. But in real life, if it isn't a woman, it's generally a brick or a banana peel that changes a man's destiny." Sure enough, the banana peel arrives with the force of a train wreck as Beth and Robert exit the station. It lands on the sidewalk in close-up, while, in another frame, Beth and Robert march blithely toward the inevitable. The fall renders Robert unconscious. Beth takes him home to nurse him, and in his delirium Robert sees her as the wife he never left. Though Sally dramatically comes to blows with Beth over Robert's unconscious body, she withdraws her claim once he returns to consciousness.

To arrive at the conventional happy ending, it remains only to restore Beth to the negligee. Now comfortable in the once disturbing garment, she floats down a staircase to join Robert in their evenly lit living room. As she gazes up into his eyes, he bends to kiss her slightly parted lips. In this final scene, various alluring commodities are indeed brought home and domesticated, as Sklar, May, and Higashi argue. Not only does Beth adopt the style of the Maison Chic, she also encourages consumer "vices" she had earlier forbidden: smoking, drinking, and dancing to the "Hindustan Foxtrot." But in order to annex the trappings of consumption to wifely virtue, the film reproduces a visual structure that could as easily demonstrate the necessity of shedding those trappings.

Just so, Lois Weber's *Sensation Seekers* (Universal, 1927) rehabilitates the dissolute seductive woman (Billie Dove) by stripping her of filmy garments and a vampish demeanor. Only then can she find happiness with the handsome local clergyman (Raymond Bloomer). In a similar vein, D. W. Griffith's *Way Down East* (United Artists, 1920) establishes the general desirability of country cousin Anna Moore (Lillian Gish) by demonstrating that her legs provoke the same erotic fascination in villain Lennox Sanderson (Lowell Sherman) as the modish flappers who surround him.[13] Before finally joining her eyeline with that of a more appropriate partner, moreover, it famously splays her sparsely clad body across a floating block of ice. Although historians typically represent DeMille's sexy Jazz Age films as superceding Griffith's gentrifying melodramas, *Way Down East* and *Why Change Your Wife?* were released the same year. More importantly, they share an imperative to make the desirable female object and marriageable female subject appear to be one and the same figure. *Why Change Your Wife?* simply makes more explicit than most of its contemporaries, first, that the woman must see herself as reproducible picture in order for this equation to occur, and second, that a properly functioning private space had to include her.

The old-fashioned wives of the Famous Players–Lasky remarriage films were not themselves Victorian ladies, in other words, but the type of woman cinematic culture imagined as traditional, with all the virtues and drawbacks "tradition" entailed. When these movies represent the power of outrageous outfits to transform wives from scolds to sweethearts, they may or may not have cajoled viewers into adopting such garb. But they must have counted on audiences to recognize the socially valuable woman in images that indicated her capacity to choose her outfit as she chose her man. There was not one but several ways for such a woman to be defined by consumption—a fact amply demonstrated by those historians who have examined closely contemporary writing by and about women moviegoers.[14]

Accordingly, one misses the forest for the trees in employing the concept of "influence" to explain how movies affected their audience. It would be more accurate to say that they popularized "influence" itself as an explanatory strategy. When Beth recognizes herself in her pictorial objectification, the moving image that renders that relationship implies that she precedes this picture, resists it, and, in the same stroke, that she can be influenced by it. She herself cannot be a source of influence, however. That power resides in the picture. Numerous commentators invoke just this type of scene when they employ the figure of the consuming woman as an allegory for cinema's audience as whole. They thereby suggest that cinema affects audiences by getting them to dress in one way or another or by providing what Sklar calls "practical hints on contemporary ways to behave." Instead, cinema constituted an audience by promulgating codes and conventions that made choices about outfits and behaviors intelligible and, more importantly, subordinate to acts of arrangement that could not possibility be conducted from an individual point of view. In this way, Hollywood's rise promoted a wholly new type of argument over when, how, and by whom an American public could be represented.

"WHAT THE PUBLIC WANTS"

To understand why the film industry found "influence" so very useful, it helps to know how its managers established that their business was one. Particularly revealing are the explanations they supplied to a general business readership. In 1918, *System: A Magazine of Business* asked Henry Ford to explain the most recent miracles of factory organization and distribution. It called upon Adolph Zukor to explain the public; he had an "instinctive feeling—common to great managers—for what the public wants just a little while before the public knows what it wants."[15] Founded in 1900, *System* paved the way for such general-interest business magazines as *The Nation's Business* (1912), *Forbes* (1917), *Administration* (1921), and *Fortune* (1930).[16] Unlike more specific trade publications (e.g., *Moving Picture World, Variety*) but like emerging university business programs, these periodicals explained conditions supposed to affect all businesses, promoted the application of managerial procedures to any enterprise whatsoever, and addressed problems purportedly faced by managers in all lines of work.[17] They provided a rising class of managers with a shared vocabulary and gave them a common enemy in older, less systematic, approaches. Eager to find "sound business methods" anywhere it could, this type of business journalism also promoted specialization by presenting individual business leaders as specialists on particular problems. In accordance with this strategy, *System* and its competitors established that the motion-picture industry was a business like any other while defining movie managers as experts on the public's unvoiced desire.

From the perspective these business magazines afford, it becomes abundantly clear that movie managers did not seek bourgeois respectability on a nineteenth-century model so much as strive to define their endeavor as a cutting-edge twentieth-century enterprise. The magazines supplied accounts of industrial organization, profitability, and business practice fully commensurate with the sources on which historians of the industry typically draw (the 1927 report of the prestigious Chicago investment banking firm of Halsey, Stuart, and Co., for instance, or the series of lectures by industry leaders that Joseph Kennedy organized for students of Harvard's business school that same year). To a greater degree than these canonical sources, however, the comparative emphasis of the business magazines reveals that movies required and promoted a substantially new set of assumptions about what an industry was. Despite frequent claims that motion pictures were already America's "fourth largest industry," it took some doing to make the business intelligible to readers likely to consider "industry" synonymous with railroads, manufacturing, and steel.[18] Commentators inside the industry and out began to explain why studios were comparable to other large corporations in the late 1910s. By the end of the 1920s, they still could not take the comparison entirely for granted. The problem did not lie simply in understanding what made this form of popular entertainment a profitable one, although that was a major difficulty. Rather, discussions of the motion picture industry required investors, regulators, and businessmen— the very people responsible for managing and financing the movies— to accept cost accounting, scientific management, and public relations models that were just beginning to prevail and that, even so, needed modification to be applicable to moviemaking.[19]

Accounting practices provide a particularly telling example. Max Prager (of the New York accounting firm Prager and Fenton) described "Some Accounting Problems of the Motion Picture Industry" for the readers of *Administration* in 1921. In characteristic fashion, he establishes that movies are analogous to other kinds of business by describing the film industry's main divisions in terms a general readership could readily understand. "Production" may be compared to manufacturing in other industries, and "exhibition" resembles retailing or "sales." "Distribution" is likened elsewhere to wholesaling.[20] Given this functional division, Prager explains, accounting methods in the motion-picture business are "to a very great extent the same as those prevalent in other manufacturing industries."[21] Although such basic comparisons tend to be taken for granted by historians of the industry, the recurrence of similar overviews in business writing throughout the 1920s suggests that they would not have been self-evident to contemporary readers.[22]

The reason why they would not have been becomes clear as Prager takes up "peculiarities of the motion-picture business to which methods of accounting must be made to conform."[23] He notes three in particular: how to account for the "large overhead during the period of idleness between the production of pictures," how to compute the depreciation of films, and how to post transactions between distributors and exhibitors. To these problems, he offers three prosaic solutions. The cost of "unproductive overhead" should not be apportioned to the cost of particular films, but segregated and noted on the books as such. The cost of films should be depreciated at a variable rate, perhaps set by a standard formula, over a fixed period of time. Film rentals should not be posted as income by the distributor until the contract has been fulfilled (i.e., the film has been delivered to the exhibitor). The most revealing of these proposals is the second. The depreciation formula quickly became essential to motion-picture accounting, and subsequent commentators emphasized it when introducing the industry to students and potential investors.[24] They lingered over the formula because it effectively explained how to account for a "manufacturing industry" that sold no product.

Although films resemble commodities, they did not fit the traditional profile of the consumable good. Within the logic of bookkeeping, the sale of a product both offsets its production costs and represents a transfer of value to the purchaser.[25] But films, once "sold," still remain in inventory. Accountants had to find some way to quantify the transfer of value, otherwise the cost of production would remain on the balance sheet as a large inventory of expensive films, skewing the books. It is not easy to compute the write-off, however, because "costs have practically no bearing upon the sales or rental value." The usual methods of depreciating assets held over time do not apply. Prager makes plain that accounting practices of the day were eager to find value in cost, both for the purpose of setting prices and for that of depreciating assets. But one cannot liken the studio's inventory of films to a manufacturer's "fixed assets"—that is, machinery. To begin with, films are a producer's "stock in trade" and not a part of the apparatus of production. But perhaps more importantly, "the life of fixed assets can be approximated fairly," whereas motion pictures are not "susceptible" to "the same degree of approximation."[26] That is, one can know the useful life of a piece of shop equipment and depreciate its "value" (cost) over this life. With a picture, however, the principle by which "cost" could be related to "value" and therefore depreciated had yet to be established.

The solution lay in the rhetorical construction of a capricious public that could nonetheless be studied and predicted. Prager declared: "The value of the picture is purely speculative, depending upon its quality and the very changeable fancy of the public."[27] Once he had established that a film had no value except what the public gave it, Prager could accommodate the disjuncture between cost and value simply by depreciating production cost according to an arbitrary formula.[28] Based on the conviction that the longer a film has been in circulation the less it will interest viewers, this formula assumes that films are worth most at their premiere and decrease in value exponentially thereafter. Two years after its debut, Prager proposed, the studio should carry a title on the books at a value of one dollar. Depreciation in motion picture accounting thus resembled depreciation in any other industry. But to establish that resemblance, Prager had to turn accounting's model of value on its head. Rather than imagining the commodity's worth to have its roots in the cost of production, the depreciation formula retrospectively defines value in relationship to the habits of consumption.

In order to see filmmaking as a business like any other, then, one apparently had to accept an argument that made the value of its wares totally dependent on the whims of their buyers. The rationale behind the depreciation formula illustrates how difficult it must have been for bankers, investors, and other businessmen to understand Hollywood's product as such. It also marks the difference between the vertically integrated corporations of the 1920s and the business models prevalent two decades earlier, when producers sold to pictures to distributors (exchanges) for a fixed price per reel. In fact, the public's "very changeable fancy" was more predictable than this novel argument made it appear. The conventions of feature filmmaking themselves stabilized it. Irrespective of the particular combination of excellence and circumstance that made a film a hit, filmmakers and audiences alike could assume that a Hollywood movie would have a certain form. Business writing did not dwell on that fact, however. It did not find value in the ability to produce a successful variation on an established formula. Rather, it praised producers for their ability to anticipate, as if directly, the public's volatile fancy. In this way, rhetoric transformed a public constituted by cinema into a general public that preceded it. To profit from this public would require meticulous management and not a little inspiration.

Numerical data supplied a necessary, but not sufficient, element of this explanatory strategy. Quantities of tickets sold measured hits and flops, provided weekly averages, and allowed assets to be valued and depreciated. In addition to box office statistics, a 1919 report on Famous Players–Lasky commissioned by investment bankers Kuhn, Loeb, and Co. revealed a fan magazine circulation of 950,000 and growing, an aggregate theater seating capacity of over 8 million, dramatically rising annual sales of Simplex projectors, and an expected annual income of $800 million industry-wide.[29] Such figures were impressive, but they could not have been persuasive without a corresponding discourse that characterized and interpreted them as reliable indications of future returns. In 1927, Halsey, Stuart, and Co. reprised that discourse by invoking a dubious investor: "The average man may have been led to believe that pictures of even large companies are produced on a 'hit-or-miss' basis; that a certain amount of money is spent in the mere hope that it will come back when the film is released." Following in the footsteps of the Kuhn, Loeb, and Co. report, the firm then refuted this view:

> Many of the pictures are even contracted for [i.e., leased to exhibitors] before production starts on them, so the company actually knows fairly well what its return is going to be before the filming gets under way. This being the situation, there is constant progress toward cost control, and budgets become increasingly significant. The money plans for a picture not only prescribe its maximum cost allowances, but they reflect a conservative estimate of its minimum net earning capacity.[30]

The Halsey report thus reproduces a line of argument that would have been familiar to Prager's readers. Responsible budgets, cost containment, and monopolistic booking practices allowed companies to set "maximum cost allowance" below estimates of "net earning capacity." A balance sheet could be considered as reliable in this line of business as any other. Yet in order for the numbers to add up, one had to accept that predicted earnings were in fact as stable a quantity as cost allowances. Investors placed their money on the "estimate," one may assume, because this type of rhetoric persuaded them of its difference from "the mere hope" of return.

The need to establish that difference accounts for the exuberance with which Hollywood's promoters extolled managerial discipline. Witness *System's* 1917 report that the "careful checking of actual cost against the original estimate has aroused keen rivalry among the directors. Each strives to keep strictly within the prescribed figures."[31] A decade later, Samuel Katz, President of the Publix Theaters Corporation, issued his own encomium to standardization, proclaiming that "everything happens on charts" in a Publix theater. Katz describes schedules for moving audiences in and out of different venues in various cities. The timing had been calibrated down to the second. Moreover, "We know the number of janitors it should take to clear a given floor area. The amount of cleaning material used is checked carefully, because experience has taught us how much material each kind of a floor should take."[32] To ensure systematic functioning at this level of detail, managers must be trained to supervise themselves as well as their employees. Katz explains that during the six-month training program in New York City, "A great deal of time is spent in building up personality with an appreciation of the responsibilities to the community the man will have when he is sent out into the field."[33] Any number of businessmen would have found this a familiar description of managerial competence and what it takes to produce it. Not only does it resemble Taylor's scientific management, which business school students were likely to encounter, but the general interest business magazine had published countless similar celebrations of discipline, training, and rationalized procedure in numerous lines of work.[34]

Still, differences in the kind of work moviemaking involved required explanation. Like the depreciation formula, star salaries were repeatedly discussed. To businessmen in other lines the large, widely publicized sums paid such stars as Mary Pickford seemed to indicate "unproductive overhead" badly managed and out of control. This objection followed logically from the analogy between filmmaking and "any other" industry. The comparison would seem to define the star as an employee, who ought to submit to the same demands for efficiency and cost-effectiveness as any other worker (including managers themselves). Actors did describe themselves as employees.[35] But executives tended to justify star salaries by taking labor out of the equation. Precisely because she brings "her" public to whatever film she is in, they argued, the star enables the studio to estimate a film's salability and hence its value. As the Halsey, Stuart, and Co.

report explains it, the star has "'production,' 'trademark,' and 'insurance' value."[36] Producers rely on the star to shape, predict, and stabilize the public's "changeable fancy." Thus, star salaries should be conceived not as compensation for work, but as a kind of capital investment.

When Adolph Zukor made the case for movie stars to the readers of *System* in 1918, for instance, he declared that "a star who is popular in Maine will be equally so not only in Arizona but also in England, China, and the Argentine." Global popularity, however, required that the star be recognizable as such: "The whole world likes Mary Pickford, but she must be Mary Pickford and she cannot have her identity lost in the character; likewise the world likes Douglas Fairbanks but only if he does athletic stunts and wears 'sports clothes.'"[37] Historian Richard de Cordova demonstrates that the movie star came into being during the 1910s when fan magazines, newspapers, and various other types of publicity began to produce accounts of her "private-life" that dovetailed with her performances onscreen. In this way, the star acquired a persona that transcended any particular role and far exceeded consideration of the performer's technical abilities.[38] One could hardly find a better instance than Pickford. Zukor personally orchestrated many of the appearances that defined "America's Sweetheart" offscreen and on.[39] Yet even when he claims credit for propelling Pickford to stardom, as he does in his 1953 biography, *The Public Is Never Wrong*, Zukor does so in terms that attribute success to "public" fascination with her "identity." The work of directors, costumers, publicists, even Pickford herself recedes into the background until one is left with what Halsey, Stuart, and Co. call "that unnamable capacity to grip the public imagination."[40] Executives took credit for cultivating this preexisting capacity. But to explain its value, and hence its cost, they resorted to the public's fancy. Through this rhetorical slight of hand, an "identity" that existed only insofar as a sophisticated corporate apparatus could reproduce it acquired a value that appeared to precede its reproduction.

There were no limits to cinema's public, yet it was American. To give movies a boundless audience, various spokespersons insisted on their fundamental appeal. Actor Milton Sills, for instance, asserts that the motion picture "satisfies a fundamental human appetite . . . it is a commodity as essential to the physical and mental health and well-being of the human animal as lumber, wheat, oil, steel, or textiles . . . in short, it is a staple product in constant demand."[41] More succinctly, public relations chief Will Hays declared movies "a great social necessity, an integral part of human life in the whole civilized world."[42] He invoked the proposition that cinema speaks in a universal language: "The roots of the motion picture run back into the unrecorded beginnings of human consciousness." As a visual medium, he claimed, movies offer the "best way of telling things, the most direct route alike to the emotions and the intelligence."[43] During the 1910s, the "universal language" metaphor had conceptually subordinated disparate groups to a standard cinematic address. It thereby equated a particular form of national culture with the generally human.[44] Writing at the end of the 1920s, Hays took advantage of the assumption that America had indeed incorporated various populations to explain why movies arose where they did. It only makes sense that a universal form would evolve in the United States because

> America is in a very literal sense the world-state. All races, all creeds, all the manners of men that exist on the globe, are to be found here—working, sharing and developing side by side in a reasonable degree of understanding and friendship, more friendship among greater diversities of tribes and men than all the previous history of the world discloses. America's people do not speak of themselves primarily as Germans, Englishmen, Greeks or Frenchmen, as Catholics, Hebrews, Protestants, but as Americans.[45]

A world cinema developed in America because America was already the world. Nonetheless, America remains distinguishable from other nations and from the various internal differences it encompasses. While few have been able to reproduce this paradoxical logic with the unselfconscious bravura of Hays, it crops up again and again. One finds it in Terry Ramsaye's pioneering 1926 history of the film industry, for instance, and it has ramified through subsequent discussions of the nickelodeon's immigrant audience and Hollywood's Jewish entrepreneurs.[46] Assertions of Hollywood's simultaneously universal and American character doubtlessly belong to a more general argument over who and what would define U.S. national identity. For the moment, however, I would observe that they also participated in an argument about cinema's commercial viability. By turning American movies into a universal staple, various commentators demonstrated the stability of an industry where no goods trade hands. They also made its audience the de facto model for the consuming public in general.

COMMERCIAL AESTHETICS

That Hollywood businessmen claimed to found their business on the ability to discover, anticipate, and satisfy a limitless public's desire would not be so remarkable if they had not also insisted on their ability to alter that desire. Joseph Kennedy voiced a familiar refrain when he told Harvard students that there was "no sure rule, no standardization of the product. Every picture must stand on its own merits. Every producer sits on his anxious seat till the voice of the people, the final arbiter, is heard." And he echoed an equally commonplace assertion when he declared that the motion picture's "potential social influence cannot be doubted."[47] But he did not explain how movies might influence "society" while waiting anxiously upon its approval. Much like their counterparts in public relations, Kennedy and his colleagues learned to live with the logical contradiction by crafting a rhetoric that equated an influenced "society" with "the people" to be influenced and discovered a positive social mission in the number of tickets movies sold.

One would be hard pressed to find a more telling instance of this rhetoric of influence than Adolph Zukor's 1929 article for *System*, "Looking Ahead a Decade or Two." Zukor explains that filmmakers "must know what principles, what psychology, a typical audience will accept as a starting point. Then we must know what theses can be presented with little or no preparation or support." He credits movies with promoting harmony in labor relations by drawing on such knowledge: "Pictures, by depicting the true basic relation between labor and capital, have educated workmen to the fact that their functions are mutual and inseparable." But his defining example is unquestionably that of domestic consumption. "There is no doubt that the great multitudes of purchasers of all things are demanding higher and higher standards of taste and design," he declares. Filmmakers "realize this with extra force because, we, ourselves, are helping to make it come true. Our own industry—motion-pictures—propagates and will propagate good taste." Zukor defines "good taste" as "unity," the "omission of superfluities." He boasts that "out of scores of settings included in a year's feature pictures, you will scarcely discover any article that does not belong in the picture." Simply by being exposed to such films, "Spectators carry home with them the new habit of unity. When they glance around their own living rooms, they object to things which do not belong in the home picture."[48]

When Zukor chooses home decorating as his case in point, he selects a privileged location both of consumer demand and of socialization: to carry a habit home is to internalize it and to reproduce it through the family. Motion pictures thus usurp the powers of the family's traditional aesthetic guide, the domestic woman, even as they implicitly retain her as their ideal addressee. "Past generations," he explains, "might not have been aware of this unity because they read their stories in books, but the present generation sees the story photographed on the screen and cannot miss perceiving its visual artistic unity."[49] He reminds readers that this special visual power is distinctly American in character: "Literature is defined as a criticism of life. Motion-pictures are a criticism of American life, its surroundings and its possessions." Lest the business reader fail to draw the logical conclusion, he notes that movie "audiences, our consumers, are consumers for all other businesses. Effects upon other businesses will be the same. . . . Esthetic improvement is sweeping alike through the homes of Third Avenue and Tenth Avenue, through the east side and the west side, the suburbs and the farms. We are about to market to a nation of artists." In the near future, he predicts, "No one will have anything to do with what they perceive is bad taste. . . . The weird, the monstrous, the awkward, and the freakish are marked 'out'—out of pictures, out of homes, and out of factory catalogs."[50] Zukor thus makes aesthetic elevation commensurate with commercial success. He contrives to demonstrate that Hollywood champions a national sales effort through its unique ability to elevate taste. And he equates the mechanism of aesthetic uplift with that of promoting less volatile labor relations. With Ciceronian deftness, taste assimilates profit and production; movies appear paragons at once of social and commercial virtue.

Zukor opposes the suasion of "influence" to rational argumentation. Movies "propagate" ideas "presented with little or no preparation or support." Other commentators gender this opposition even more explicitly when they describe the object of influence as a woman consumer. For instance, the director of the United States Bureau of Foreign and Domestic Commerce justified his claim that "motion pictures are the latest form of silent salesman, not so much perhaps for the goods of some individual firm as for classes and kinds of goods as a whole" by pointing to the movies' function as a "fashion show" for the latest woman's styles.[51] Similarly, Samuel R. McKelvie, publisher of *The Nebraska*

Farmer, credits motion pictures with "bettering living conditions" because they encourage farm girls to dress in contemporary styles.

McKelvie's celebration of feminine consumption is all the more notable for its subordination of other tropes of democratic inclusion. He explains, "With the advent of the moving picture, it may be said that the last barriers which separated the man on the isolated farm from his neighbors in the cities were hurdled." By dint of the movies, "the man on the farm may keep abreast of the times as surely as any man anywhere."[52] Similarly, cinema promises to heal religious divisions within the rural community, as the theater provides an ecumenical meeting place for Lutherans and Methodists alike. Yet women's fashion provides the only concrete example of what it means for different types of Protestants to meet or for farmers to "keep abreast of the times." Inspired by movies, shared practices of consumption place farm daughters on an even footing with one another and with their urban counterparts, bridging city, country, and religious difference to produce a single America.[53] McKelvie suggests that this mechanism also works upon the "man on the farm" and will allow his sons to blend in at university. So strongly gendered is his example, however, that it implicitly raises the question of how movies can promote a common America without emasculating it. A similar implication strains Zukor's comparison between improving the "home picture" and educating "workmen." Those who sought to reform the industry did not fail to consider its feminizing effects. But in so doing, they tended to strengthen the impression that an audience that could be influenced could also be understood as feminine.

To succeed with this imaginary woman, influencers had to avoid the appearance of imposition. Zukor starts from the premise that consumers themselves are "demanding higher and higher standards." A similar, but more delicate rhetorical maneuver may be found in repeated claims that "business follows the film much more dependably than it follows the flag."[54] Here an implicit contrast between Hollywood persuasion and state imposition allows cinema to seem the more reliable promoter of American business interests abroad. Yet insofar as it sets itself up as a superior alternative to state power, Hollywood could be assumed to have effects of a political as well as economic character. The proposition was useful because it allowed filmmakers to advocate two positions that might otherwise seem contradictory: Hollywood promotes American interests; the movies supplant government's authority to represent America. They are able to supplant it because they promote commerce through aesthetics, a category that could be distinguished from "politics" and at the same time assimilate it. By expanding the purview of aesthetic influence to include all of civilization, in other words, this type of discourse strove to convince businessmen and state regulators that the hegemonic form of filmmaking was at once socially desirable for global audiences and commercially desirable for American businesses. It sought to install as common sense the proposition that what was popular with American moviegoers would be good for consumers everywhere.

Having staked cinema's ability to be a commercial leader and promote "America" to its aesthetic power, industry spokesmen faced the challenge of proving that "good" aesthetics were "good" business. They supplied the proof by staging mock battles between art and industry. Movies are "a peculiar industry," Jesse Lasky explained to Harvard students, "I call it an industrial art or rather an art industry, for I put the art first and I am always going to." The executive vice president of the Paramount–Famous Players–Lasky Corporation invokes a dilemma familiar to anyone who had been reading about the movies for the past decade: while financial adepts are conservative with respect to artistic experimentation, those with real imagination are careless of capital. It takes the right sort of manager to reconcile the demands of industry with the ambition of art. Film companies, he advised, should "try to retain an executive at the head who has sympathy for the artistic side of production but who also has a lot of good common business sense."[55] The entrepreneur-executives of Lasky's generation often presented themselves as "half business man," "half dreamer or visionary" types, and Zukor was no exception.[56] Given his contention that "to act as a source of taste, motion-pictures, themselves, must have constantly better taste," it was only logical to conclude:

> Individual picture makers who do not possess good taste will be forced into acquiring it by repercussion from audiences constantly more sophisticated. Or else they will be forced out of the industry by managers' reports of giggles, titters, and other criticisms, including the very effective criticism of lower box-office receipts.[57]

This fear of "giggles" ought not to be confused with the strivings of the parvenu. As Zukor describes it, "good taste" is less a personal quality than a professional skill. One must constantly update it to stay ahead of an audience made "constantly more sophisticated" by films themselves. Thus Zukor sets in motion a rhetorical seesaw on which the public's desire sits opposite Hollywood's ability to influence that desire. As in Lasky's account, to balance the two would require a manager skilled in reconciling business with art (and everything that could be assimilated to it).

Unlike Zukor, Lasky indicates what the production of commercially viable taste actually involved on screen. He relates an anecdote about the film *Rough Riders* (1927), which depicted Teddy Roosevelt's famous troupe. One might assume that the topic alone would prove popular with viewers, he reasons. After all, the story of San Juan Hill was well known and had a scale that would lend itself to the screen. Moreover, the studio had guaranteed historical credibility by engaging Roosevelt's official biographer, Herman Hagedorn, for the screenplay. Unfortunately, the completed scenario got bogged down in detail. It "lacked every essential of romance to hold it together," Lasky asserts, and had to be substantially altered to bring out "the drama, the heart interest." A love story was added. Lasky opposes himself to a hypothetical executive who would have released the film on the strength of its subject matter and screenwriter alone—and invariably produced a flop. He takes credit for striking an inspired balance between art and commerce, in other words, when he repeats the formula that established Hollywood movies as corporate art form.

Business discourse neither conceals nor reveals some hidden truth about Hollywood movies and their audiences. It promotes its own agenda, and that agenda is obvious enough. Above all, a highly metaphoric rhetoric of "the public" provided Hollywood businessmen with a way to legitimate their jobs and their industry. Through this rhetoric, they strove to explain that movies were manageable, profitable, and conducive to any number of beneficent endeavors. They turned the inherent unpredictability of hits and flops into proof that careful management would be required to give the public's fancy any stability at all, and thus make a profit. And they promoted an allegory between moviegoer and feminine consumer in order to argue that such management served the commercial and social interests of the nation. To be sure, their claims of positive influence had counterparts in predictions of moral danger. Celebrations of supremely American appeal inspired accusations of un-

American influences. And advocacy of feminine consumption prompted concern that masculine reason was at risk. Joseph Kennedy gestured toward such objections when he acknowledged that cinema's "esthetic standards, wavering between intrinsic quality and commercial value, have revived ancient and seemingly interminable controversies."[58] One might pause to marvel at how neatly the supposed hoariness of the controversies mitigates cinema's responsibility for them. But more clever still is the proposition that "esthetic standards" are bound to waver. When Kennedy defined controversy as a problem of balancing "intrinsic quality" and "commercial value," he picked a fight some version of corporate management was bound to win.

THE BUSINESS OF REFORM

Although the twenties are commonly depicted as the heyday of Hollywood licentiousness, they are better understood as the period when the project of regulating the movies reached professional maturity. To be sure, that project began much earlier. A direct line is often drawn from the campaigns of the 1920s back to the Christmas closing of New York City's nickelodeons in 1908 amid fears of moral pollution. From there, it has been all too easy to insinuate that those who decried the movies spoke in the repressive voice of nineteenth-century gentility. Lary May identifies early reformers more precisely when he describes them as "men and women aligned to rising business, professional, and political groups" who were "primarily interested in public welfare and industrial regulation as a means to order the new corporate system through the creation of a powerful state."[59] During the 1920s, industry critics developed divergent positions on what the role of the state should be, as various reformers opposed demands for federal censorship legislation while insisting that the social good would require some mechanism for improving film aesthetics. The major achievement of the decade, however, lay in the formation of institutions capable of incorporating critics in a nationwide public relations apparatus.

A number of transformations were involved. The industry itself developed production guidelines capable of satisfying various state and local censorship boards as well as censors abroad. The National Board of Censorship (later the National Board of Review) had inaugurated a voluntary postproduction approval process in 1909. But with the founding of the Motion Picture Producer's and Distributor's Association

(MPPDA) in 1922, the industry sought ways to forestall objections during the planning and production phases. Examinations of the association's internal documents reveal that it considered from its inception the full panoply of concerns later included in the Production Code of 1930. In addition to the representation of sex, crimes, and violence, for instance, producers were cautioned against the defamation of clergy and cruelty to animals. Portrayals of various types of foreigners and foreign locations were also a concern.[60] To calibrate its sense of the permissible, the MPPDA created an advisory committee of representatives from a wide range of national organizations, including, for example, the American Federation of Labor, the Camp Fire Girls, the Federal Council of Churches of Christ in America, and the War Department.[61] Among censorship and reform advocates themselves, meanwhile, national campaigns by national organizations increasingly subordinated local and regional efforts. If the National Catholic Welfare Council is any indication, this required that spokespersons be hired specifically to explain and advocate a position on the movies. Substantial authority to represent the organization as a whole was transferred to that office.[62] Finally, the first national studies of Hollywood's effects on young people began to appear in the early 1920s.[63] An application of the emerging discipline of social survey research, the studies supported reformers in their contention that movies influenced impressionable minds, and they provided producers with information about the audience demographics. In sum, these developments provided a framework that allowed businessmen, censorship advocates, and reformers to collaborate as well as compete in determining what the acceptable contents of commercial mass entertainment would be.

To authorize themselves, however, reform advocates and censors alike adopted a rhetoric that set business interest in opposition to moral value. Censorship advocates condemned the greed of producers who catered to base desires in hopes of realizing a quick profit. Reformers equated artistic merit with moral elevation and made commerce the opponent of each. Much like Hollywood executives, in other words, censors and reformers set influence and profit at odds in order to claim that they alone could strike the proper balance between the two.

For their part, censorship proponents asserted that "decent" pictures were in the long-term interest of the industry. The exemplary procensorship tract of the 1920s is undoubtedly Reverend William Sheafe Chase's

Catechism on Motion Pictures in Inter-State Commerce. President of the New York Civic League, Chase begins with what has been the perennial censorship question: "Who is to blame for the menace of the movies, the producer or the public?" To answer, Chase identifies a disagreement among executives themselves. While "B. B. Hampton, the President of four motion picture companies," answers "'The Public,'" "Mr. Sidney S. Cohen, President of the Motion Picture Theaters Owners of America, contends that producers are to blame for the indecent, rotten, putrid films which are defiling our land, 'because they have misjudged the tastes and demands of the public.'"[64] Here Chase takes advantage of a contemporary industrial dispute, just as these executives apparently turned to procensorship rhetoric to strengthen their respective positions. Exhibitors (such as Cohen) warred with producers (such as Hampton) for control of national theater chains in the early twenties (and were losing). But the manner in which Chase sets up the question is more notable than either position alone. On the basis of answers given, one must conclude that neither "the public" nor *good* executives want "smutty pictures." Thus, "an effective law, which requires every motion picture to be examined by competent inspectors and compelled to come up to the standards of the morality of the general public" would liberate the majority of producers "from the control of the few degenerate producers. It will enable honorable producers with big profits to themselves furnish clean movies to the public." The contention that "clean movies" are desired by public and producers alike would seem to contradict the censor's contention that audiences need protection from "putrid" films. Chase finesses that contradiction by declaring: "Curiosity, not real, lasting desire to see licentious films, accounts for the first drawing power of vile pictures. But in the end filth disgusts and repels the crowd." Only an unscrupulous businessman would build his enterprise on such a shaky foundation.

Historian and Pennsylvania censor Ellis Paxson Oberholtzer echoed Chase's reasoning in his 1922 volume, *Morals of the Movie* when he elaborated a vision of the "clean film" as

> drama which is light and pleasant and romantic, coming with nice humor and sound psychology close to our daily life, plus a little idealism. . . . There is a place in the "movie" world for plots which abound in good natural sentiment, dealing with the eternally interesting theme

of honest love, drawing the mind to pleasant relationships between men and women. If producers would set more stories of this kind before the people a great deal of the "sex rot" in pictures would automatically be driven out of existence.[65]

It is essential to note that Oberholtzer's distinction between "sex rot" and "honest love" provides a poor description of contemporary filmmaking. In fact, contemporary films of celebrated sexiness, such as *Why Change Your Wife?*, typically dealt with the "eternally interesting theme of honest love" and often did so in a "light," "pleasant," and "romantic" manner. Moreover, films beloved by conservatives, such as *Way Down East,* called to mind the hazards and thrills of unchecked lechery with leaden explicitness. Here and throughout the book, Oberholtzer does not specify how we may distinguish "sex" from "love" on-screen so much as he insists, first, that the difference is all-important, and second, that censors like himself were in a better position to adjudicate it than industry executives.

The proposition that "sex sells" thus cuts two ways in censorship writing. It provides a commonsense explanation for why censorship should occur, but it also supplies the rationale behind the prediction that "decent" films will incite even more profitable desires. Censorship writing reproduced a thoroughly modern discourse on sexuality. It made the difference between the moral and the immoral equivalent to the difference between the normal and the deviant; it suggested that a healthy society would require the regulation of individual desire; and it confirmed heterosexual monogamy as the normative state of that desire.[66] It also promoted the notion that movies had a unique power to upset that norm by exploiting a depraved "curiosity" already present in the public. The medium made it especially easy to collapse the difference separating love from lust, and worse, sexualized aggression. As the censorship debate progressed, it became increasingly clear that detailed prohibitions of specific topics or scenes could not provide practicable regulation. Rather, general principles interpreted on a case-by-case basis by qualified experts would be required to distinguish corruption from "real, lasting desire."[67]

Where censors began with the premise that an indecent picture would defile the public, other critics started from the assumption that commercial mass appeal degrades taste and intelligence. Movies dragged those who might otherwise have higher standards down to the level of the lowest common denominator. This supposition underwrote a number of the articles published by the *Annals of the Academy of Political and Social Science* as a 1926 special issue on "The Motion Picture in Its Economic and Social Aspects." To open the issue, no less an authority than journalist-turned-historian Terry Ramsaye contrasted the dramatic rise of motion pictures as an industry with their "accidental" and "incidental" development as an art.[68] Ramsaye believed that movies had "reached the ceiling of popular understanding." In a similar vein, writer Charlotte Perkins Gilman emphasized their wasted potential. She wrote:

> Part of our failure to see new and enormous values in this medium is due to the coarse misuse of it by commercial interests seeking only to appeal to the most people, and to the lowest tastes of the most people at that. We have not only the novelty of this young art to confuse us, but its degradation, the repellent anomaly of a corrupted child. Efforts at "uplifting" are ridiculed. Censorship, so far, has rather added to the ridicule. Against the introduction of the motion picture in the schools stands the entrenched book system and the question of expense; and against demand for better films in general is the opposition of the box office.[69]

There is no mistaking the moral character of such arguments for aesthetic reform. The deference between high and low taste is every bit as charged, and every bit as slippery, as the distinction between "decent" and "filthy" in censorship writing. Just so, Gilman's "corrupted child" implies that readers in social and political science are right to recoil from Hollywood. But it also urges them to adopt the wayward waif. Gilman confirms that corruption derives from "commercial interests" but works to redefine the antagonists of those interests as contributors to the problem. "Entrenched" reliance on books in education and ineffective censorship and uplift campaigns will not correct the "coarse misuse" of the medium. To correct it will require reformers to abandon traditional approaches and find a way of turning the "opposition of the box office" into an advantage.

There were several proposals. Gilman suggests that public libraries make generally available the very best films. As these quality films begin to stimulate the "imagination" of library patrons, she predicts, a general elevation of taste will occur, which will in turn inspire a market for better films and spur the artistic development of the industry.[70] Where

Gilman hopes that better art might prevail if only the general public were led in the right direction, others anticipated the public's segmentation into an aesthetic hierarchy. For instance, Arthur Edwin Krows, freelance scenario writer, film editor, and author of *Play Production in America,* proposes that filmmakers would profit by cultivating the highbrow audience as a distinct market.[71] Yet another tactic for reconciling commerce and taste may be found in the work of movie critics Morris Ernst and Pare Lorentz. They attributed cinema's aesthetic failings to censors, and not filmmakers.[72] Just as Chase accused a "few degenerate producers" of betraying the public trust, they cast "self-appointed" censors as petty Victorians out of step with the public's values.[73] Captions and illustrations make the case in their 1930 book, *Censored: The Private Life of the Movie.* Underneath an artful and apparently unobjectionable still, we read: "'Love.' Greta Garbo and John Gilbert playing the lovers in a dramatization of Anna Karenina. Note: They had to be married before they could love in Pennsylvania."[74] Here and throughout the text, Ernst and Lorentz expose what they clearly assumed would be self-evident hairsplitting and hypocrisy. They inform readers that studios avoid re-editing films to meet the specifications of various states only by accommodating the standards of the most restrictive censorship boards. The industry is compelled to enforce the nebulous rules of a conservative minority in exasperating defiance of the artistic work of screenwriters, directors, and actors. In this way, *Censored* suggests that commerce, the public, and art would be on the same side if not for the meddlesome influence of a backward few.

The stakes were high because so many commentators reproduced the claim that American movies had a special power and a universal appeal. Reformers and censorship advocates appropriated for their own purposes the same assertions about cinema's visual properties that business writers employed. Gilman, for instance, assured readers that movies were in fact "the long sought 'universal language,'" which "spreads communication world-wide and swift as eye can follow." This contention allowed her to explain why cinema, if properly administered, offered "inescapable supremacy" as an agent of "social progress."[75] Chase gave this power a more sinister construction:

> A film cannot be put in the same class as a book. A gun and a razor are
> both dangerous weapons. But New York requires one to be licensed and

not the other. In order to be injured by a bad book one must be able to read the language and have mind and imagination enough to picture the evil to himself. When a bad book is dramatized on the screen, its vividness and effect upon the mind are multiplied a hundred fold.[76]

Chase's metaphor collapses a difference of kind (gun vs. razor, movie vs. book) into a quantitative difference (a movie has one hundred times a book's influence). He implies that a mind affected by the movies cannot be expected to be fully aware of its own best interests, while a mind affected only by books has superior powers of discernment. For this reason, movies posed a special hazard to public morality. But also for this reason, they offered unprecedented opportunities to "educate" the public, to reveal its true interests, and thus bring about positive change.

It comes as no surprise, therefore, to find reformers repeating the trope of the feminine consumer. Gilman appropriates the rhetoric of the motion picture as fashion show to advance her own reform proposal: "Women of sluggish minds, who care for nothing in dress but the newest invention of their dictators, could see the pitiful exhibition of what we used to wear, the skillfully intensified absurdity of things we do wear, and a startling array of things we might wear—if we chose." She argues that were her library plan to prevail "some nascent power of selection might be developed among the sheep."[77] Her position is unique—and perhaps uniquely feminist—in accepting the diagnosis of a mind-numbing feminization while advancing a cure that did not abandon the conception of the public as a woman. She takes the full weight, one might say, of the paradox posed by Beth's self-actualization through fashion in *Why Change Your Wife?* More often, solutions to the problem of a sheep-like public predicated the restoration of purportedly masculine reason on the rejection of purportedly feminine consumption.

But remasculinization took a telling turn in reform writing. It tended to render the desirable type of audience not as a self-governing man but as a studious schoolboy. "Motion picture audiences must be consciously trained to know good pictures as a boy must be trained in a knowledge of the classics," asserted sociologist Donald Young in an essay on "Social Standards and the Motion Picture."[78] Ernest L. Crandall, Director of Lectures and Visual Instruction for the New York City Board of Education, agreed and proposed that public schools should teach film as a form of literature.[79] Editor of *The Educational Screen* Nelson L. Greene explained that such efforts were especially necessary because "theatrical films themselves are already a colossal force in world education, unmeasured and probably immeasurable." The lack of concrete data, however, does not prevent Greene from characterizing the education movies provide as "lawless and uncontrolled . . . quite accidental and without aim." "Education" and "influence" become interchangeable terms as Greene describes the motion picture's all-pervasive effects: "For the audience beyond school age, it influences opinion, attitude and conduct in every phase of human living. For the school children themselves, it has an influence, largely adverse, which carries over into the classroom to a degree little realized as yet by the rank and file of the teaching profession."[80] Greene defines motion pictures the "competitor" and "dangerous opponent" of the educator, then, by arguing that movies and teachers exercise comparable kinds of influence.[81] As in business writing, the professionally crucial move was to distinguish a socially desirable version of influence from that which threatened disorder. Young, Crandall, and Greene collectively make such distinction by contrasting the "lawless" and "aimless" education of the movies with the faculty of discrimination film appreciation classes might provide. To make the case that this second type of education would in fact serve the public, however, they contend that every aspect of its "opinion, attitude, and conduct" has already been influenced by the movies. They rhetorically deprive the public at large of the very capacity they hope to inculcate at school. To "educate" the public on the schoolboy model, then, amounts to essentially the same sort of process whereby the taste of a feminine consumer might be improved. Those who promoted this view did not aim to turn the public into a reasonable paterfamilias, in other words, but to arrogate his authority for themselves.

The feminization of the public gave professionalism a masculine voice, but it did not equate it with a male body. True, the new professional logic displaced the nineteenth-century argument that authorized the middle-class woman to influence the nation through her supervision of a domestic sphere. Historian Alison Parker provides a case in point. She describes what happened to the Women's Christian Temperance Union (WCTU) as it took up the project of regulating the movies during first decades of the century. Often depicted as the quintessential crusade of Victorian ladies, the WCTU in fact "welcomed experts and celebrated every legislative and regulatory advance as a victory for mothers and their children." That strategy produced a contradiction, however. Campaigns based on "petitions and voluntary actions" clashed with "calls for government regulation, which removed the site of 'mothering' ever farther from the home."[82] During the 1920s, efforts to mother a nation through the movies finally became obsolete. Rather than a hypothetical lady of the WCTU, one might better imagine this decade's woman reformer as a social scientist. She conducts survey research at the Russell Sage Foundation, for example, which in 1923 presented the first major national study of moviegoing children (i.e., teenagers).[83] This professional woman did not face the same double bind that her Victorian counterpart did. It was not a matter of explaining why her sex qualified her to influence America even as it precluded political and economic participation in the nation. The rhetorical equation of "women" with an unselfconscious state of society at large produced a different conundrum.[84] The public-as-woman figured diverse demographic elements, including children, and demonstrated that a purportedly neutral science would be required to apprehend their common features. This presented the professional woman with the challenge of representing the public without appearing to personify it; to personify it would define her as the object, rather than the subject, of professional activity. The "we" in Gilman's "things we might wear—if we chose" should be understood as consequence of this double bind. Gilman must both mark her distance from the "women of sluggish minds" and acknowledge her similarity to them in order to argue on their behalf.

Whether they were men or women, critics of the movies and industry advocates tended to described cinema's public in similar ways. They did so because they were trying to establish similar kinds of authority over it. In fact, reformers often proposed mechanisms the industry had already instituted. Gilman, for instance, does not mention how her 1926 proposals would differ from the public library campaign the industry had sponsored since the late 1910s.[85] Similarly, when Young called upon "churches, women's clubs, civic associations, governmental agencies and philanthropic foundations" to promote an "Enlightened public opinion" through movies, he does not acknowledge that the MPPDA had already invited "great national citizen organizations with millions of members interested in social service, education, religion, civics, to associate themselves with the organized industry" on its Public Relations Committee.[86] Censorship advocates proposed a kindred arrangement: a new federal censorship agency would be headed by six commissioners, including two lawyers, two teachers, one member of a local censorship board, and one representative with experience in the film industry (but without a current financial stake in it).[87] The MPPDA's public relations apparatus was certainly a way of coopting the criticism behind such proposals. But it was also a way of coopting the power of those who made them. By including national spokespersons who could collectively claim an even broader expertise than the censors' six commissioners, the industry attempted not only to secure its professional autonomy but also to enhance its ability to define, predict, and shape as many diverse constituencies as possible.

This is not to say every type of organization could be included or that all who were had equal standing. The NAACP had proved itself capable of a highly coordinated national censorship campaign against *The Birth of a Nation,* for example, yet did not win a spot on the MPPDA's Public Relation's Committee. My point is simply that arguments over who could and should "influence" America through the movies abetted an institutional model that entrusted decisions about content to salaried professionals.[88] Studio executives, not investors, would make the day-to-day decisions of the art industry, just as official spokespersons would represent the members of national organizations. Alongside the hierarchy of specialists responsible for making the movies stood growing ranks of women and men who wrote survey questions, developed production guidelines, sold advertising, and edited fan magazines. Although they disagreed with one another on any number of issues, they collaborated to maintain, update, and extend cinematic culture.

"Influence" supplied a rationale for this project, but it does not describe how movies remade the nation. Those who competed to regulate motion picture content used the language of influence to establish that the future security of the nation's markets and members depended on their efforts. In the process, they defined the public as a locus of contradictions. Though capricious and unpredictable, it could to a certain extent be molded and anticipated. Although it could not immediately distinguish "depraved curiosity" from "real, lasting desire," it could be expected to thrive on the latter. It was both the inviolable agent of the market and innocent victim of its moral depredation. Fundamentally human, it was also supremely American. Composed of diverse components, a woman best represented it. These contradictions do not indicate the persistence of the nineteenth-century America movies supplanted. They are abiding features of the America movies mediated. They result from attempts to make mediation intelligible as a "message" from those who produce information to an audience imagined to precede the form in which the message occurs. It made sense to fight over who would influence the nation through the movies only after a large and stable audience shared information in the form of the feature film. Influence rhetoric succeeds by failing to acknowledge that predication. Those who employed it vied to extend and update the categories of cinematic culture by misrecognizing the novel form of mediation that authorized them to do so. Hollywood's historic role cannot be found in its supposed power to promote sexual license, degrade taste, banish critical thought, and make a nation of women consume. It may be found in the ability to envision a woman who can be influenced: although her existence as an alluring and reproducible picture at first seems at odds with her subjective vision, the two fall into harmonious alignment once sightlines and space have been properly arranged, not always by men, but almost always by professionals.

4. Ethnic Management

In their compulsion to depict the romantic couple as a white one, silent feature films accorded white persons a normative status they denied the nation's other inhabitants. But the movies also demonstrated that no embodied person, no matter how white, could see and arrange spaces well enough to secure the couple. Such supervision depended on an ability to stand aloof from any particular population, to distinguish types of individuals from one another, and to place individuals in social space. In this final chapter, I address the logical question of how a culture can persist in both beliefs. To locate "America" both in a white body and in an invisible management team, I argue, ultimately required a collaboration between two distinct ways of categorizing identity: one that sought to standardize visible differences among populations and another that purported to specify psychic conflicts between native and foreign ways of life. Social science generally distinguishes the first of these as a residual nineteenth-century scheme of "race" and the second as the emergent early-twentieth-century form of "ethnicity." Although such a chronology helps to explain the persistence of racial thinking among ethnicity's key proponents, it also sets the two terms in opposition and therefore misses their novel partnership. Ethnicity neither eclipsed nor preserved race. Rather, it reconfigured race and made it part of a productive new combination. Corporate America employed the conjoined concepts to establish how members of marginal populations might depict and regulate a mainstream public. In parallel, not in tandem, race and ethnicity answered the question of who should orchestrate the appearance of a loving white couple on Hollywood's silver screen.

No figure better illustrates why professional managerial America required the concept of ethnicity than the movie mogul. By the end of the 1920s, journalism had delineated the mogul's features and made him the motive force behind the industry. As his myth grew, it attributed the rise of Hollywood to a markedly Jewish desire to succeed on American terms. It became a critical commonplace that Jewish movie managers won authority by conserving America's most WASPish features. The distinction between ethnicity and race made it possible to imagine that foreigners might move from the margins of American culture to its managerial center without ceasing to be Jewish or altering the nation's racial makeup. This narrative of relatively smooth transition belies a far more fundamental shift. That shift occurred during the first decades of the twentieth century as a new type of pluralism competed with an especially vicious racial nativism to determine whom "America" would comprise. In history, philosophy, and sociology, such key figures as W. E. B. Du Bois, Horace Kallen, and Robert Ezra Park began to make an ethnic account of American populations possible by offering distinct amendments to the race concept. Crucial though these revisions were, they make little sense in the absence of the more general convictions, first, that race was a visible fact, and, second, that its very visibility concealed an identity race would not suffice to define. This twofold proposition is a preeminently cinematic one. In 1927, it achieved what remains its most noteworthy audiovisual formulation.

THE AUDIOVISUAL AMERICAN

The surprise hit of 1927 and harbinger of the talking pictures, *The Jazz Singer*, tells an exemplary assimilation story. Those who have chronicled the themes, characters, and plot lines of the "ghetto film" typically make *The Jazz Singer* the culminating example of that genre, which arose with the feature film, thrived during the 1920s, and largely disappeared after 1930.[1] The film uses sound to perfect the tale related by any number of early-twentieth-century films, novels, and plays, in which a first generation of Jewish immigrants, characterized by their Lower East Side neighborhood life, religious traditions, and foreign heritage, vie with a second generation, who desire nothing more than to leave the ghetto, fall in love with a blond man or woman, and live the American dream. As early as 1909 Israel Zangwill offered such a narrative as a parable of American national identity in his controversial play *The Melting Pot.* For many, Zangwill's title invokes the liquidation of mama, papa, and everything they stand for. Yet we would do well to recall how hard his play and its successors strive to redefine New World ambition and Old World tradition as compatible entities. To produce a happy ending for its young couple, for instance, the film *Abie's Irish Rose* (Paramount, 1928) restages a scene of reconciliation between Irish and Jewish parents that dates back at least to *Becky Gets a Husband* (Lubin, 1912).[2] By the same token, *The Younger Generation* (Columbia, 1929) reminded moviegoers that the arriviste who disavowed his ghetto background would end up alienated, abandoned, and alone.

The very prevalence of assimilation narratives during the 1920s perhaps explains why reviewers largely ignored *The Jazz Singer*'s New York premiere. They were all too familiar with the hackneyed stage melodrama on which it was based. An about-face in the tone of reception occurred months later, when, as historian Donald Crafton puts it, critics "retroactively transformed the release of *The Jazz Singer* into a cultural, industry, and personal monument" by calling attention to its protagonist's remarkable voice.[3] This revision recast an otherwise typical movie as an exceptional one. *The Jazz Singer* became the film that established a curiosity—the talkies—as the future of American cinema. It attained this status despite the fact that no technical breakthrough had occurred. While ambitious in its use of existing techniques, the film was hardly the first to synchronize a recorded voice with an image, nor does it do so throughout.[4] One must look elsewhere to distinguish *The Jazz Singer* from contemporary part-talking features and to explain why historians of U.S. film and culture continue to find it such a key example.

The film is exceptional because it uses sound to organize space according to the pattern silent features had established strictly by manipulating the visual field. The Jewish voice supplements the visual love story to resolve the predictable struggles of its protagonist through the then unconventional technique of the musical number. In fact, *The Jazz Singer* employs two numbers to achieve resolution. In the first, Jack Robin takes his dying father's place as cantor in the synagogue next to the family's Lower East Side home. Clad in robe and shawl, the gleaming Jazz

Singer does not so much perform as inhabit Kol Nidre. The motion of his expressive face and body are wholly synchronized with Aramaic words that seem to come from deep within. When this voice travels to his father's death chamber, it moves Cantor Rabinowitz to acknowledge the son he had disowned in the first reel. When its sound wafts through the outer room of the Rabinowitz apartment, it enraptures Jack's gentile romantic interest Mary Dale (May McAvoy), who stares out the window toward the synagogue next door. The "tear" or "cry" ascribed to this voice marks an audible similarity not only to the voice of Cantor Rabinowitz (Warner Oland/Joseph Diskay), with which it is explicitly compared, but also to that of another cantor (Josef Rosenblatt) whose public performance Jack attends while away from home.[5] These auditory resemblances endow Jack's voice with a Jewishness irreducible to his ritual performance of Kol Nidre. As this irreducible quality, Jewishness persists despite everything that indicates Jack's assimilation into gentile America. His rendition of Kol Nidre speaks to the Jewish father even as it wins Mary's heart.

A still more complex orchestration of ethnicity occurs in the second of the film's concluding numbers, when the Jazz Singer takes the Broadway stage to perform "Mammy" and his Jewish voice animates the blacked-up face of American minstrelsy. Where the visible contrast between burnt cork and an apparently foundational whiteness underscores the importance of racial classification to national identity, sound overcomes the strict separation that for most of the film makes the American stage seem incompatible with the synagogue and Jewish home. Linguistically, rhythmically, and melodically, "Mammy" could not be more different from Kol Nidre. Familiar English supplants foreign Aramaic; up-tempo triumphs over dirge; the major key defeats the minor. But we hear Robin's inheritance of Jewish suffering in each. The very contrast serves to underscore the fact that the same voice—and thus the same body—sings these two very different songs. As in the prior number, synchronization with the image serves to give this voice a source in Jack's body and thus to locate it concretely in space. When the voice continues over images of Mama Rabinowitz (Eugenie Besserer), who beams at Jack from the audience, and Mary, who looks yearningly toward him from the wings, it redefines the formerly antagonistic relationship between these two women. Mary and Mama do not occupy exactly the same space. Here as elsewhere the film maintains a distinction between their separate spheres.

Seen in relationship to the voice, however, they occupy overlapping spaces with a common center. By thus using pictures and sounds to assure us its white protagonist might embrace American success and survive intermarriage without ceasing to be Jewish, *The Jazz Singer* gives ethnicity an ideal form.

All sounds that contribute to visual narrative may be said to have something in common with this voice. James Lastra calls "voice like" any use of film sound that emphasizes "its origin, identity, and comprehensibility." In order for sound to appear synchronized with the image in the first place, he explains, "The essential problem was to produce the effect of appropriate and recognizable sounds emanating from the objects on the screen, as if the sounds were, like the voice, a property of the depicted object."[6] Even before the predominance of speech, films employed noises and musical instruments to this end. *Sunrise* (Fox, 1927), for instance, was among the first feature films to offer a recorded soundtrack and makes a characteristic honk the audible property of pictured car horns. More ambitiously, *The First Auto* (Warner Bros., 1927) uses musical instruments to represent human speech and to give voice to the spasmodic flicking of ash from a cigar. Unrecorded musical accompaniment for silent films undoubtedly included similar "vocal" effects. This minor component of the silent film's audiovision became a defining component of the sound film, then, once the human voice claimed a relationship to a visible body and began to participate in film narrative. To be sure, the musical score persists and continues to function in ways it had throughout the silent era—underscoring the menacing nature of one scene and the safety of another, lending its tempo to the competition between the two, and so on. But only when music acquires vocal properties does it begin to supplement the definition of its source by placing that source in a particular space.[7]

Sound that appears embodied locates itself in a space irreducible to the frame. Whether heard over one shot or several, whether the source is pictured or not, a voice represents the particular location from which it emanates.[8] In Hollywood film, a variety of techniques ensure that sound collaborates with the image to define that location. Filmmakers manipulate the sound's "spatial signature," for instance, to guarantee that it does not contradict the picture. A voice that places its speaker in a large reverberant room, for instance, will never accompany an image that locates him in a more intimate setting.[9] Accordingly, the voice may always be placed within a larger visual story, even when the dialogue provides its own narrative information. This use of sound distinguishes the fiction film from those documentaries in which the narrator's disembodied voice claims god-like authority to explain the image from elsewhere.[10] It also distinguishes the sound feature from early "canned" vaudeville acts, which used the synchronization of speech and image to represent a singular, theatrical space and thus subordinated sound and picture alike to the performance they represented. In contrast, feature films employ sound most deftly when they make it contribute to the process of distinguishing, relating, and transforming spaces. This is why *The Jazz Singer* seems ahead of its time. Although director Alan Crossland and his team synchronize sound and image in only a handful of sequences, they employ that technique to move Jack Robin's voice from the synagogue to the Broadway stage and to place his auditors, Mama and Mary, within a single American space. Neither *The Jazz Singer's* immediate predecessors (e.g., *The First Auto*) nor its immediate successors (e.g., *Noah's Ark, Abie's Irish Rose, The Younger Generation*) use sound in this manner.[11]

Sound technology did not restore voice to a silent body, in other words. Rather, particular uses of that technology created a new, distinctly cinematic, version of the speaking body. Lastra notes, for instance, that film's audible voices have a good deal in common with the type of writing that had previously represented cinematic speech: "Changes in typeface, use of italics, quotation marks, exclamation points, deviant syntax . . . as well as bracketing of intertitles by shots of the same pair of moving lips, served to assign a source to an utterance and to make the utterance as expressive of the character's emotional state as possible."[12] Similarly, Hollywood developed techniques to ensure that sounds would be readily intelligible as linguistic signs and could be combined with images to lodge a particular voice in a particular body. These techniques define the point of origin in the individual body, rather than the other way around. The audible voice differs from prior cinematic uses of words and pictures not because it gives the body an interior they denied it but because it simultaneously thickened human interiority and allowed it to travel across spatial boundaries, detached from the body image.

Audibly embodied, the properties of Jazz Singer's voice defy simple description. What intertitles identify as a "tear" or "cry" may be heard as a sharp, almost gasping attack on accented notes then held with a tremulous sustain. This quality classifies Jack Robin's voice as Jewish, but it also gives the voice a distinct, individual grain. In contrast, the voices of the anonymous cantor and Papa Rabinowitz, each of whom sings only once and not in English, are nearly indistinguishable from one another. Their voices have a tear, but no grain.[13] Because Jack's cry differs while remaining similar to these others, it signifies a unique interior volume. Images make the sound visible as a physical force that contorts the Jazz Singer's frame. The outgoing song cocks his torso and thrusts his arms away from his shoulders. The intake of breath snaps the body back into position. Moving pictures conspire with sounds to lodge Jewishness in Robin's body and define it as his very own. This effect carries over to the body of the star. Asa Yoelson may well have been understood as a Jewish vaudevillian despite his stage name, Al Jolson. *The Jazz Singer* made him an inescapably Jewish one because of it. Tellingly, the producers of the 1939 musical tribute film *Hollywood Cavalcade* (Twentieth-Century Fox) asked Jolson to reprise Kol Nidre and not "Mammy" or "Blue Skies," both of which had been in his stage act.[14]

When *The Jazz Singer* represents Jewishness as a vocal quality, it makes intelligible a type of difference audiences cannot have found easy to characterize. In this film and others, intertitles refer to Jews as a "race." Far from clarifying matters, however, that term pointed to problems of classification raised by a wide range of arguments over differences that would later be called "national," "racial," and "ethnic." If film Jews were a "race" in the 1920s, for instance, there is no confusing them with the caricatures that had prevailed little more than a decade before. Such films as *Cohen's Fire Sale* (Edison, 1907) and *A Gesture Fight in Hester Street* (Biograph, 1903) had populated the ghetto with swarthy, bearded men equipped with enormous wax noses.[15] This Jewish type had been prominent on the American stage for at least a decade (but not before the 1880s) and no doubt participated in a more general trend to link racial difference and foreignness as the joint objects of derision. Beginning around 1908, however, filmmakers modified the type in such a way that these two qualities, formerly so intimately entwined, became distinct. Such films as *Romance of a Jewess* (Biograph) and *Old Isaacs, the Pawnbroker* (Biograph) reduced the Jew's exaggerated features. They placed him clearly within the visual range that defines whiteness while continuing to portray him as a little bit foreign. This shift was relatively sudden. As Miriam Hansen points out, film historians sometimes judge the Jewish husband of *Romance of a Jewess* by its contemporaries and mistake it for an early narrative of Jewish-Gentile intermarriage.[16] In a matter of years, then, the caricatured alien Jew became the protagonist of a slightly modified Hollywood love story.[17]

As a feature film genre, the ghetto film told substantially the same sort of visual story about Jews as Hollywood features in general told about any number of other white couples. Surveys of the genre typically stress the conventional character of its romantic narratives, which often, but not always, concern the difficulties of Jewish-Gentile intermarriage.[18] A staple of the genre such as *Humoresque* (Cosmopolitan, 1920), for instance, does not depart dramatically in structure from tales of non-Jewish lovers separated by war and eventually reunited (e.g., *The Big Parade*). Considered as stories of spatial transformation, the notable feature of these films is their imperative to extract the couple from the teeming sidewalks and tenements of New York's Lower East Side. Yet it is important to note that narrative resolution is as likely to occur by carving out an oasis of domesticity within the ghetto as it is by removing the couple from the Jewish neighborhood entirely. *The Jew's Christmas* (Rex, 1913) provides an early instance of the former option, while at least one late example, Frank Capra's *The Younger Generation,* strongly presents it as the preferable alternative. Capra isolates the son who turns his back on the ghetto in the dim, cold, cavern of his uptown apartment. Even his Mama leaves him. She goes to live in the modest music shop on Delancey Street that his sister and her Jewish husband share. But the space inhabited by the Jewish family at the end barely resembles the crowded streets of the film's opening. It approximates much more closely the unmarked middle America of small businesses and domestic bliss made familiar by countless feature films. As this example suggests, the ghetto film did not aim to eliminate the Lower East Side entirely or wall it off from the rest of nation—in the manner, for instance, of the absolute segregation of African America mandated by *Birth of a Nation.* Rather, it defined the Jewish neighborhood as a less-than-ideal part of America, a place from which ordinary Americans might emerge and that could itself be transformed in accordance with normative principles.

Yet despite everything that would place Jews in the white American mainstream, versions of the older caricature persisted. The ghetto film itself updated the Jewish type to provide a pictorial distinction between the assimilated and unassimilated Jew. *The Jazz Singer's* Moisha *[sic]* Yudelson, "the kibitzer," echoes the turn-of-the-century comedic figure in his appearance as well as his use of gesture (as when he tilts his head and shrugs his shoulders, hands out, palms up). To this type, ghetto films added the stern, bearded, Jewish father and his plump, fastidious wife.[19] Because these three figures are readily distinguishable from a younger generation, some critics describe them as indicating the persistence of a racially foreign Jew and thereby equate the assimilation of their sons and daughters with the project of blanching them.[20] Judged strictly according to ranges of skin tones and body types, however, both generations appear to be already white, in contrast to turn-of-the-century film and stage Jews. Jewish typing took a similar turn in films with only minor Jewish characters. For example, Jewish jockey Izzy Macfadden provides comic relief in an otherwise unnoteworthy vehicle for child star Jackie Coogan. Released the same year as *The Jazz Singer, Johnny Get Your Hair Cut* (MGM) stages a scene at the horse races in which members of a crowd see "Macfadden" blazoned above a shamrock on the back of Izzy's jersey. They call out (in a title) to this "Mick." He does not immediately respond, and intercutting builds anticipation for the moment when he turns to face the crowd and camera in close-up. Dark curly hair, dark eyes, and a prominent (though hardly huge) nose cause crowd members to double over with laughter. Clearly, the filmmakers anticipated that the dissonance between Irish patronymic and Jewish face would provoke a comparable reaction in the movie's audience. Yet, with equal clarity, the film makes Izzy just as pale-faced as the other jockeys. Nowhere does it compare him with the black groomsmen who dot the film.

Intertitles continued to mark Jews as a foreign race, plot lines made intermarriage an ongoing problem, and gags mocked Jewish inheritance. At the same time, feature films placed Jews within the visual category of whiteness and took the achievement of their safety and happiness as a narrative aim. This can only have raised questions of what Jewishness was, how exactly it related to racial whiteness as a visible category, and what the inclusion of Jewish difference meant for American national culture.

The Jazz Singer addresses these questions by presenting Jewish inclusion as a spatial problem with an auditory solution. The film begins by placing the Rabinowitz home in the Lower East Side and by telling us, via intertitles, that bearded Cantor Rabinowitz "stubbornly held to the ancient traditions of his race." The next sequence represents a space dramatically different from the Jewish neighborhood and home, as young

Jakie (Bobbie Gordon) begins to sing the ballad "My Gal Sal" in a café. The scene proleptically establishes the ability of the voice to transcend spatial division and presents such transcendence as a twofold problem. First, the elevated platform on which Jakie and a piano player perform implies a slight boundary that separates them from the audience. The boundary exists only to be crossed by his song, which continues as a series of shots reveal the fashionably dressed patrons arranged in discrete clumps around café tables. This audience differs sharply from the Lower East Side crowds shown in the opening sequence. Fair-haired women are prominent within it. Subdivision of space promises to bring Jakie's body across the minimal boundary traversed by his voice and thus to locate it among the American audience. But the same scene redefines such vocal movement as a violation. In a barroom adjacent to the café but separated from it by swinging doors, the avuncular Moisha Yudelson (Otto Lederer) looks up from his beer and, as if following his ears, moves toward the source of song. Smiling at first, he is soon horrified to discover the cantor's son. Yudelson stops short of entering the café himself and then races through ghetto streets to tell papa. The show comes to an abrupt end in the midst of the ragtime "Waiting for the *Robert E. Lee*" as the father bursts through the front door to catch his terrified son in the act and drag him home. We know from the outset that the problem is neither the rebellious child nor the spaces he inhabits, but the Old World ways of the Jewish father and his attempt to make America into an extension of the Jewish home.

The narrative proceeds to turn this spatial antagonism inside out. Jakie runs away from home in the next scene to become Jack Robin, the Jazz Singer. Following the progress of Jack's career, the film defines "the outside world" as a series of secular, white audiences in relation to which the Jewish home seems an insulated exception. While Jack's surroundings are never the same from one scene to the next, "home" is as an unchanging interior: the cantor has found a substitute pupil, and Sara continues to worry about her son. While "America" now surrounds the ghetto, the two will not be able to interpenetrate, and "assimilation" cannot occur.

The film must transform both the Jewish home and the American audience in order to soften the boundaries between them, yet preserve the essential character of each. A redoubling of the visual love story drives that transformation, and all of Jolson's musical numbers relate either to the bond he shares with Mary or to that he shares with his mama. Jakie's flight from home sets the latter plot in motion. His departure is represented as a painful separation from the mother; close-ups of Jakie's tearful face are dramatically intercut with hers, inaugurating a familiar spatial drama of eyelines separated and rejoined. Their eyelines meet in exaggerated reconnection when Jack returns to New York for his Broadway debut—his eyes spring open as the unheard declaration "Mama!" reshapes his entire face. This dramatic reunion spurs an extended sound sequence, as Jack sits at the piano to sing "Blue Skies." The performance is addressed to his mother, and when he interrupts it to solicit her approval we hear synchronized dialogue for the first time in the film. Jack launches back into the song, this time "jazzy"— syncopated and up-tempo—but mother and son are forced apart by the father's entrance. The cantor's infamous "Stop!" banishes recorded voices from the soundtrack and sunders once again the look Jack and his mother share. Jack's voice will cease to seem a foreign contaminant within the Jewish home only when the father hears that voice as Jewish. On this, the stability of his relationship with Mama depends.

A corresponding problem vexes Jack's relationship with Mary. From the moment he sings as an adult, the Jazz Singer's audience includes Mary, who returns his look in characteristic romantic fashion at the end of the "Dirty Hands, Dirty Face" number. Once established, their shared gaze is broken and reestablished over the course of several scenes. It is steadier and longer in duration than the look indicating Jack's maternal attachment, and Mary's wide eyes and slightly parted lips reproduce the face of the iconic heroine. Moreover, Jack's face presents a more conventionally masculine demeanor when juxtaposed with Mary's; it undergoes fewer and less dramatic alternations than it does in scenes with his mother. True, Jack and Mary's love is somewhat tepid, and Jack's love for Mama, a bit ardent—a combination that signals Oedipal troubles for some critics and causes others to attribute a "suffocating" quality to maternal love.[21] As the visual narrative sets up the problem, however, it is not Jack's mother that threatens his affair but a contradiction posed by the incompatibility between the Jewish and American spaces the two women in his life occupy. During most of the film, Sara is seen at home, and Mary, in theatrical spaces. Jack's choice between family and career, Old World and New, therefore seems to be identical with a choice between the two women. They are placed in competition precisely in order to insist that Jack loves them both and thus should not have to choose. By extension, then, he should not have to chose between home and the theater, between Jewishness and Americanness.

When the inevitable moment of decision comes—should Jack open the Broadway show or take his father's place in the synagogue?—he is physically placed between Mama and Mary as each pleads with him to do what is "in his heart." In competing shot-reverse-shot sequences, Jack turns his head from side to side as images of Mary's, then his mother's, returned looks are intercut with those of his anguished face. Also incorporated in the reverse shots are male adjuncts who plead on behalf of the women. Yudelson supports Sara, and Jack's Broadway producer advocates for Mary. These additions prove crucial to the substitution with which the scene ends. The last round of exchanges replaces a close-up of the producer for the image of Mary we have been led to expect. This reduces Jack's vexing decision to a choice between love and career. Though he decides to sing in the synagogue, this return to his roots provides no resolution to the persistent struggle between Jewish mother and gentile lover.

Indeed, the resulting Kol Nidre number demonstrates Mary's desire for Jack more powerfully than any other scene. Before this moment, the film had represented the separation of the romantic couple by means of Jack's searching looks out of frame "toward" Mary, who was pursuing her own career elsewhere. Now she is enthralled by a voice whose source she cannot see, as she stares out the window of the Rabinowitz parlor toward the synagogue. Kol Nidre proves no less moving for its other auditors. Before we see Mary, we see the visibly pleased cantor father reinstate the son. He then expires, but death does not eliminate him and the tradition he symbolizes. As if both to ratify Jack's return to the fold and to bless his relationship with Mary, Cantor Rabinowitz reappears in ghostly double exposure behind his son, placing a solemn hand on Jack's shoulder just before we see Mary's reaction to his voice. The opening number showed that a Jewish son could not sing to an American audience so long as a foreign neighborhood surrounded the American stage. Subsequent numbers invert that relationship by making the Jazz Singer's performance seem an American intrusion in the Jewish home. Kol Nidre redefines it once again by placing the voice in the synagogue and locating its American audience in the Jewish parlor, and "Mammy" reiterates the new arrangement by seating the Jewish mother in the theater to hear her son.

The impossible choice in *The Jazz Singer* (Warner Bros., 1927). Still photographs courtesy of the Academy of Motion Picture Arts and Sciences.

Critics generally agree that *The Jazz Singer* arrives at a happy ending in which Jack "gets the girl" without appearing to renounce his heritage, but they seldom acknowledge the degree to which this resolution depends on the manipulation of his voice.[22] From the moment Kol Nidre begins until the end of the film, no one of the three characters appears in the same frame with any of the others. Absent sound, viewers might well conclude that Jack, Mama, and Mary remain separated. In both final numbers, Mary and Mama look out of frame toward Jack. His look out of frame possibly addresses Mary in Kol Nidre and certainly addresses Mama in "Mammy." Although none of these looks exactly reprises the shared gaze of a romantic couple that marks completion in films throughout the silent period, *The Jazz Singer* takes full advantage of the synchronized sound-image to achieve a remarkably similar sense of closure. Audiovisual manipulation anchors Jack's voice in a particular body and thus in a particular space. When this voice travels to adjacent spaces, it makes the slight boundary that separates Mary and Mama from Jack and from each other seem inconsequential.

That boundary actually matters a great deal. Without it, the film could not sustain both love stories right up to the end. Sparing use of the voice, limited largely to Jolson's performances for one or the other of the women, only enhances the sense that we have arrived at an America when he can sing simultaneously to both. By the same token, such use of the disembodied voice allows for the preservation of distinctions within that national space. The stage, wings, and audience and synagogue, parlor, and bedroom retain their differences even as they are shown to be compatible with one another. Thus, *The Jazz Singer's* final numbers resolve the competition between spaces with which the movie began by redefining it as collaborative relationship. No longer can the encroachment of the ghetto put a halt to the Jazz Singer's Jewish voice. No longer will American success demand that he forsake his parents. The relationship among the two sets of final spaces appears to be strictly parallel, the consequence of a common transformation that yokes the American stage to the Lower East Side and allows the two to interpenetrate in such a way that never fully dissolves the distinction between them. Mary's inclusion redefines the home as a place for a gentile auditor. Sara's inclusion redefines the theater as a place for a Jewish one. In bringing together these differences, it appears, the Jewish voice enriches America without losing its identity.

As had been the case throughout the silent feature period, however, incorporation of the Lower East Side hardly occurs on its terms.[23] "Old World tradition" is doomed from the moment it is identified as "old"— that is, from the very first scene. This is a contest entirely within American culture, one designed to reclassify the Jewish home and synagogue as less than entirely American parts of American space. For Jews to be Americans, they must come out of the synagogue and away from their homes and neighborhoods to inhabit a common space with other Americans. To do so does not require white America to conquer and re-segregate Jewish space in the same way that *Birth of a Nation* insists on the strict separation of black and white. Yet *The Jazz Singer* shares with that nationalist epic an obsession with establishing the "proper" relationship of the subject population to the clean, well-illuminated space of the Hollywood happy ending. Neither Jewishness nor African American-ness, in other words, is represented as self-evidently American. It takes film narrative to establish the relationship between the two.

When *The Jazz Singer* employs the sound-image to make Jewish mother, gentile lover, and the spaces they occupy seem distinct and yet harmonious parts of a single America, it extends cinema's power to narrate into the audible domain. As in a silent film, the narrative implies an agent that cannot belong to pictorial space. The addition of sound further demonstrates that this agent cannot be a voice that emerges from a body and travels across spatial boundaries. To chart the career of a disembodied voice requires an agent of an entirely different order. In *The Jazz Singer,* it requires an entity capable of lodging that voice within a particular body, comparing it with other voices to classify it as Jewish, demonstrating a problem with the way that Jewish voice travels, and resolving that problem by making the voice accompany two distinct images of devoted women. The agent that docs all this cannot logically address the movie's audience in the same manner that Jack Robin's song addresses its own audience within the film. Rendered by the incipient form of the sound feature, Robin's voice is no more capable of specifying its unique grain than Robin's body is of envisioning its relationship to unseen auditors. Seen and heard on this model, national unity does not occur when one disembodied voice responds to another—as nineteenth-century advocates of print conversation assumed it could. To unite diverse populations requires more deliberate arrangement. In the abstract, it presupposes an incorporeal agent capable of coordinating sounds and pictures to render and manipulate spatial distinctions. In concrete practice, the addition of sound required an even more elaborate professional hierarchy, and more intensive participation by finance capital, than had existed before.[24]

Nonetheless, audible ethnicity exists in a quite different relationship to the body than visible race. As Michael Rogin most clearly shows, the use of blackface in *The Jazz Singer* ensures that we will see the body underneath it as white.[25] So typically American was this maneuver, he contends, that it simultaneously established the Jew's racial identity and gave him a home in national tradition. When blackface made the Jazz Singer American as well as white, it reprised a dynamic that was at least a century old.[26] Yet to succeed on film in the 1920s, this blackface strategy apparently required a supplement. It took a voice to make sense of a Jewish strangeness *The Jazz Singer's* contemporaries had persisted in representing, even after locating Jews within the visible range that defined racial whiteness. Unlike the black mask that conceals a white foundation, vocal performance made Jewish difference a locus of internal contradictions. The plaintive Kol Nidre anchors Jewish heritage, but Jack Robin also sings tunes in the tradition of the Irish ballad (e.g., "Mother of Mine").[27] Such quintessential examples of Jewish jazz as "Toot, Toot, Tootsie, Goodbye" and "Blue Skies" make audible a complex, if unequal, encounter between African, European, and American musical styles.[28] And critic W. T. Lhamon finds Jolson's performance of "Dirty Hands, Dirty Face" to include "stock poses from popular theater on both sides of the Atlantic that many blackface songs had absorbed, modulated, and relayed for nearly a century."[29] An audience attuned to this tradition, he suggests, would not have needed burnt cork to recognize the postures of the minstrel show in this number. To trace the history of musical performance in the film is invariably to reveal legacies left by the diverse traditions that became America's races, ethnicities, foreigners, and natives. Yet the movie's audiovisual narrative hardly presents the possibility that any one of those traditions might compete with America as if from outside it. It is the movie's contention that they have already been incorporated within it.

Lhamon finds that the Jazz Singer "is frankly speaking the contradictions within one self."[30] His description could not be more apt. But to appreciate those contradictions fully, we must remember that the Jazz Singer's voice does not precede the diverse materials he sings and speaks.

Rather, their variety contributes to the impression of an elusive, continuous, individual grain. Sounds conspire with images to define the voice as a Jewish American one, to make that identity appear more than merely one stylistic performance among the others. They do so by representing the self as a site of conflict between musical traditions as much as between mother and gentile lover. Interior contradiction confirms the univocal cry and vice versa. In this way, the supplement of sound made the body's white exterior an insufficient measure of identity even as it insisted on the continued importance of racial classification.

ETHNICITY

To grasp *The Jazz Singer's* significance requires an appreciation for just how controversial Jewish identity was at the time. Little more than a decade prior to the film, philosopher Horace Kallen had launched his famous pluralist argument against the melting pot by promoting a decidedly Jewish American Jew.[31] Contemporary with it, sociologist Robert Ezra Park made the Jewish "marginal man" the test case for his influential contention that racial prejudice would invariably decline as Americans mingled with one another. Although they are now considered to be key developers of the ethnicity concept, Kallen and Park each continued to use the language of race to describe Jewish difference. And so did their powerful antagonists. As historian John Higham was the first to explain, their respective varieties of pluralism emerged in logical contradistinction to a virulently racist turn-of-the-century nativism. This nativism had a stridently antisemitic dimension. Clubs, resorts, and hotels had closed themselves to Jews beginning in the late 1880s, and redlining displaced the segregation of the ghetto onto the rising suburb. In the late 1910s, colleges, universities, and medical schools started to restrict Jewish admissions (they continued to do so until the 1950s). And during the 1920s, perhaps 90 percent of New York City office jobs excluded Jews.[32] The infamous 1914 Georgia lynching of Leo Frank indicates the lethal potential of anti-Jewish agitation. But Higham notes a telling disparity between denunciations of Jews in print and the violence visited on them relative to other immigrant groups. While Italians arguably suffered greater physical harm during the 1920s, nativist discourse singled out Jews and "reckoned them the most dangerous force undermining the nation."[33]

The great virtue of Higham's 1955 account remains its refusal to accept that nativism was the inevitable reaction to the wave of Italian and Russian (mostly Jewish) immigration that peaked in 1907.[34] Even if one grants that these immigrants were self-evidently strange in appearance and custom, Higham contends, one must still look to turn-of-the-century racial discourse to explain, first, why they were supposed to present such a threat to the nation, and, second, how their strangeness was extended to taint members of long-resident populations. The answer to both questions lies in theories of the essentially Anglo-Saxon or Nordic character of American civilization. Such commentators as Madison Grant popularized nineteenth-century racial science in order to define anyone "outside the charmed Nordic circle" as a contaminant to the national body.[35] This was the period when American English borrowed the term "antisemitism" from avowed German antisemites who sought to distinguish their views from those of traditional religious bigots.[36] While subsequent commentators have questioned the novelty Higham claims for anti-Jewish sentiment in the period, there is no mistaking the patina of racial science it acquired.[37] Yet the science was not certain; arguments within the fields of biology, anthropology, and sociology had begun to critique the race concept.[38] Moreover, histories of U.S. racial categories typically treat the 1920s as the period when the turn-of-the-century jumble of racialized Irishmen and Mediterraneans, mulattos and Anglo-Saxons, began to give way to new categories of white, black, Oriental, and, more nebulously, Latin.[39] In this context, it seems clear that an emerging definition of Jews as "white ethnics" could have neither swept away race nor eliminated Jewish difference. Rather, it provided a pivotal term in a much broader argument over how to order American populations.

In late-twentieth- and early-twenty-first-century parlance, "race" typically indicates a scientifically suspect inheritance visible on the skin, while "ethnicity" designates a more palatable cultural difference defined by kinship rules, culinary habits, religious practice, and dialect. Such a distinction fails to convey the complexity of the historical relationship between these two categories in the 1920s. More importantly, it continues to reproduce the principal dilemma this period of redefinition bequeathed. Social scientists Michael Omi and Howard Winant have been among the leading critics of what one might call the racism of ethnicity. They describe how an "ethnicity paradigm" of U.S. race relations prevailed after World War II by presenting ethnic assimilation as the solution to scientifically discredited racial difference. Its opposition to race notwithstanding, this paradigm continued to reproduce a distinction between populations considered nonwhite and those Irish-Americans, Italian-Americans, and other white hyphenated Americans considered exemplary ethnics. It tended not to locate comparable ethnicities within the black population, for example. By calling attention to the difference, Omi and Winant make the case that ethnicity reinforces, rather than replaces, racial classification. In contrast, critics so different as literary historians Walter Benn Michaels and Werner Sollors and philosopher Kwame Anthony Appiah contend that the argument against a paradigmatic ethnicity must at some point validate the racial essentialism it sets out to critique.[40] In the process of demonstrating the interdependence of race and ethnicity, such arguments invariably make race seem the more fundamental fact of American life. The solution for these critics involves an even more emphatic rejection of race in favor of one culture-based account of difference or another. My point is this: although the argument dividing these prominent late-twentieth-century critics appears to have race at its center, ethnicity may be regarded as the main bone of contention. When both sides agree to describe race as a historically produced category, the question becomes whether ethnicity competes or collaborates with it.

A partial explanation for why ethnicity and race appear both to collaborate and to compete may be found in the work of Robert Park, who retold the story of the Jewish immigrant to make visibility the measure of racial prejudice for all American populations. "The Jew," he writes in 1926,

> emerges finally from the ghetto and with the natural vivacity and intellectual virtuosity which is his heritage, enters into all the varied interests of this modern cosmopolitan life. The old, haunting memories of his racial history grow dim. He loses his characteristic type, his cast of countenance, and sometimes even his soul. In the vast tide of cosmopolitan life the Jewish racial type does not so much disappear as become invisible. When he is no longer seen, anti-Semitism declines. For race prejudice is a function of visibility. The races of high visibility, to speak in naval parlance, are the natural and inevitable objects of race prejudice.[41]

Park makes prejudice "a function of visibility." The more visible races, such as "Negroes" and "Orientals," are "natural and inevitable objects of race prejudice." Yet Park also makes a rhetorical distinction between actual "disappearance" and perceptual "invisibility." He offers the Jew as proof positive that difference can persist without being "seen" as different. A Jewish heritage of "vivacity and intellectual virtuosity" somehow endures despite the loss of a distinct "cast of countenance" and hazard to the soul. On the basis of this distinction between disappearance and invisibility, Park suggest that racial difference tends to become less prominent over time and predicts that Negroes and Orientals, like Jews, will eventually pass unnoticed by cosmopolitan America.

When he gives racial prejudice an assimilationist telos, Park inaugurates a line of argument that runs from Gunnar Myrdal's *An American Dilemma* (1944), to Nathan Glazer and Daniel Patrick Moynihan's *Beyond the Melting Pot* (1963), and finally to the neoconservative opposition to "special group rights" at century's end.[42] One finds Park's rhetoric of "disappearance" versus "invisibility" reprised in any number of proposals to make a willful "color blindness" the solution to racism.[43] As Omi and Winant suggest, this model needs race to mark the difference between those who have been assimilated and those who have yet to be. The metaphoric "invisiblity" of the assimilated may all too readily be understood as a virtue conferred by their definition as white. But Park's early formulation of this model makes clear that race does more than mark the limits of a purportedly diverse America. It inhabits the very heart of the ethnic alternative as the "soul" that Park fears may be lost through the process of assimilation.

The Jewish soul becomes the focus of Park's famous 1928 essay "Human Migration and the Marginal Man." There, Park draws examples from contemporary Jewish autobiographies (e.g., Lewisohn's *Up Stream*) to explain assimilation as an internal conflict: "The conflict of cultures, as it takes place in the mind of the immigrant, is just the conflict of 'the divided self,' the old self and the new." The Jew, Park explains, is "historically and typically the marginal man" in that he simultaneously belongs to two different groups: one foreign, racially visible, and "old," the other American, racially invisible, and "new." Whereas "something of the same sense of moral dichotomy and conflict is probably characteristic of every immigrant during the period of transition, when old habits are being discarded and new ones are not yet formed," for the marginal man the "period of inner turmoil and intense self-consciousness" is likely to be a permanent condition and often "terminates in a profound disillusionment."[44] Although Park presents assimilation as a change in habit anyone might undergo, the process differs for those migrants the host culture perceives as racially distinct. The perception of the father's difference continues to haunt the son, who strives to overcome it and fears that it will be seen once more in him. Once Oedipalized in this manner, "assimilation" can never be total. An internalized sense of difference from the host culture becomes the son's inheritance from the father down the generations. Park thus rewrites what had been a biological difference as a psychological matter and fractures the very concept of race. Whereas nineteenth-century racial science strove to make typologies of heritable (nonenvironmental) physical characteristics determine temperament and mental capacity, Park pries the racial exterior from its interior and sets the two in competition.[45] Even as a primarily psychological, rather than primarily biological concept, however, race remains a heritable quality. In this way, Park explained that Jewishness would abide, despite its metaphoric "invisibility," as a foreign element within an American psyche.

Horace Kallen made an earlier move in this direction when he inverted the rhetoric of assimilation to argue that ethnic difference was good for America. In his 1915 *Nation* article, "Democracy vs. the Melting Pot," Kallen critiques not only Zangwill but Jacob Riis, Edward Steiner, Mary Antin, Edward Bok, and "numerous other recent imitators mostly female and Jewish."[46] This set collaborates with the establishment, he maintains, when it equates American democracy with "Anglo-Saxons," the English language, and the principles expressed in the *Declaration of Independence*. True democracy resides neither in a national language nor in the means by which the original colonists secured their political and economic rights. Rather, Kallen asserts, democracy "means self-realization through self-control."[47] It thrives on the sense of identity immigrants develop in the new country. Accordingly, Kallen finds that America flourishes when its Jewish inhabitants develop their own theater and press, speak Yiddish and Hebrew, and found distinct educational, religious, and civic institutions.[48] Kallen takes full advantage of the stereotypical wandering Jew to suggest that in America he finally finds a home. Like Park, moreover, Kallen uses Jews to model all other immigrants, from Anglo-Saxons, Germans, and Irish, right down to Slavs, "Latins—Spanish, Mexican, Italian," and Asiatics. Because "Negro" haunts the bottom margin of Kallen's hierarchy, subsequent commentators have been quick to decry its racism.[49] A closer look complicates that assessment. Kallen plainly includes groups that would not be considered

"white" by most twentieth-century measures, and the conceptual relationship between biological race and ethnic "self-realization" remains
murky throughout. While Kallen describes the Irish as "an approved
ethnic unit of the white American population" in one modern-sounding
passage, he elsewhere critiques the idea of a new "American race" on the
grounds not of conceptual incoherence, but of practical impossibility—
he reasons that biological mixture increases diversity.[50] In other words,
race not only resides in the exclusion of blacks from Kallen's America,
it also saturates Kallen's perception of what America's component populations are, and were, before they arrived on U.S. shores. Like Park,
Kallen uses Jews to address a problem posed by racial definitions of
American identity, namely, how members of foreign races might occupy an American body. More explicitly than Park, he also raises the question of what would make America cohere, if not the continued predominance of Anglo-Saxons.

When Park and Kallen looked for the solution to a racist America in
psychological conflicts and competing projects of self-realization, they
had everything in common with W. E. B. Du Bois, who, like them, had
studied with William James.[51] Indeed, it is difficult not to hear in Park's
"historical and typically" Jewish marginal man the echoes of Du Bois's
famous description of life inside "the veil" from *Souls of Black Folk* (1903).
There, it is the Negro who "feels his twoness—an American, a Negro;
two souls, two thoughts, two unreconciled strivings; two warring ideals
in one dark body, whose dogged strength alone keeps it from being torn
asunder." We will fail to understand why the American soul wars with
the Negro one, Du Bois insists, if we attribute their scission only to racism. Negro thoughts, strivings, and ideals are irreducible to the "one
dark body" America typically sees. In an oft-cited passage, Du Bois
makes the necessary relation between these two senses of "Negro" crystal
clear. The "American Negro," he explains,

> wishes neither of his selves to be lost. He would not Africanize America,
> for America has too much to teach the world and Africa. He would not
> bleach his Negro soul in a flood of white Americanism, for he knows
> that Negro blood has a message for the world. He simply wishes to
> make it possible for a man to be both a Negro and an American, with-
> out being cursed and spit upon by his fellows, without have the doors of
> Opportunity closed roughly in his face.[52]

This American Negro anticipates the hyphenated Americans of the 1920s. In the wake of Park's argument, however, Du Bois's substitution of "African" for "Negro" and "Negro blood" for "Negro soul" must be read as metaphoric. Authoritative American discourse found it increasingly difficult to present "blood" as the solvent fluid of souls and continents. And yet, I am proposing, this shift is not well understood as movement from "nature" to "culture." Rather, what runs from Du Bois through Kallen to Park is a new type of descriptive language. In similar, though hardly identical, fashion, the three borrowed the rhetoric of race and supplemented its conceptual distinctions. They proposed that America might embrace racial difference by redefining that difference in psychological terms as "strivings" and "profound disillusionment."

This insight complicates not only Omi and Winant's critique of the ethnicity paradigm but also Kwame Anthony Appiah's contention that a decidedly nineteenth-century conception of race persists in Du Bois's oeuvre, and, by extension, throughout American black nationalism and Pan-Africanism. Appiah does identify an important contradiction in *Dusk of Dawn,* Du Bois's 1940 "essay toward an autobiography of a race concept." Here, Appiah explains, Du Bois makes his own intellectual development coincide with the critique of racial biology and claims to have arrived at a fully sociohistorical conception of race. The volume pithily defines the "black man" as "a person who must ride 'Jim Crow' in Georgia," for instance.[53] Yet, Appiah also points out, Du Bois continues to write that African heritage marks him "in color and hair." True, he makes this "badge of color" into the marker of a shared history: "The real essence of this kinship is its social heritage of slavery; the discrimination and insult; and this heritage binds together not simply the children of Africa, but extends through yellow Asia and into the South Seas." But this history is entirely collapsed into the "badge" that designates it, leveling differences between the experience of slavery in Africa and in the United States, not to mention Asia. Since "what Du Bois shares with the nonwhite world is not insult but the *badge* of insult," he at this moment substitutes a biologistic explanation for a historical one. Appiah, in other words, applies to the badge of "skin, hair, and bone" the same critique of racial science that Du Bois himself purports to embrace. In this way, he urges us to finish the job Du Bois began and rid African American ethnicity of its race once and for all. We should admit that "race" really is nothing more or less than a badge, understand that it has a largely European history, and define the historical contributions of Africans and African Americans "not by genetics, but by intentions, by meaning."[54]

Although Appiah describes race as a lingering nineteenth-century residue, I believe his argument reveals a major difference between Du Bois's 1940 "badge" and the "Negro blood" of 1903. Whereas "blood" gives skin and soul a common source, the "badge" defines identity through the act of concealing it. Once conceived as a badge, race could be understood both as an Anglo-American lie about biological essence and as a maker of the shared habits and feelings that might inspire one to change America (and/or "Africa"). By his own admission, Appiah's argument remains indebted to this conception. He maintains that there are good reasons why one might believe oneself to be African American even as he insists that hereditary connection to "Africa" is not one of them. As a psychological legacy, African American identity abides when blood ties are unclear (Du Bois) or irrelevant (Appiah). In this, it is an ethnicity akin to that of Park's Jewish marginal man. There is a crucial difference. Whereas Park makes Jewish American ethnicity something that does not disappear when it becomes (racially) invisible, Du Bois and Appiah describe African American ethnicity as something that disappears because it is (racially) hypervisible. As conceptual categories, race and ethnicity have a comparable relation to one another in each case. As terms in a hierarchy of American populations, however, the African American interior of a black body has a very different standing from the Jewish American interior of a white one.

When Appiah, following Du Bois and Park, finds that race persists as a visual category, he reiterates a proposition established first and foremost by the movies. At a time when social and biological science was beginning to debunk racial biology, the Hollywood love story gave twentieth-century racial types clear parameters and privileged whiteness among them. The rise of cinematic mass mediation intervenes between the racial blood that coursed through turn-of-the-century Negroes and Hebrews and the racial badge that concealed a conflicted African or Jewish American subjectivity.[55] No film of the silent era renders more precisely than *The Jazz Singer* the collaboration between racial hierarchy and ethnicity that cinematic culture ultimately promotes. The film reprises familiar tropes of assimilation when it makes Jack Robin reject the name "Rabinowitz" and gives him a love of jazz, a zeal for ham and eggs, and a yen for Mary the shiksa. Critics often point to these tropes to explain what makes the Jazz Singer Jewish. If transgression of traditional rules implies Jewishness by negation, however, the voice establishes it as a positive fact. As a uniquely embodied voice, the properties of which are irreducible to musical style yet testify to group membership, Jewishness acquires a permanence and classificatory power comparable to the whiteness visible on the skin. Here, in contrast to Jack's culinary and romantic preferences, one may even say that ethnicity marks him more profoundly than race does. While appearance may render the Jazz Singer indistinguishable from all the other white men in blackface— so much so that his mother fails to recognize him in one key scene— his voice reveals an inalienable Jewish inheritance. Ethnicity hardly supplants race, however. Rather, it supplements it. The voice provides Jack with a psychically fraught Jewish American identity. In the process, it endows the category of whiteness with an irreducible internal complexity. It allows us to understand whiteness as a permeable-yet-inelastic border enclosing heterogeneous populations, or what Micheal Rogin calls a "magic circle."[56] While sociology tortured the term "race" to make it render this sort of relationship and thereby generated the impression that race would need to disappear in order for ethnicity to truly emerge, *The Jazz Singer's* audiovision made plain that race and ethnicity can and must be distinguished, as it made the one category unintelligible without the other. This explains why *The Jazz Singer* became so important in the twenties and continued to animate so many late-twentieth-century arguments over American racism.[57]

Properly understood as a supplement to visible race, ethnicity cannot provide just another word for white power. The metaphor of the "magic circle" does capture a historically specific relationship between race and ethnicity. But that metaphor obscures matters by suggesting that placement within the circle empowered people according to the same logic that authorized "free white persons" at the founding of the Republic, and thereby disenfranchised, excluded, or exterminated everyone else. The distinction between ethnicity and race made it possible to define all immigrant and native-born populations as more or less American and launched arguments over how, and by whom, the "more or less" would be determined. Kallen proposed a logic that questioned the placement of WASPs at the top of the hierarchy by making them "a" rather than "the" American group. A similar conception of American was employed to very different ends in the Immigration Act of 1924, which replaced the haphazard mid-nineteenth-century port tax system for discouraging immigrants with a centralized approach. Lawmakers hoped to maintain America as it was by limiting European immigration relative to the percentage of the American population particular national groups already comprised. Asian immigrants, on the other hand, were excluded entirely.[58]

As Du Bois and Park each in his own way insisted, racial difference continued to delimit America's component populations. Under these circumstances, a particular sort of double bind emerged for the spokespersons who staffed such new organizations as the American Jewish Committee (1906), the Anti-Defamation League of the B'nai B'rith (1913), and the National Association for the Advancement of Colored People (1909).[59] They were, by turns, accused of being not black or Jewish enough to represent their particular groups and of being too black or too Jewish to represent the American whole.[60] To speak for hyphenated America, in other words, meant shuttling back and forth between a racial explanation and an ethnic one. It meant acting out the inner split between African and American, or Jew and American, that shaped the psychology of the ethnic subject. It required the ability, furthermore, to describe the relationship between a particular group and an unmarked, "invisible" American majority.[61] Of logical necessity, the social scientist, ethnographer, literary critic, or lawyer who provided an authoritative representation of this sort could be wholly identified with neither the particular group nor the public at large. Such an expert could, however, be partly identified with each.

Therein lies the connection between the emergence of ethnicity and the contemporary changes in national governance wrought by a rising professional managerial class. If the ideological equation of white male property-owner with self-governing citizen supplied the defining contradiction of the liberal democratic state at its inception, the professional managerial class strained that equation beyond its breaking point by arguing that the capacity for reasoned self-interest, debate, and electoral decision could not possibly suffice to secure the national good. Accordingly, Walter Lippmann and John Dewey redefined the mid-nineteenth-century problem of the "tyranny of the majority" as one of minority control over the semiotic machinery of public opinion. By their logic, the dramatic expansion of the franchise in the constitutional amendments of

1870, 1913, and 1920 could be said to advance a process of cooptation and regulation as much as correct prior exclusions.[62] To solve the problems of an entrenched order required a more thorough overhaul of American institutions. Lippmann proposed that professional skill, training, and technique would allow social scientists to suspend group affiliations, identify common interests, and adjudicate competing ones. American management throve, and thrives still, on this sort of claim. In the avowed service of private property and democracy, professional authority displaced the type of authority inheritance and election conferred. This presents its defining contradiction, according to Dewey. If experts must disavow membership in the publics they objectify in order to be experts, professional administration can only abridge the democracy it purports to reform.[63] The Janus-faced concept of ethnicity, one might say, offered an imaginative resolution to this very contradiction when it showed that any single person could not help but be defined in two different ways at once. Understood as ethnic, a manager's psyche embodied the conflict between the biases of the majority and the parochialism of the minority. Understood as raced, a manager's body took up position in a hierarchy of populations to be specified and arranged, advocated and opposed. This twin conception proved essential for a culture trying to explain the authority of Hollywood's executives.

THE MOVIE MOGUL

Since the late 1920s, *The Jazz Singer* has been read as an allegory for the lives of its star, writers (Alfred A. Cohn and Samson Raphaelson), producers (Harry, Jack, and Sam Warner), and by extension all of Hollywood's Jewish executives. Such allegorical application of the Jazz Singer's story makes the struggle of Jewish businessmen for wealth and power isomorphic with their struggle to assimilate as Americans. It thereby generates a paradox for the story of Hollywood filmmaking, one Irving Howe calls by its proper name when he describes Hollywood's "Moguls" as "semiliterate men, ill at ease with English, but enormously powerful in their intuitive grasp of what American—indeed, international—audiences wanted."[64] Neither the first not the last to offer special intuition as the explanation for how a bunch of foreigners produced the most supremely American of media, Howe follows precedent in implying that this intuition is itself a Jewish quality. Just as the Jazz Singer's foreign interior animates the minstrel show, so too does the mogul's authority to reproduce U.S. culture through the movies appear both hyperbolically American and alien to the core.

Although the term "movie mogul" dates perhaps to the mid-teens, the sort of character Howe describes is barely discernable in accounts of the movie industry before the great wave of successful vertical integration at the end of that decade.[65] In 1912, for instance, *Munsey's Magazine* ran an article entitled "The Magnates of the Motion Pictures" that typifies then-current narratives. The piece charts the development of the motion-picture industry according to the accomplishments of individual men. It begins with Thomas A. Edison, "who made possible the first practical and commercial moving-picture machine," and brings the reader up to date with the battle between "the Trust" (the Motion Picture Patents Company) and "the insurgents" (independent film producers such as Carl Laemmle, Patrick A. Powers, George K. Spoor, and William N. Selig).[66] Some of the entrepreneurs mentioned (Laemmle, Adolf Zukor, and Marcus Loew) will later be described as moguls, but this article makes no explicit mention of their Jewishness, nor does it present the motion-picture magnate as in any sense at odds with American life.

Munsey's does consider the immigrant backgrounds of the new magnates to be important, however. It uses them to signal a contrast not between the American and the foreign, but between self-made men and established elites. Trust insider Jeremiah J. Kennedy is described as a studied professional, a "master organizing genius of the business— a forceful and compelling personality, whose firm hand has been felt along the whole line of industry," while his "rough-hewn" competitors are "men of obscure origin, who give the enterprise its flavor of real adventure." Information about "obscure" origins tends to establish comparisons among the newcomers rather than to differentiate them. Powers is "an energetic and muscular young Irishman"; Edwin S. Porter comes from Fayette County, Pennsylvania, "the district that produced [Henry Clay] Frick, Senator Clark, and Secretary Knox"; Loew had a "strenuous boyhood" as an "East Side gamin"; Laemmle is identified as a "poor German immigrant."[67] In each case, *Munsey's* chronicles the talent and determination that lead from humble beginnings, through other trades, to a chance encounter with the movies, and finally to wealth and power.

While this type of narrative did not single out the Jewish magnate as presenting a special problem for American culture, it did contribute two key features to mogul lore. First, the magnate's personal background promises to provide inside information about the movie business. *Munsey's* frames its article as an exposé: "Some of the most powerful forces remain behind the films—silent, obscure, yet dominating factors in a business which is brimful of human interest and replete with spectacular fortune."[68] Second, the "rough-hewn" upstart is a man of the people who has made good through determination and hard work. His success, by no means certain in 1912, is partly attributed to a first-hand knowledge of movie audiences that the established interests of Edison and company are supposed to lack. The writing of the 1920s first opposed and then developed these two themes to produce the movie mogul as Hollywood's mythic founding father.

Henry Ford's *Dearborn Independent* made a particularly decisive contribution by defining the Jewish movie executive in accordance with its broad nativist program.[69] Distributed through thousands of Ford dealerships nationwide, the newspaper began in May 1920 to publish a series of articles on "the Jewish question." In February 1921, articles on the "Jewish control" over motion pictures characterized that "control" as part of a broad, international Jewish conspiracy to dominate America's financial, cultural, and political institutions.[70] The *Independent* borrowed rhetoric from contemporary censorship writing to denounce "the cesspool which the most popular form of public entertainment has become." It identified this licentiousness as "an Oriental ideal—'If you can't go as far as you like, go as far as you can.'" Such ideals are "essentially different from the Anglo-Saxon, the American view," the paper explained. In particular, urban Jews are held to be ignorant of rural America and its "home life." The reader learns that "American life is bare and meager to the Eastern mind. It is not sensuous enough. It is devoid of intrigue. The women of its homes do not play continuously and hysterically on the sex motif." While Americans value "interior qualities of faith and quietness . . . these, of course, are ennui and death to the Orientally minded."[71] In representing the foreign danger as one of excessive sensuousness and feminization, the newspaper simply attributed to racial mentality the dangers contemporary censorship advocates decried.[72] But the problem ultimately has less to do with the version of "home" circulated by cinema than it does with the Jewish producers themselves, who are "racially unqualified to reproduce the American atmosphere" and exert an "influence which is racially, morally and ideal-istically foreign to America."[73]

Although the *Independent* mounts similar criticisms of the "Jewish Song Trust" and the financial sector, the availability of a distinct rheto-ric of cinematic suasion allowed it to make a particularly hyperbolic case against movie producers:

> When you see millions of people crowding through the doors of the movie houses at all hours of the day and night, literally an unending line of human beings in every habitable corner of the land, it is worth know-ing who draws them there, who acts upon their minds while they quies-cently wait in the darkened theater, and who really controls this massive bulk of human force and ideas generated and directed by the suggestions of the screen. . . . The motion picture influence of the United States— and Canada—is exclusively under the control, moral and financial, of the Jewish manipulators of the public mind.[74]

The darkened theater, the quiescent spectator, and the unending line were tropes common to any number of discussions of Hollywood's in-fluence over the "public mind," but again, the *Independent* differed in identifying this influence as Jewish manipulation. The newspaper had borrowed its story of Jewish conspiracy from the *Protocols of the Elders of Zion*. Manufactured by the Russian Czar's secret police in the late 1890s, the *Protocols* purport to be the plans of a secret assembly of Jewish lead-ers for an international conspiracy to "split society by ideas," to corrupt and eventually to overthrow all existing governments and institutions in order to secure Jewish domination over all non-Jews.[75] The paper used this late-nineteenth-century tale to spin the rhetoric of motion picture influence in a new direction. Marshalling anecdotes and statis-tics to show that "85 per cent of [the industry's] parent concerns are in the hands of Jews," it claimed that Jewish executives "constitute an in-vincible centralized organization which distributes its products to tens of thousands of exhibitors, the majority of whom are Jews of an inferi-or type." A distinctly foreign Jewish plan, on this logic, inspired most every film and lurked just beneath the surface of every argument against censorship.[76]

Along with the language of "influence," the *Independent* coopted the story in which humble beginnings foretold popular success. *Munsey's* "rough-hewn" men behind the screen became sinister manipulators of a public whose best interests they could never appreciate. Because Jewish executives were "former newsboys, peddlers, clerks, variety hall managers and ghetto products," they could "hardly be expected to understand, or, if they understand, to be sympathetic with a view of the picture drama which includes both art and morality."[77] Yet Ford's paper described a different type of industry than *Munsey's* had. The "invincible centralized organization" was no mere Trust. Sketches of the industry emphasized the size and complexity of its corporate organization.[78] And a more general emphasis on Jewish "financial control"—particularly in banking— left no doubt that the corporate form was itself part of the conspiracy: it authorized shadowy figures who produced nothing tangible.[79]

Higham, for one, argues that the *Independent* series "excited nation-wide attention and met with much *sotto voce* approval."[80] And certainly the narrative of a Jewish conspiracy to control America through the movies continued to be circulated right through the 1930s by such figures as radio priest Charles Caughlin. It still reverberated at century's end.[81] But such conspiracy stories can hardly be made to characterize all national discourse on the Jewish executive. Throughout the 1920s, business writing compared movie producers to managers in other lines (including Ford).[82] Major national magazines and newspapers reported, but did not support, the *Independent*'s stance. Even procensorship writing sought to distance itself. In the *Catechism on Motion Pictures,* William Sheafe Chase agreed that "Mr. Fox, Mr. Zukor, Mr. Loew, Mr. Laemmle and Mr. Lasky . . . control almost the whole of the motion picture business of the United States." "Clean pictures," he wrote, "can never be obtained so long as these few unclean men hold a despotic control over the motion picture industry." But he also declared that "the author of this book has absolutely no anti-Jewish spirit but a profound admiration for the real Hebrews"—by which he means "patriotic American Hebrews who protest against men of their race" responsible for unsavory films.[83] Throughout the 1920s, the national magazine *American Hebrew* published sympathetic portraits of Jews working in Hollywood.[84] National Jewish organizations publicly opposed the *Independent* series, which was also denounced by a group of over one hundred prominent Americans, including presidents Woodrow Wilson and William Howard Taft; by the Federal Council of the Churches of Christ; by a meeting of four hundred ministers in Chicago; and by the Wisconsin state legislature. Several exposés of the *Protocols* as a fraud were published.[85] And there was a boycott of Ford cars. In July 1927, Ford issued a public retraction drafted by Louis Marshall of the American Jewish Committee.[86] Some indication both of the prominence of the controversy and of the film industry's disposition toward it is given by a *Moving Picture World* story published that same month: "Despite Henry Ford's recent apology, Jewish patrons of the West End Lyric Theater, St. Louis, Mo., objected to pictures of Ford shown in a news reel exhibited at the theater and as a result of their complaint the objectionable sections of the news film were deleted at subsequent shows."[87] The accusation of antisemitism was apparently so familiar as to need no further explanation. The *Independent* was closed later that year.

The problem of "Jewish control" over the movies proved durable, however, among those who dismissed conspiracy. The first book-length history of the industry, Terry Ramsaye's 1926 *A Million and One Nights,* mocks Chase, the *Protocols,* the *Independent,* and censorship campaigns in general as inconsequential to the development of the motion-picture business.[88] Although Ramsaye makes no specific mention of their antisemitism, he reworks the idea of Jewish control these sources promoted to produce what would become the prevailing narrative of the mogul. "It is not an accident," he writes, "but rather a phase of screen evolution which finds the American motion picture industry, and therefore the screens of the world, administered rather largely by our best and most facile internationalists, the Jews." The racially alien "international Jew" of the *Independent* becomes "our" cosmopolitan Jew:

> The American motion picture theater definitely took its rise out of the opportunity presented by the confusion of tongues and races in the Babel centers of concentration for imported labor, notably Pittsburgh, Chicago, Cincinnati, St. Louis, Milwaukee, and New York. From this beginning of service to seekers of fortune in the New World the motion picture took its still sustained keynote of ornate opulence and optimism. The screen chieftains of today are the industry's own elections from the store show and arcade exhibitors of the nickelodeon age.[89]

The success of the specifically Jewish executive and that of Hollywood cinema thus become the same story—a mighty American industry grows from humble foreign roots. Ramsaye further posits a similarity between the "psychology" of the garment industry, where several of the executives got their start, and that of motion pictures. He cites Abraham Cahan's novel *The Rise of David Levinsky* for support and implies, as Park will later argue using similar sources, that the immigrant's very marginality provides a psychological advantage. The struggle to assimilate requires him to identify and appropriate the defining features of the host culture.[90] Unique facility with this basic immigrant project explains Jewish superiority in retail businesses that rely on assessments of public taste or fashion. Ramsaye's "screen chieftain" thus encapsulates a paradoxical explanation of cinema's progress that would persist into the twenty-first century: because the prominent movie executives won American authority by overcoming their Jewish difference, the movies became supremely American through the intuition of foreign Jews. The American movie industry thus took on a hyphenated quality analogous to that of the Jewish-Americans who ran it. To be a truly American enterprise required a corporate psychology modeled on that of the ethnic subject.

Such honorifics as "screen chieftain" are unlikely to offer early-twenty-first-century readers the same delicious irony they must have held for Ramsaye in 1926. The racial connotations of "chieftan" and "mogul" have perhaps come to outweigh their administrative ones. In the context of late-twenties writing about the movie industry, however, the implication of primitive despotism would have clashed provocatively with Ramsaye's history of a thoroughly modern business endeavor. *A Million and One Nights* follows the pattern *Munsey's* employed a decade before. It narrates the progress of the industry as a series of contributions by and disputes among great men, beginning with Edison. Like that earlier history, Ramsaye attributes greatness to hard work, determination, inventiveness, business sense, and lucky timing. He adds Jewishness to the list. But he does so only in the final chapter, to retrospectively characterize an industry that scarcely resembles the one *Munsey's* describes. In Ramsaye's treatment, the epic battle between "the Trust" and its "rough-hewn" opponents simply inaugurates the real campaign, namely, the series of mergers, takeovers, stock issues, and pell-mell expansion that results in a large and complex industry dominated by a handful of vertically integrated corporations. It was this corporate authority to represent all America that Ramsaye retrospectively attributed to Jewish intuition.

Interestingly enough, identification of the Jew's ethnic intuition allowed for a reversal of the *Independent's* conspiracy story. The *Dearborn Independent* made executive William Fox "one of the men who can pretty nearly determine what millions of movie fans shall think about certain fundamental things."[91] In contrast, Upton Sinclair's 1933 Fox biography describes how a shadowy group of antisemitic, WASP investment bankers, abetted by Fox's rivals in the industry, conspired to wrest control of the Fox Film Corporation from the hard-scrabble, but basically honest, executive Fox. Sinclair provides a chronicle of shareholder meetings, stock manipulation, backroom deals, and battles over assets personal and corporate. Nonetheless, he describes Fox as a fundamentally good executive because of his ability to separate his personal interests from those of the corporation and its shareholders. The market requires unscrupulous behavior, but "an honest executive or director" stretches his principles only "for the benefit of [his] corporation, using the profits to increase the corporation's surplus," while "an ordinary executive or director" does things "for [his] own profit."[92] Sinclair appeals to Fox's humble Jewish roots to explain both his work ethic and his sense of responsibility to competing interests—a sense that socialist Sinclair had found more than lacking in his prior novelistic exposés of finance capital. Where the *Independent*'s Orientalist conspiracy defined the movie managers as the hidden controllers of an America to which they were utterly foreign, Sinclair lays despotism at the door of entrenched elites in order to put the immigrant executive on the side of the public.[93]

Precisely because Ramsaye and Sinclair succeed so well in making the "screen chieftain" appear the logical successor to "rough-hewn" populists who busted Edison's Trust, more recent histories can count on the movie mogul to give corporate moviemaking a populist flair. Robert Sklar explains that immigrant "entrepreneurs and showmen" were derided for their "foreignness, their language, their alleged ignorance," but were uniquely capable of "restoring cultural unity to American society" through mass culture.[94] Lary May writes that "as immigrants with bourgeois values, the Jewish film moguls were ideal middle men for realizing a fusion with styles."[95] Sklar and May follow Howe when they make the Jew's immigrant intuition the key to understanding cinema's popular success. Tellingly, however, the novelty of corporate culture becomes less pronounced that it is in Ramsaye and Sinclair. Even when a new middle class arises, as it does in May, we are left with a "fusion" of abidingly populist and "bourgeois" values. The ability to yoke these supposed antimonies has been the great virtue of the mogul as a mythic explanation. If they are controlled by such a figure, runs the often unstated argument, the movies must capture something of the struggles and aspirations of the public they address even through they are manifestly made for profit by a select few. Similarly, Hollywood films must indicate something of America's internal diversity, even as they insist that the socially reproducible couple comprises a white man and woman.

The need to make the mogul at once a populist and a powerful businessman explains why his success so often has a tragic dimension. In his 1988 book *An Empire of Their Own: How the Jews Invented Hollywood,* Neal Gabler provides a comprehensive synthesis of decades of mogul narrative. He builds a composite portrait of the Jewish executive from the novels, biographies, social histories, and journalism that established Adolph Zukor, William Fox, Carl Laemmle, Louis B. Mayer, Jack and Harry Warner, and Harry Cohn as legendary figures. Following Ramsaye's lead, for instance, he quotes a lengthy first-person passage from the novel *The Rise of David Levinsky* in order to observe that "Zukor certainly would have understood these pangs" and thus make his story an archetypically Jewish one.[96] To describe the mogul's revolt against the culture and personal failures of his father, he borrows tropes made familiar by two novels of 1941—F. Scott Fitzgerald's unfinished *The Last Tycoon* and Budd Schulberg's *What Makes Sammy Run*—and recirculated by Howe in the 1950s.[97] The mogul is convinced that respectability and status require that he remake himself in gentile terms. The antisemitism voiced by the *Independent* only strengthens this conviction and spurs on his quest to assimilate. As the realization of this quest, Gabler explains, Hollywood cinema represents an idealized America that the world learns to recognize as America itself. But the very marginality that drives the mogul mars his personal success and his appropriation of American culture. Much as it had for Park's "marginal man," a deep-seated guilt accompanies the mogul's Americanization. Perhaps more importantly, the American culture he reproduces remains, by definition, a gentile one. The movies succeed in redefining how America sees itself and the world, but they remained predicated on a subordination of Jewishness to Americanness that, if anything, hyperbolizes America's image of itself as a gentile nation. Thus, for Gabler, the mogul successfully remakes America in his image only to find that he has reproduced his alienation from it.

I do not dispute that the men described by the above-mentioned sources were Jewish, encountered antisemitism, and achieved success. I am simply noticing that when the figure of the mogul is called upon to explain where cinematic culture comes from, it does so by mediating two otherwise incompatible explanations of national authority. In one, American power is the prerogative of native-born, white, Protestant men who own property and control capital. In the other, the authority to represent America derives from nothing more than the ability to specify the American ideal and give it a reproducible form. The mogul figure reconciles these logically incommensurate notions of where American authority comes from by turning them into halves of a single psychological process. He thus offers a logical tool for distinguishing the racial mission of the movies from the race and ethnicity of those who manage them, while insisting that there must necessarily be some relationship between the two.

Since its inception, the writing that limns this figure has been in dialogue with arguments over how to classify America's component populations. There is thus no hard and fast distinction to be made between the rise of the mogul and rise of the particular concepts of "race," "ethnicity," and "assimilation" through which his historical role has been debated. To understand what authorized Hollywood's pioneering Jewish executives, moreover, one might equally well consider their own writing as businessmen. The mogul's reputed difficulty with English is not in evidence when William Fox, for instance, explains that early movies "appealed mainly to the foreign born, who could not speak or understand our tongue, who had no theater where he could hear his own tongue."[98] Throughout the 1920s, businessmen, whether Jewish or not, used such accounts of the early days to define movies as a distinctly American universal language and to establish their own authority to explain, and thus to supervise, the mature motion picture industry. Only in the case of Jewish businessmen do historians insist on seeing a hidden ambition to assimilate in such descriptions. Constant reminders that motion picture executives faced a problem of "respectability" that was equivalent to the problem of antisemitism thus promote a compound historical error. First, they obscure the mogul figure's participation in arguments over what a Jewish-American was (and to whom this model could be extended). Second, they occult the difference between the "respectability" of America's traditional WASP rulers and the type of authority a rising professional managerial class strove to win. In both ways, finally, such formulae set the cart before the horse and ask us to take at face value an origin story that could be produced only after corporate filmmaking mediated national culture.

The movies transformed America, I have argued, by allowing a mass audience to understand it as internally subdivided space managed by an incorporeal agent outside the frame. Through myriad repetitions of the love story, motion pictures showed that one type of spatial unit defined everything worth preserving about the others. So long as disparate spaces could be transformed into a haven for a white man and woman in love, they yielded to appropriation by this narrative form. Because this visual story persists, the talkies may be considered a continuation of the silent feature, even through they employed new techniques to tell it. Sound supplements feature film form, however, when vocal properties enter into the dialectic of visible spaces. Just so, *The Jazz Singer* employs the voice to produce an unusual relationship of three: two couples with a single common member, a Jewish-American who sings both to the synagogue and to the Broadway theater. Later sound features employed vocal sound in the service of a more conventional resolution. In *Sleepless in Seattle,* for instance, the sound of Sam's disembodied voice accompanies a close-up of Annie's entranced visage to establish a connection between the two. Because this voice sounds in one location (Annie's car on the East Coast) while having a source in another (Sam's house on the West Coast), this audiovisual tactic sets the love story in motion by defining the problem of distance it must overcome. When the two finally meet, however, the lovers hardly speak to one another. Vocalization would be superfluous; it would even detract from their mutual stare. Similarly, Sam's son Jonah, who completes the incipient nuclear family and has provided a pretext for its formation, is all but ignored by the couple.

The sense that *The Jazz Singer* is a transitional or liminal film derives from its use of the voice to render a much more complicated relationship between parent, lover, and son.[99] In combination with the images it accompanies, the Jazz Singer's voice shifts the conflict between the ghetto and rest of America to the interior of Jack Robin's body. It thereby creates the Jewish-American whom silent cinema had found it difficult to produce by simply locating the Jew within the visual range delimiting whiteness. Once Jewish difference was made audible, the ethnic could be shown to speak at different times in different styles and thus to address any number of different Americans. There are at least two good reasons, then, why the rise of the sound feature coincided with the demise of the ghetto film. First, *The Jazz Singer* finally succeeded in solving the principal problem posed by that genre, namely, how Jews could continue to exist as such and be white. Second, it demonstrated that to make the Jewish-American the audiovisual protagonist of a ghetto film story would require a coordination of bodies and spaces that departed from formal habit: it was necessary to render three not-quite-separate spaces, as opposed to collapsing distinctions to produce a single space for lovers. For these very reasons, however, *The Jazz Singer* lived on as an example and provided an allegory for a Jewish-American type with which national culture has remained preeminently concerned.

The mogul figure demonstrated that American culture could be administered by those it defined as marginal or even alien—provided they possessed the skill necessary to intuit a national public's desires. It did so by positing an antagonism between the Americanness of cinema and the Jewishness of its producers and by moving that antagonism inside the mogul's psyche to be his motive force. When we mistake this problematic as the cause, rather than the consequence, of Hollywood cinema, we forget that the mogul himself does not speak to us from the screen any more than Al Jolson does. Jewish executives, rather, made the screen speak. In the process, they did not exempt themselves from contradictory American definitions of Jewishness so much as resolve a problem past decades of filmmaking had generated.

The terms of this resolution favored them as managers as well as white persons. When *The Jazz Singer* demonstrated that the Jew's white exterior only acquired meaning when considered in concert with its complex interior qualities, it also demonstrated that it would take sophisticated manipulation of sound and picture together to establish a proper relationship between inside and out. As musical films of the 1930s tested the new rules of propriety, the problem of Jewish sound was eclipsed by the question of which types of bodies black sounds could legitimately come from and where, once made a property of a black body, they could safely travel within nation space.[100] The continued prominence of Jewish-American movie managers relative to African-Americans owes everything to their preservation of the white couple as a norm, despite new attention to blacks on screen. But the two types of managers are not as dissimilar as a Manichaean view of U.S. history would suggest.[101] When and if each wins authority to address a national whole, this occurs not despite, but on condition of an exclusion. *The Jazz Singer* and the movie mogul naturalize that paradoxical formulation when they demonstrate that there can be no final escape from racism, only its internalization and displacement. In this way, they consolidated a revision to America's categories of population that proved amenable to a less than entirely white class of professional managers. So thorough a cultural change cannot have been inspired by a single immigrant group. Nor can it have resulted from a concerted master plan by its eventual economic beneficiaries. It required, rather, the rise of a historically new form of national mediation.

Conclusion: Hollywood in the World

It may well seem peculiar to have deferred the problem of Hollywood's global reception to these final pages. U.S. cinema, after all, often provides the archetypal example of global culture, with all the arguments about cultural imperialism that entails. Moreover, the process of incorporation in general was predicated on businesses of transnational scale and scope. A wide range of histories finds that the rise of managerial capitalism coincided with ascendancy of the United States as a global political and economic power.[1] In the introduction, I echo Richard Abel's observation that the project of defining the movies as American only made sense in light of international competition: before there could be Hollywood, U.S. filmmakers and critics had to unite in opposition to the French imports of the nickelodeon era. It is equally important that the tables turned after World War I, when the films of U.S. studios came to dominate European markets.[2] By the end of the silent era, the Motion Picture Producers and Distributor's Association could treat international and domestic public relations as comparable kinds of endeavors.[3] There is no doubt that Hollywood's ability to mediate an American audience entailed the capacity to address audiences outside the United States. If, however, its national audience was in some way coextensive with a transnational one, this begs the question of why Hollywood movies remained discernibly American as they traveled the globe.

The proliferation of the Hollywood feature film did not edge out so much as inspire national alternatives. Study after study shows that the film industries of Europe and Asia developed their own distinct approaches by working with and against the U.S. model.[4] Clearly, nebulous declarations that cinema provided a "universal language" will not explain this variety. Nor will a stylistic opposition between "classical Hollywood" and various forms of modernism.[5] While it may be appealing to imagine that aesthetic sophistication is both anticapitalist and anti-American, it is more likely the case that various filmmaking institutions cultivated artistic distinctions in order establish their own versions of what Jesse Lasky called the "art industry."[6] By the same token, economistic models also fail to explain why alternatives took the particular form they did. The fact that American firms had superior capitalization and more efficient organization may illuminate the process whereby Hollywood thwarted such rivals as Germany's Universum Film Aktiengesellschaft (UFA). But it will not reveal why American movies proved appealing and therefore salable outside the United States and, at the same time, in need of domestication by other cultures. True, the feature film traveled a globe already linked by capitalist economy, imperial administration, and print communication. It makes some sense, then, to attribute Hollywood's success to its ability to address widely shared problems, to give order to the upheavals of modernity, to explain a world that seemed smaller, faster moving, and more interconnected than ever before. Yet even if we allow that American movies did so in a manner uniquely conducive to the rise of corporate capital, this still does not explain on what basis various groups of filmmakers resisted their imposition, borrowed their techniques, and developed alternative forms. The shift to a transnational perspective, in other words, does not obviate the need for an account of national culture. On the contrary, such a perspective must distinguish among localities even more clearly if it hopes to explain what makes them part of a common formation.

I propose that American movies addressed a global audience and yet continued to be perceived as American precisely because various groups of filmmakers modified the spatial logic of its love story. Each encounter of this type constituted Hollywood cinema as the foreign part of a new domestic assemblage. Each assemblage of this type reproduced the managerial imperative of American films while sanctioning a distinct permutation of it. This was not a unidirectional process. New approaches to the problem of manipulating spatial difference returned to update and extend Hollywood's own strategies for arranging territories and populations. Global cinema developed through a deterritorialization and reterritorialization of the Hollywood love story as a managerial technique.[7] Although a thoroughgoing account of this process would far exceed the scope of the present work, I can suggest how it produced some of the better known developments abroad.

As popular convention would have it, Hollywood's international fate may be discerned in the refusal of its happy ending. The great European art films do not simply result in tragedy, however. Rather, they deny viewers even the bittersweet resolution of the American tearjerker. My favorite example comes from France. Typically described as an avant-garde rendition of the lowest sort of melodrama, Jean Epstein's 1923 *Coeur fidèle* (Pathé-Consortium) ranks alongside Abel Gance's *La Roue* (Pathé-Consortium, 1922–23) as a classic of the 1920s.[8] The film's simple plot can be encapsulated in terms that make it seem indistinguishable from an ordinary Hollywood product: a saloon keeper's daughter, Marie, is trapped by circumstance into marriage with Paul, a brutish drunk, and saved years later through the persistence of her true love, Jean. Here, as in the typical American feature, love begins in the furtive glances shared by hero and heroine and abides in their longing stares out of frame. Similarly, danger is plain when the heroine recoils in close-up from the villain's menacing advance. Nevertheless, it would be extremely difficult to mistake this for an American film.

In its most famous scene, *Coeur fidèle* traps Marie with Paul on a spinning carnival ride. Increasingly rapid cuts emphasize the acceleration of the suspended airplane on which they sit and establish an unstable relationship with its surroundings. As the airplane flies upward with outward momentum, the background begins to blur behind the couple. The ground whizzes past. Elsewhere, a merry-go-round also picks up speed. When Paul struggles to kiss an unwilling Marie, the off-kilter framing of their faces recapitulates the ride's upward arc. The outboard support wire slices across the upper-left corner of the frame. Marie clings to the wire. The side of her face presses against it as her eyes desperately seek the empty space beyond it. Paul's face, in profile and shadowed by the brim of his hat, encroaches upon hers from the opposite direction. His hand grabs her chin at the bottom of the frame. Meanwhile, Jean walks the country road that leads to the fair; his pace and manner seem placid by comparison to the spinning machines. Up to this point, the scene establishes a situation that might exist in the Hollywood feature. It provides a nested series of spaces, the innermost of which includes a glowing woman in danger and the outermost of which offers the possibility that she might be saved. But Epstein's film goes on to define the problem of rescue in very different terms. Here, as critics have observed, the centrifugal movement of the whirligig prevails.[9] As if by sympathetic vibration, the woman's discomfort propagates outward to define all spaces. There is no inward rush to the rescue, and Jean does not arrive in the nick of time. Instead, a nearly catatonic Marie descends the ride with the smug villain by her side. Although they have been restored to the perpendicular, the carnival around them seems a continuation of the airplane's uncomfortable enclosure. When Jean cries out to Marie from across the carnival, rapid images of spinning, thrusting, noisy machines thwart a connection. Within the logic of Hollywood film, such interruptions exist as obstacles to be eliminated. Here, however, they do not stand between the unhappy woman and her lover so much as define the space they share. This space cannot be definitively changed because its attributes are in constant motion.

After Paul's death and Jean and Marie's reunion, a reprisal of the carnival scene indicates that the fundamental problem persists. Now it is Jean who clings to the outboard wire. He stares forward with a furrowed brow as Marie, smiling for the first time in the film, turns to kiss him in profile. As the airplane arcs upward, a series of rapid cuts and dissolves provide wedding images, fireworks, and a close-up of the happy pair. No viewer schooled in the conventions of American filmmaking could fail to grasp the ambiguity of this resolution: where, after all, is this couple going to live? How long could it possibly survive against a constantly shifting background? A viewer familiar with the conventions of French films, however, might well understand this ambiguity to stem from a dissatisfaction with those very questions. *Coeur fidèle* presents the problem of spatial difference in a fundamentally different manner. As in Hollywood, embodied vision is limited within space. To arrange space will thus take an agent that does not belong to it. Unlike in an American movie, however, visual narrative does not progress through a process of differentiation, juxtaposition, and eventual collapse to yield (or deny) a single stable space of safety. Rather, spatial change occurs as if via a shockwave that redistributes elements while leaving principle distinctions intact. Thus, it would be imprudent to equate the shared look of any individual couple with spatial stability; such a look at best indicates a fleeting moment of happiness amid a world in constant motion.

Of course, French films are not the only ones famous for refusing the Hollywood happy ending. The cinema of Weimar Germany provide numerous well-known examples of suicidal heroines *(Nosferatu, Hinter-treppe),* insane couples *(Cabinet of Dr. Caligari),* and doomed mantraps *(Pandora's Box).* For the sake of argument, one might consider a rare case in which the couple does come together at the end. Fritz Lang's canonical 1921 *Der müde Tod (Destiny)* typifies the stylized mise-en-scène and contrasty lighting Lotte Eisner famously identified with German Expressionism.[10] It includes one of the many tyrannical figures Siegfried Kracauer saw as the cinematic precursors to Nazi authority.[11] Like *Cœur fidèle,* moreover, it may be said to straddle two genres: while plainly an allegorical fantasy in the *Caligari* tradition, it also features the sort of female protagonist associated with the melodramatic *Kammerspiel,* or street film.[12] And like the French example, it generates a spatial logic different from, but related to, that of the Hollywood romance.

In *Der müde Tod* (Decla-Bioscope), Death separates a young woman and her true love no fewer than four times. The film draws to a close with the young man laid out along the bottom edge of the frame, the heroine collapsed over his chest. Death, personified in the figure of a pale, lanky man in black robes, stands in ghostly double exposure behind their solid, insensible bodies. The corpses remain as he lifts their translucent likenesses one by one. Draping a robed arm over the woman's shoulders, he pivots away from the camera to embrace the man in the same manner. With Death in the middle, the three walk toward a wall in the background. The scene changes around them, and they acquire solidity. A "V" shaped mask blackens the bottom third of the frame as they slowly climb toward the arced horizon of a small grassy hill. Once they reach the top, Death disappears from between the lovers, and the two turn to face one another before resuming their walk over the summit. The man raises his hand to touch the heroine, and for an instant the crook of his elbow repeats the "V" at the bottom of the screen. The gesture suddenly combines with the frame lines to complete the outline of a heart. If there could be any doubt about the desirability of their union, such symbolism banishes it—despite the fact that the angle is too oblique, and the camera too distant, for their faces to be legible. Thus, by making Death disappear, *Der müde Tod* completes the couple, isolates it, transforms it into a symbolic figure, and implies its eternal happiness.

The space from which Death can and does finally disappear exists as a wholly separate one. In no way does the film suggest that its other spaces have been, or can be, rearranged so that the couple might thrive within them. One might think that such would be the case whenever the couple is united beyond the grave, but *Home Sweet Home* (Contintental/ Mutual) shows otherwise. Directed by D. W. Griffith in 1914, this movie prefigures *Intolerance* (Wark/Road Show, 1916), with which *Der müde Tod* is frequently compared, in its story of a love thwarted through several lifetimes. In its conclusion, the heroine's radiant face fills the screen as she urges her lover to climb to Heaven from the smoking pit of Hell. He must fend off the men in blackface who seek to restrain him, while she floats through the sky surrounded by a chorus of angelic women. Here allegory depends on the division of the visual field into areas of light and dark, clarity and obscurity, above and below, white and black, feminine and masculine—opposed spaces saturated by social significations, in other words, that mimic and confirm those repeated throughout the film. In contrast, *Der müde Tod*'s humble hillock implies a boundless area emptied of everything but the couple. Only in this way can the film provoke the shift in the relationship between ground and figure that allows the lovers to be legible as lines that form a symbolic heart. Where the American case provides a permeable boundary separating Heaven from Hell, *Der müde Tod* makes its afterlife an ideal zone noncontiguous with any other.

Death himself cannot walk out of this zone; something must make him fade away. His final disappearance reassures in the same measure that his materialization menaces. In this regard, the film is strictly symmetrical. It opens with Death's magical appearance at the crossroads, where he first intrudes upon the lovers by climbing into their carriage. There is no question of keeping Death out. When Hollywood wants to introduce a complication, it establishes a boundary. But in *Der müde Tod,* the narrative relationship among spaces has less to do with adjacency than it does with shifting graphic elements, fungible characters and objects, disparities of complexity and scale. This is especially true of the three Oriental episodes embedded in its framing narrative. Persian, Venetian, and Chinese surroundings lack clear borders, contributing to a highly elaborate and mutable mise-en-scène that makes Death impossible to elude. In China, for instance, we alternate between the lovers' lumbering elephant (transformed from a pagoda in a previous scene) and the Emperor's pursuing army. They travel through a series of distinct settings, but the precise geographic relationships are impossible to determine, nor is it clear that one party gets farther from or closer to the other. The chase progresses more through the graphical transformation of the mise-en-scène than through the overcoming of successive borders within it. It comes to an end when the heroine fixes the pair in place by transforming herself into a statue and her true love into a tiger who guards it; Death, appearing in the guise of an archer, shoots the tiger, who again becomes a man, while a tear falls on the statue's alabaster cheek. The sleepy German hamlet of the frame story does not present such dramatic problems of appearance and essence. Nonetheless, in classic Orientalist fashion, there is a bit of the East at home. Death's domain appears as an unbroken wall that fills the frame. Because it has no limit, the nature of the relationship between the village and the other side of the wall is impossible to discern. It may surround the village or be surrounded by it. When a high, arched opening finally appears, it reveals a staircase without end. Little wonder, then, that here, as in so many Weimar films, we sometimes see the heroine staring past the camera with catatonic intensity. She is mesmerized by a complex, indeterminate space with no stable features. Under such circumstances, romantic resolution can hardly occur through a collapse of boundaries. Nor does the film depict an outward motion that redistributes elements within established spaces, after the fashion of *Coeur fidèle*. Rather, its resolution requires that the couple be located in radically simplified, abstract, and apparently unbounded "elsewhere."

To define spatial complexity as a problem in need of so drastic a solution, Lang and his colleagues at Decla-Bioscope perform the amazing technical feats for which the Wiemar studios are justly famous. Here, as in France and the United States, spatial transformation implies an narrative agent that is distinct from an embodied point of view. True, Death is a domineering and ubiquitous figure. But no character could have the power to regulate his own appearance and disappearance within a film, let alone to define spaces of relative menace and safety on that basis.[13] Although institutional models differ in the United States, France, and Germany, to produce this noncorporial narrative address in each case required hierarchies of experts who did not themselves own the means of production. It only makes sense that teams of French and German filmmakers would revise Hollywood form in order to define problems of spatial arrangement in ways that would make specifically French or German expertise necessary to the solution.

Perhaps this insight could help to answer a question that has been with us since Kracauer's landmark 1947 study of German film and national character. *From Caligari to Hitler* describes a "cinema firmly rooted in middle-class mentality" and observes that the "paralysis of minds spreading throughout Germany between 1924 and 1929 was not at all specifically German." Yet Kracauer's overarching objective is to find "behind the overt history of economic shifts, social exigencies and political machinations . . . a secret history involving the inner dispositions of the German people."[14] This raises the question of what international shifts in the composition, definition, or psychology of the middle-class during the 1920s had to do with a supposedly more fundamental German psyche. Part of the difficulty, Thomas Elsaesser points out, is that Kracauer himself is more interested in accounting for the rise of German fascism than he is in explaining what distinguished German culture between the wars. Where Kracauer sees Hitler foretold in Weimer cinema's mad doctors and vampires (not to mention Death himself), Elsaesser asks: "Why not assume that the films were 'looking back in banter' rather than forward in *angst,* that they made a bonfire of Wilhelmine Germany's eclectic tastes and historicist pastiches with their ham-theatrical acting, their camera wizardry and spectacular special effects?"[15] If Wiemar cinema did contribute to fascism, he effectively points out, it cannot have done so simply by reiterating or exaggerating national character via cinematic character. Rather, it must have inaugurated a new epoch in national mass culture, with a number of different results. Not unlike Kracauer, however, Elsaesser tends to veer between describing a modern culture industry that nearly beat Hollywood at its own game and an art cinema that remains distinctly German. One might explain how it can be both, I am proposing, by describing the distinct manner in which the two film industries gave the purportedly universal problems of the human psyche a spatial form and in the process promoted the different national components of a rising professional managerial class.

My French example would rather reiterate spatial distinctions than collapse them, and my German example abandons adjacency in favor of figural manipulation. In each, however, the separation and reunion of the couple animates narrative progression. Such films remain intelligible to audiences schooled in the conventions of Hollywood film, but are different enough in structure to estrange the logic of those conventions. To find a cinema that neither repeats the Hollywood love story nor refuses it in this manner, one might turn to early Hollywood's most traditional aesthetic adversary: the Soviet avant-garde.

Among the many admirable Soviet films of the 1920s, Sergi Eisenstein's 1929 *The General Line (Old and New)* perhaps best demonstrates the alternative structure I have in mind. This film works to define the difference between prosperity and poverty as the difference between a spatial whole and its internal subdivision. It introduces destitute peasants in the act of splitting their house in two. These images are followed by rapidly intercut close-ups of a saw being pulled through one of the timbers, first from the top left corner to the bottom right corner of the screen and then on the opposite diagonal. In turn, the saw strokes yield to rolling hills—fields on which fences appear in double exposure. Through a montage that links together several ways of subdividing the visual space, Eisenstein defines the problem of social division at a relatively high level of abstraction. We are to understand the splitting up of families, houses, and natural resources, as well as the use of technology to that end, to be aspects of the same fundamental problem. That problem implies its own solution: a unified space inhabited by a collective workforce. Accordingly, at the end of the film a brand-new tractor triumphantly pulls the wagons of the entire village up and down the hilly fields, and the villagers give chase on horseback. In an American film, this could only appear as a spatial competition, a race to rescue the wagons or perhaps the heroine atop the tractor.[16] But the Soviet filmmakers provide synecdochic close-ups that juxtapose, for instance, the engine's internal operation with horses hooves, thereby rendering horsepower not as a mathematical but as a social concept: one tractor does the work of many horses. The relationship among villagers it treated in a similar manner. A series of portraits represents the cheers of various individuals as aspects of a single collective action within a shared space.

This narrative movement from division to unity sublates the Hollywood romance. Granted, "lampoon" might better describe what happens to the love story in the film's famous marriage of bull and cow. The wedding is meticulously staged for an audience of villagers dressed in their finest. Bovine eyelines meet in alternating close-ups as the bull is led from his stable toward the cow's pasture. The pace of alternation increases as he picks up speed, and finally gives way to the bull's eye view of his headlong rush to mount the cow from behind. Displacement onto animal sex makes a joke of the type of scene that brings Jim and Melisand together at the end of MGM's *The Big Parade* (to pick one example). The film's own ending, however, is not played for comedy. On a sunlit country road, the heroine, behind the wheel of the tractor, encounters the driver who first brought it to the village. Their gazes meet across framelines, and the two come together. Unlike its American manifestations, however, this happy ending in no way advances our sense that prosperity depends on a particular organization of space. The space in which land, animals, machines, and workers can be seen as interdependent aspects of a whole has already been produced in the climactic montage of cheers, horses, and tractor parts. That montage ends with images of ranks of tractors spiraling outward to fill the screen with circular furrows and arcing through the frame toward the distant horizon. In the wake of such representations of ideally productive social organization, the romantic postscript arrives to demonstrate that no further feats of narrative transformation are required to make it occur. And not much depends upon it. *The General Line* makes the couple all but irrelevant, in other words. In this, it apparently departed from the melodramas of thwarted romance popular with Soviet audiences of the 1920s.[17] The film neither destroys the Hollywood love story nor preserves it by other means, but rather redefines it as one harmonic element within an abstract and apparently all-encompassing spatial dialectic.[18]

The dialectic only appears all-encompassing. The film's narrative movement from dissonant fragmentation to a cohesive unity implies, but cannot include, an agent that makes abstraction coincident with social transformation. To see the Soviet state and realize it, one must grasp the imbrications of part and whole. It takes the mediation of a particular form of film to render them visible. Like its American counterparts, then, *The General Line* arguably authorizes a class of intellectual workers—filmmakers and party bureaucrats—charged with the production and mass dissemination of the information that allows a modern nation to exist as such.[19] Indeed, when the film elicits delight in the formal manipulation that, for example, transforms the mechanical success of a whirling milk separator into an event of orgasmic intensity, it arguably makes the virtuosity of expertise more desirable than Hollywood ever could.

It would be absurd to think that any one example could sum up the cinema of an entire nation or that a few European countries could stand in for "the world." I have selected some telling cases from among the canonical works in order to describe them from the perspective of my argument about American movies. At the very least, I believe the films I have chosen reveal just how seriously alternatives to Hollywood must have taken its spatial logic. At most, they begin to indicate the contribution film studies might make to a comparative history of professional authority. They also suggest a new type of explanation for how one sort of cinema encounters another. We are too accustomed to describing such encounters as a procession of styles. One familiar stylistic history, for instance, leads from low-key "Lasky lighting" in the 1910s (e.g., *The Cheat*), to strong patterns of light and dark in German Expressionism, to the American style that the French retrospectively termed *film noir*. Soviet montage travels in a kindred manner. In film appreciation classes, for example, the Odessa Steps sequence of *The Battleship Potemkin* provides a staple example of "good" editing, quite apart from a consideration of why one might require montage to represent a revolution, let alone of what happened to this content when American filmmakers adopted the technique. Because filmmaking style is generally treated as different from conceptual structure, it has been possible to show that various borrowings have not perturbed the norms of "classical" Hollywood.[20] If, however, Hollywood is best recognized in its visual love story, if this form of narrative set a global standard, and if films made outside the United States achieved national exemplarity by articulating distinct logics of spatial transformation, then it stands to reason that American filmmakers would have attempted to secure their standing and even extend their purview by incorporating those different models. Insofar as they really were different, furthermore, one would expect their assimilation to alter Hollywood form.

The rhizomatic movement of spatial narrative may eventually explain some of the more characteristic developments in mainstream American filmmaking during the 1930s. In Busby Berkeley's musical numbers, for example, a well-nigh Soviet approach transforms silent Hollywood's most cherished visual object. Editing and mise-en-scène conspire to dissociate the woman's face from her body and render them graphic elements of a more abstract whole. One number from *Gold Diggers of 1935*, for example, presents identically costumed women who move not only in perfect unison with one another but also in intimate coordination with the animated grand pianos that constitute the main elements of the mise-en-scène. The women's swaying torsos appear permanently connected to the whirling pianos, which form various geometrical figures before combining, as if they were puzzle pieces, to form a single giant square.

Such images call to mind Kracauer's contention that teams of chorus girls exemplify the hollow rationality of American mass culture. The Tiller Girls, he declared, were "no longer individual girls, but indissoluble girl clusters whose movements are demonstrations of mathematics."[21] But Berkeley's work at Warner Bros. represents a dialectical leap forward in geometrical abstraction. It gives us neither "individual girls" nor "indissoluble girl clusters" exactly, but interchangeable elements that collide and combine to yield an inhuman unity. The enlarged face of one frame may belong to any one of the miniature bodies that form a shimmering line in another. In the decades before Berkeley, American features strove to connect the woman's legs with her face as parts of an individually unique (although conventional) body. The face signified an interior that corresponded to the legs' alluring surface. Just so, the camera ogles Beth from ankle to thigh in *Why Change Your Wife?* precisely to define her visage as the seat of satisfaction. Her legs catch Robert's eye, but it is her face he desperately wants to discover behind her shielding parasol. Through this upward displacement, the film prefigures an ending in which sexual desire, heterosexual monogamy, and spatial stability neatly coincide: nothing impedes the lovers' reciprocal stare. In *42nd Street* (1933), however, endless pairs of legs are famously disarticulated from any torso whatsoever. They make a corridor of doorways through which the camera passes. One cannot underestimate the peculiarity of this lewd gesture; it evokes a penetration and denies it. The camera appears to move "inside," but finds there only the "outside" of another pair of legs. Eventually, it arrives at the grinning faces of the leading man (Dick Powell) and his dance partner (Toby Wing), who stare directly at the camera.[22] In *Why Change Your Wife?* movement from leg to face concretizes and individuates the desirable object. This makes it possible to recognize a secure social space in the woman's loving look at her desiring male partner. In the Berkeley number, a similar movement abstracts the conventionally desirable object. It sunders legs and faces and sets them in endless new graphic combinations. Surely it cannot be too far-fetched to suggest that a cinematic model so plainly antagonistic to Hollywood romance would have a partly foreign origin.[23]

Only with difficulty does feminine virtue survive geometrical abstraction in the Berkeley musical to sanction the customary union of white heterosexual lovers by the end. To do so required some means of relating the logic of the musical numbers, which pose the problem of interchangeable parts imbricated in a whole, with that of a more conventional framing narrative, which strove to individuate the lovers, unite them, and organize space around them.[24] Of the early Berkeley films, *Gold Diggers of 1935* is perhaps the most successful in exempting its leading couple from the geometry of the chorus. *Gold Diggers of 1933*, on the other hand, exemplifies what is at stake in that gesture. The film places its multiple heroines within the musical assemblage and also makes them protagonists of a story in which America can survive economic depression by putting the right (impoverished) woman together with the right (wealthy) man. By the end, pairs of lovers are united backstage and their happiness secured. But the film's final number ("My Forgotten Man") reopens the problem of spatial arrangement by questioning the adequacy of this solution. The number substitutes an endless line of male soldiers for the chorus line, and transforms them, via montage, into a breadline that stretches through the frame. This anonymous mass of men stands in contrast to a series of individual women who look dejectedly out of frame, among them the song's main performer (Joan Blondell).[25] What is missing in "My Forgotten Man" is not "a man" so much as it is the possibility of seeing social relationships as a series of romantic pairings. Once war and depression are presented as problems of endless lines of men detached from isolated women, it seems improbable that simply securing individual couples could resolve them. To restore that possibility, later Berkeley musicals apparently required the chorus to be feminine, plastic, happy, disciplined, and, above all, separate from the romantic couple.[26] In this way, perhaps, Hollywood domesticated the Soviet strategy of representing "the social" as an abstraction made visible through the juxtaposition of individual elements. If such a domestication in fact occurred, it would mark a particularly significant extension of the corporate model, and might go some way toward explaining Hollywood's role in what Michael Denning calls the "laboring of America" during the 1930s, when organized business came to have a serious rival in organized labor and when the corporate state pioneered under Wilson's New Freedom developed into the social welfare state of Roosevelt's New Deal.[27]

Before we can understand what happened to various national cultures as the visual love story migrated and developed, however, we must appreciate the degree to which it altered the nation form itself. That alteration occurred in the United States during the silent feature film era, and it explains what I regard as the most vexing problem of twentieth-century authority, namely, why eighteenth- and nineteenth-century categories of privilege outlive the juridical, political, economic, and scientific models that sustained them. Twentieth-century America, after all, witnessed the triumph of private wealth through public ownership. It saw traditionally male party leadership thrive on universal suffrage. It allowed racism to prosper despite the abolition of slavery and devastating critiques of racial science. And it made the nuclear family seem more important than ever before, despite unprecedented control over fertility, the rise of the professional woman, and a sexual revolution or two. The explanation for such paradoxes, I have argued, lies not in some mystically capitalist, racist, or sexist essence of the modern state but in the way cinema appropriated and revised earlier forms of mediation.

The modern state came into being through the medium of print. If its ruling class ever represented itself for itself, print provided the means by which it did so. At a time when the ability to alienate labor displaced the ability to coerce it, print established the qualities of mind that fitted a man to rule others. It was through this medium that a rising bourgeoisie worked out the rules of sexual conduct, protocols of gendered behavior, and categories of kinship that set it apart from a late feudal order and allowed it to reproduce itself. Once printed, such rules, protocols, and categories took on a life of their own. During the long eighteenth century, they came to pass for everyone's ideas. In another half century more, their universal quality could be unmasked as particular, as in Marx and Engels's observation that "the ideas of the ruling class are in every epoch the ruling ideas."[28] Thus, print allowed a proportionally small group of readers and writers to represent nations, genders, and races and did so in a manner that infamously equated the white, male, property-owning head-of-household with the self-governing citizen. There is a reason why novels and newspapers—as opposed to, say, printed poetry or the Bible—exemplify this print culture. These forms, with their characteristic subject matter of current events, marriage and seduction, national character and commerce, had the ability to suggest that any member of the reading public might become an author, if not of novels and editorials, at least of his or her own relationship to the social whole. The novel and newspaper did not authorize a particular sort of man to rule simply by excluding everyone else. In a very real sense, it took an entire ensemble of characters to privilege the reasonable, male citizen: the man of property requires the woman of feeling; the father needs the son; the European, the savage; the cultured, the rustic; the productive man, the aristocrat; the American, the Englishman; and the Englishman, the Frenchman. Print defined the bourgeois individual as a many-faceted entity.

The movies pictured those many faces. They appropriated and revised the rules of sex, gender, and kinship through which the modern ruling class had distinguished and then universalized itself. They found ways to make heterosexual romance seem more satisfying, natural, and important than ever before—and thus mandated the proliferation of a now-familiar range of deviant options. They began to tell visual stories in which words were inferior signs of love and in which safety depended on an arrangement of space its protagonists, by dint of their embodiment, were powerless to see and affect. In the process, they transformed the imaginative relationship between the individual and nation. When *The Crowd* transports the couple from the safety of their home to the raucous public sphere, it imagines a relationship between person and place, private and public quite different from that established by print culture. Just as a series of secure private units compose a larger public, the mass comprises any number of alienated individuals. To see either is to place individuals within a larger spatial whole. Novels and newspapers, in contrast, aspired to a metonymic relationship between individual and group. The private and public guaranteed one another because an individual consciousness could be associated with each—private thought goes public in writing, and returns, through reading, to the private sphere. By these lights, "public" and "mass" amounted to different names for much the same sort of entity: a "many-headed multitude" that either governs itself or fails to do so. When cinema transformed the problem of associating many heads with one body into a problem of locating many bodies in a single space, it extended the mediating function of print while altering the relationship among those it mediated. No matter how much they talk to one another, the heads no longer govern the body. This explains why the problematic of "mass culture" is so strongly associated with American cinema, despite the fact that it has clear antecedents in print forms. The form of the Hollywood love story divorced techniques for representing, arranging, and transforming relations among individuals and groups from any particular body. It made them the prerogative of a necessarily impersonal narrative agent. To produce this type of narrative address historically required and sanctioned a hierarchy of experts working within corporate institutions.

A broad coalition of censorship advocates, reformers, professional spokespersons, and movie managers embraced the project of influencing a moviegoing public by controlling the sorts of pictures it would see. Although these would-be influencers disagreed among themselves over which particular institutions should regulate cinema and what exactly the governing principles of that regulation should be, they spoke univocally on behalf of three key principles: Hollywood cinema was a supremely American form; it should promote heterosexual romance and the nuclear family; it should elevate social and aesthetic values as commercial values. By the 1920s, arguments over regulation had set in place a new, now regnant paradox. On the one hand, they accorded the interests of an American public an objective existence prior to and apart from its constitution as a moviegoing audience. On the other, they implied that this public learned to know itself largely through mass produced and circulated images. By midcentury, this ever-inarticulate public inspired, among intellectuals especially, a powerful yearning for a time when reading and writing were supposed to have allowed better thinking and more democratic participation. The problem with such a model, Walter Lippmann was perhaps the first to explain, lies in its eagerness to believe its own press—to embrace the stereotypical distinction between measuring opinion and manufacturing it, to segregate the process of opinion formation from that of social symbolization, and thus to conceal the self-authorizing character of any successful representation of the public. For this very reason, John Dewey argued, radical experimentation in the production and use of signs should be the cornerstone of any democratic project.

Unlike the project of experimental education, the project of influencing a public requires a deliberate distance from its object. The rhetoric of gender provided businessmen and reformers with such a distance. When they figured the public as a feminine consumer, they implied that her needs and desires could only be anticipated, fulfilled, encouraged, and safeguarded by a more rational masculine organization. In this way, their writing drew strength from a paradox of long-standing utility: woman is both utterly alien and man's necessary other half. Nonetheless, close attention to the writing that defined and contested cinema's "influence" reveals that Hollywood's rise subtly but surely altered the terms of this paradox. Once the ideal woman had been defined as a unique consciousness trapped inside a reproducible picture—as she is in *Why Change Your Wife?*—her status as a source of influence changed. She claimed that ability not by virtue of feminine sensibility, but through her ability to manipulate the masculine discourse that reconciled image and interior. However contradictory, this was a type of authority quite different both from the middle-class woman's control over a domestic sphere and from the traditionally masculine privileges of legal rights and capital accumulation. When movies dissociated the gender of narrative arrangement from the spaces and bodies narrative arranged, they made a professional woman intelligible.

The compulsion to attribute the success of American movies to the intuition of a foreign movie mogul testifies to a similar shift. Historians and critics looked for such an explanation only after corporate filmmaking had taught audiences to see America as heterogeneous, as comprising discreet, semipermeable spaces defined, in part, by the sorts of persons who occupied them. *The Jazz Singer* reiterates the habitual lesson about how those persons and spaces should be ordered. It does not disturb the assumption that proper arrangement will secure a white, heterosexual couple. The film supplements that well-worn story, however, by employing the difference between sound and image to demonstrate that WASPs and Jews remain different from one another even as they cohabit the privileged space of resolution. To establish this type of relationship among bodies, sounds, and spaces presupposes a narrative agent even more ambitious than that of the silent feature, one that manipulates types of voices as it does types of bodies. The film thus reveals just how contingent upon invisible, inaudible management the traditional prestige of the Anglo-American individual had become. The mythic figure of the Jewish mogul allows us to grasp the fact that this change occurred, but it limits consideration of who was authorized by it. The central problem movies addressed was not that of how immigrants might join a traditionally racist America. Rather, motion pictures met the challenge of producing race and ethnicity as types of difference amenable to corporate management.

Hollywood cinema is American not because it represents America exclusively or is made exclusively by its citizens, but because it redefined the national interest for the age of corporate expansion. It is masculinist not because it is made by men or encourages prurient interest in women, but because, in using sexual difference to make sense of the world, it requires woman to be the marker of that difference and the index of what it means to love. It is a white perspective not because it is made by white people or shows others in a bad light, but because it installs a system of racial differences in which the love and safety of the white couple are supposed to be in everyone's best interest. The movies displaced print culture not because of some innate antagonism between linguistic signs and pictorial ones, but because their visual form uniquely suited the project of dethroning the embodied individual in favor of the impersonal corporation. This form serves a professional managerial class not because its themes appeal to managers or leave viewers in their thrall, but because it envisions spatial differences it takes a team of experts to narrate and secure. The movies, finally, were neither inherently good for American democracy nor bad for it. Rather, Hollywood cinema helped change who could rule and how rule would be conducted. It represented a world that professionally trained specialists would necessarily vie to depict and order.

Notes

INTRODUCTION

1. Periodizations vary according to focus on exhibition situation, length, production process, and narrative address. There is general agreement that changes in all these areas were required to produce the phenomenon of the feature film. See Eileen Bowser, *The Transformation of Cinema, 1907–1915* (Berkeley: University of California Press, 1990); David Bordwell, Kristin Thompson, and Janet Staiger, *The Classical Hollywood Cinema: Film Style and Mode of Production to 1960* (New York: Columbia University Press, 1985); Charles Musser, *The Emergence of Cinema: The American Screen to 1907* (Berkeley: University of California Press, 1990); Miriam Hansen, *Babel and Babylon: Spectatorship in American Silent Film* (Cambridge: Harvard University Press, 1991); and Douglas Gomery, *Shared Pleasures: A History of Movie Presentation in the United States* (Madison: University of Wisconsin Press, 1992).

2. Richard Abel, *The Red Rooster Scare: Making Cinema American, 1900–1910* (Berkeley: University of California Press, 1999).

3. Janet Staiger, "*The Birth of a Nation:* Reconsidering Its Reception," in *Interpreting Films: Studies in the Historical Reception of American Cinema* (Princeton: Princeton University Press, 1992).

4. On audience statistics, see Richard Koszarski, *The Age of the Silent Feature Picture, 1915–1928* (Berkeley: University of California Press, 1990), 25. On the rise of the movie palace and its place in the history of exhibition, see Kathryn H. Fuller, *At the Picture Show: Small-Town Audiences and the Creation of Movie Fan Culture* (Washington: Smithsonian Institution Press, 1996); Gomery,

Shared Pleasures; and Lary May, *Screening Out the Past: The Motion Picture and the Birth of Consumer Society, 1900–1929* (New York: Oxford University Press, 1980), 147–66.

5. Will H. Hays, *Moving Pictures: An Outline of the History and Achievements of the Screen from Its Earliest Beginnings to the Present Day* (New York: Doubleday, Doran and Company, 1929), 504.

6. Koszarski, *Age of the Silent Feature,* 67–68; Kalton C. Lahue, *Dreams for Sale: The Rise and Fall of the Triangle Film Corporation* (South Brunswick, N.J.: A. S. Barnes, 1971); Janet Wasko, *Movies and Money: Financing the American Film Industry* (Norwood, N.J.: Ablex, 1982), 11, 34.

7. For a compact survey of these developments, see Bordwell, Thompson, and Staiger, *Classical Hollywood Cinema,* 399–400. According to Wasko, "New corporate security issues during this period increased from nearly $3 billion in 1920 to over $9 billion by 1929" (*Movies and Money,* 30).

8. This is true, for example, of the body of work concerned with the relationship between the sociohistorical women in the audience and the male spectator Laura Muvley described as the ideal addressee of Hollywood form. See, for instance, Mary Ann Doane, *The Desire to Desire: The Woman's Film of the 1940's* (Bloomington: Indiana University Press, 1987); Hansen, *Babel and Babylon*; Shelley Stamp, *Movie-Struck Girls: Women and Motion Picture Culture after the Nickelodeon* (Princeton: Princeton University Press, 2000); and Lauren Rabinovitz, *For the Love of Pleasure: Women, Movies, and Culture in Turn-of-the-Century Chicago* (New Brunswick: Rutgers University Press, 1998). It may also be said of such disparate studies as Bowser, *Transformation of Cinema*; Virginia Wright Wexman, *Creating the Couple: Love, Marriage, and Hollywood Performance* (Princeton: Princeton University Press, 1993); Lynne Kirby, *Parallel Tracks: The Railroad and Silent Cinema* (Durham: Duke University Press, 1997); and Janet Staiger, *Bad Women: Regulating Sexuality in Early American Cinema* (Minneapolis: University of Minnesota Press, 1995).

9. For an intellectual history of 1970s film theory, see David Norman Rodowick, *The Crisis of Political Modernism: Criticism and Ideology in Contemporary Film Theory* (Berkeley: University of California Press, 1994). For a collection of more recent work that exposes the historical and theoretical limitations of the model, see Linda Williams, ed., *Viewing Positions: Ways of Seeing Film* (New Brunswick: Rutgers University Press, 1995).

10. Bordwell, Thompson, and Staiger, *Classical Hollywood Cinema,* 4; Rick Altman, "Dickens, Griffith, and Film Theory Today," *South Atlantic Quarterly* 88, no. 2 (1989).

11. Hansen, *Babel and Babylon,* 16.

12. The case for melodrama is made by Altman, "Dickens, Griffith, and Film Theory Today"; Linda Williams, "Melodrama Revised," in *Refiguring American Film Genres: History and Theory,* ed. Nick Browne (Berkeley: Univer-

sity of California Press, 1998); and Ben Singer, *Melodrama and Modernity: Early Pulp Cinema and Its Contexts* (New York: Columbia University Press, 2001).

13. Cooptation was not complete, however, as Sklar finds a democratic undercurrent that persists throughout the twentieth century and occasionally erupts in bursts of erotic exuberance. Robert Sklar, *Movie-Made America: A Social History of American Movies,* revised ed. (New York: Random House, 1994).

14. May, *Screening Out the Past.*

15. Ruth Vasey, *The World According to Hollywood, 1918–1939* (Exeter: University of Exeter Press, 1997); Richard Maltby, "The Genesis of the Production Code," *Quarterly Review of Film and Video* 15, no. 4 (1995).

16. For a survey of the controversy over the class composition of early audiences, see Melvyn Stokes, "Introduction: Reconstructing American Cinema's Audiences," in *American Movie Audiences: From the Turn of the Century to the Early Sound Era,* ed. Melvyn Stokes and Richard Maltby (London: BFI, 1999).

17. Roy Rosenzweig, *Eight Hours for What We Will: Workers and Leisure in an Industrial City, 1870–1920* (New York: Cambridge University Press, 1983); Kathy Peiss, *Cheap Amusements: Working Women in Leisure in Turn-of-the-Century New York* (Philadelphia: Temple University Press, 1986); Steven J. Ross, *Working-Class Hollywood: Silent Film and the Shaping of Class in America* (Princeton: Princeton University Press, 1998); Nan Enstad, *Ladies of Labor, Girls of Adventure: Working Women, Popular Culture, and Labor Politics at the Turn of the Century* (New York: Columbia University Press, 1999).

18. Francis G. Couvares, "Hollywood, Main Street, and the Church," in *Movie Censorship and American Culture,* ed. Francis G. Couvares (Washington, D.C.: Smithsonian Institution Press, 1996); Lee Grieveson, "Fighting Films: Race, Morality, and the Governing of Cinema, 1912–1915," *Cinema Journal* 38, no. 1 (1998); Grieveson, "'A Kind of Recreative School for the Whole Family': Making Cinema Respectable, 1907–1909," *Screen* 42, no. 1 (2001); Staiger, *Bad Women*; Stamp, *Movie-Struck Girls*; Frank Walsh, *Sin and Censorship: The Catholic Church and the Motion Picture Industry* (New Haven: Yale University Press, 1996); Vasey, *The World According to Hollywood.*

19. Sergei Eisenstein, *Film Form,* trans. Jay Leyda (New York: Harcourt Brace Jovanovich, 1977), 53. Italics have been removed from the original.

20. André Bazin, "The Evolution of the Language of Cinema," in *What Is Cinema?* (Berkeley: University of California Press, 1967), 28.

21. Laura Mulvey, "Visual Pleasure and Narrative Cinema," in *Visual and Other Pleasures* (Bloomington: Indiana University Press, 1989), 20.

22. To cite just a few more instances: Christian Metz, in his pioneering work on the problem of film "language," refutes the proposition that the shot be considered the minimum semiotic unit of film, despite the fact that his turn to the problem of syntax tends to reinstall it as the main analytic unit. See Christian Metz, *Film Language,* trans. Michael Taylor (Chicago: University

of Chicago Press, 1974). Michel Chion provides a lengthy demonstration of how sounds and images collaborate to signify spaces irreducible to shots, only to end up supporting the shot as a unit "that everyone . . . can agree on." See Michel Chion, *Audio-Vision: Sound on Screen,* trans. Claudia Gorbman (New York: Columbia University Press, 1994), 41. Ben Brewster and Lea Jacobs show how reliance on shots over scenes thwarts consideration of cinema's historical debt to and departure from theater. See Ben Brewster and Lea Jacobs, *Theater to Cinema* (Oxford: Oxford University Press, 1997), 3–17. Working from an entirely different direction, Fredric Jameson bases his account of late capitalist filmmaking on spatial distinctions. See Fredric Jameson, *The Geopolitical Aesthetic: Cinema and Space in the World System* (Bloomington: Indiana University Press, 1995).

23. Noël Burch, "Primitivism and the Avant-Gardes: A Dialectial Approach," in *Narrative, Apparatus, Ideology,* ed. Philip Rosen (New York: Columbia University Press, 1986). Noël Burch, "Porter, or Ambivalence," *Screen* 19, no. 4 (1978).

24. Tom Gunning, *D. W. Griffith and the Origins of the American Narrative Film: The Early Years at Biograph* (Urbana: University of Illinois Press, 1991), 114. Gunning continues, "In other words, instead of the shot being a simple container for the action, a means of recording and presenting it, it intervenes and structures it, overriding its natural unfolding." I would simply observe that the impression that a shot interrupts a naturally unfolding action depends also on the staging of that action. A distinct action must follow the cut. In Gunning's privileged examples as in so much of American filmmaking, that other action occurs elsewhere. The same effect can be achieved within the shot through a variety of techniques more characteristic of later films, e.g., rapid camera movements or changes to the plane of focus.

25. Ibid., 113.

26. Wexman, *Creating the Couple,* 44.

27. Christian Metz, *The Imaginary Signifier: Psychoanalysis and the Cinema,* trans. Annwyl Williams, Celia Britton, Ben Brewster, and Alfred Guzzetti (Bloomington: Indiana University Press, 1982).

28. In addition to the above-cited essays by Burch, see Noël Burch, *Life to Those Shadows,* ed. and trans. Ben Brewster (Berkeley: University of California Press, 1990).

29. Stephen Heath, "Narrative Space," in *Questions of Cinema* (Bloomington: Indiana University Press, 1981).

30. David Bordwell, *Narration in the Fiction Film* (Madison: University of Wisconsin Press, 1985), 50–51. This model has been written into Bordwell and Thompson's popular textbook. See David Bordwell and Kristin Thompson, *Film Art: An Introduction,* 4th ed. (New York: McGraw-Hill, 1993), 60, 67. Cf. Seymour Chatman, *Story and Discourse: Narrative Structure in Fiction and Film*

(Ithaca: Cornell University Press, 1978); and Edward Branigan, *Narrative Comprehension and Film* (New York: Routledge, 1992).

31. Here I also depart from Seymour Chatman's influential account in *Story and Discourse* (see esp. p. 96). I do not reject the analysis of narrative structure per se, but simply the postulate that the categories of "event," "character," "time," and "space" enjoy comparable relations to one another in all forms. Much preferable, in my view, is Roland Barthes's suggestion that a fundamental investigation of what the units of narrative are should precede the question of what in narrative "translates" across various forms of semiosis. See Roland Barthes, "Introduction to the Structural Analysis of Narratives," in *Image Music Text* (New York: Farrar, Straus and Giroux, 1977), 121.

32. Raymond Williams, *Keywords: A Vocabulary of Culture and Society*, revised ed. (New York: Oxford University Press, 1983), 192–97. Italics in the original have been removed. Cf. Raymond Williams, *Culture and Society, 1780–1950 (1958)* (New York: Columbia University Press, 1983), 295–338.

33. The meaning of the term "communication" itself shifted in the United States during the early part of the twentieth century. See Warren I. Susman, *Culture as History: The Transformation of American Society in the Twentieth Century* (New York: Pantheon, 1984).

34. Neil Harris, "Iconography and Intellectual History: The Halftone Effect," in *Cultural Excursions: Marketing Appetites and Cultural Tastes in Modern America* (Chicago: University of Chicago Press, 1990), 307.

35. Among the numerous accounts of this phenomenon, the most important to me have been Nancy Armstrong, *Fiction in the Age of Photography: The Legacy of British Realism* (Cambridge: Harvard University Press, 1999); Walter Benjamin, "The Work of Art in the Age of Mechanical Reproduction," in *Illuminations* (New York: Schocken Books, 1985); and Timothy Mitchell, "Orientalism and the Exhibitionary Order," in *Colonialism and Culture,* ed. Nicholas B. Dirks (Ann Arbor: University of Michigan Press, 1992). On cinema's debt to and departure from this late-nineteenth-century image boom, see Anne Friedberg, *Window Shopping: Cinema and the Postmodern* (Berkeley: University of California Press, 1993); Tom Gunning, "Tracing the Individual Body: Photography, Detectives, and Early Cinema," in *Cinema and the Invention of Modern Life,* ed. Leo Charney and Vanessa R. Schwartz (Berkeley: University of California Press, 1995); Rabinovitz, *For the Love of Pleasure*; Mark B. Sandberg, "Effigy and Narrative: Looking into the Nineteenth-Century Folk Museum," in *Cinema and the Invention of Modern Life*; Vanessa R. Schwartz, "Cinematic Spectatorship before the Apparatus: The Public Taste for Reality in *Fin-de-Siècle* Paris," in *Cinema and the Invention of Modern Life.*

36. I discuss John Dewey's early rendition of this complaint in chapter 2. Versions of it run the gamut from Daniel J. Boorstin, *The Image: A Guide to Pseudo-Events in America* (New York: Harper and Row, 1961); to Jürgen

Habermas, *The Structural Transformation of the Public Sphere,* trans. Thomas Burger (Cambridge: MIT Press, 1991); Guy Debord, *Society of the Spectacle* (Detroit: Black and Red, 1983); and Jean Baudrillard, *The Evil Demon of Images* (Sydney: Power Institute of Fine Arts, 1986). See also Martin Jay, *Downcast Eyes: The Denigration of Vision in Twentieth-Century French Thought* (Berkeley: University of California Press, 1993).

37. W. J. Thomas Mitchell, *Iconology: Image, Text, Ideology* (Chicago: University of Chicago Press, 1986), 43. Susan Stewart names the historical problem precisely when she reverses the usual causality to find that "the printed text is cinematic before the invention of cinema." Although Stewart lacks an account of cinematic culture that would allow her to explain how this retrospective inscription occurs, she rightly calls our attention to the fact that the problem of novelistic "realism," as a kind of mediation between subject and object that redefines both parties, makes most sense through the critical retrospection cinema provides. Susan Stewart, *On Longing: Narratives of the Miniature, the Gigantic, the Souvenir, the Collection* (Durham: Duke University Press, 1993), 9.

38. Thomas Carlyle, *On Heroes, Hero-Worship, and the Heroic in History (1841),* ed. Carl Niemeyer (Lincoln: University of Nebraska Press, 1996), 164; Benedict Anderson, *Imagined Communities* (New York: Verso, 1991).

39. Nancy Armstrong, *Desire and Domestic Fiction: A Political History of the Novel* (New York: Oxford University Press, 1987); Mary P. Ryan, *The Empire of the Mother: American Writing about Domesticity, 1830 to 1860* (New York: Institute for Research in History and Haworth Press, 1982); Doris Sommer, *Foundational Fictions: The National Romances of Latin America* (Berkeley: University of California Press, 1991); Michael Warner, *The Letters of the Republic: Publication and the Public Sphere in Eighteenth-Century America* (Cambridge: Harvard University Press, 1990); Ian Watt, *The Rise of the Novel: Studies in Defoe, Richardson, and Fielding* (London: Chatto and Windus, 1957).

40. I readily acknowledge that novels engage in pictorial description and depict spatial differences. Nonetheless, the ability to set figures in simultaneous spatial distribution has been considered a distinguishing gift of visual representation since Gotthold Ephraim Lessing, *Laocoön: An Essay on the Limits of Painting and Poetry (1766),* trans. Edward Allen McCormick (Baltimore: The Johns Hopkins University Press, 1984). Films employed that gift to revise the relationship between embodied consciousness and narration. This revision was the effect of a particular semiotic structure, not of the idealized distinction between spatial visual representation and temporal verbal representation Lessing describes. Cf. W. J. T. Mitchell, "Spatial Form in Literature: Toward a General Theory," in *The Language of Images,* ed. W. J. T. Mitchell (Chicago: University of Chicago Press, 1980).

41. See, e.g., Jackson Lears, *Fables of Abundance: A Cultural History of Ad-*

vertising in America (New York: Basic Books, 1994), 223; and my discussion of C. Wright Mills in chapter 2.

42. Robert H. Wiebe, *The Search for Order 1877–1920* (New York: Hill and Wang, 1967), 4.

43. Ibid., 12.

44. T. J. Jackson Lears, *No Place of Grace: Antimodernism and the Transformation of American Culture 1880–1920* (New York: Pantheon, 1981); Martin J. Sklar, *The Corporate Reconstruction of American Capitalism, 1890–1916: The Market, the Law, and Politics* (Cambridge: Cambridge University Press, 1988); Alan Trachtenberg, *The Incorporation of America: Culture and Society in the Gilded Age* (New York: Hill and Wang, 1982); Olivier Zunz, *Making America Corporate, 1870–1920* (Chicago: University of Chicago Press, 1990); James Weinstein, *The Corporate Ideal in the Liberal State, 1900–1918* (Boston: Beacon Press, 1968).

45. Richard Ohmann, *Selling Culture: Magazines, Markets, and Class at the Turn of the Century* (London: Verso, 1996). Ohmann defines mass culture as "voluntary experiences, produced by a relatively small number of specialists, for millions across the nation to share, in similar or identical form, either simultaneously or nearly so; with dependable frequency; mass culture shapes habitual audiences, around common needs or interests, and it is made for profit" (14). As he explains, this definition tends to exclude prior forms of publication (novels and newspapers). This creates a paradox. If a national culture must logically be a mass culture, as Ohmann and Wiebe suggest, American national culture begins in the 1890s. Plainly, however, the nation as politico-economic entity and idealized citizen-readership exists before this moment. Otherwise it would not be possible to describe as "national" the crisis of order that mass consumer culture helped to solve. This paradox may be partly explained, I suggest, by the fact that movies taught us to see the nation and the incorporeal force of mediation as mutually dependent structures.

46. Ibid., 363.

47. Michel Foucault, *Discipline and Punish,* trans. Alan Sheridan (Vintage Books, 1979); Bruno Latour, "Centers of Calculation," in *Science in Action: How to Follow Scientists and Engineers through Society* (Milton Keynes: Open University Press, 1987); Max Horkheimer and Theodor W. Adorno, *Dialectic of Enlightenment* (New York: Continuum, 1991); Mary Poovey, *A History of the Modern Fact* (Chicago: University of Chicago Press, 1998).

48. Burton J. Bledstein, *The Culture of Professionalism: The Middle Class and the Development of Higher Education in America* (New York: Norton, 1976); Mary P. Ryan, *Cradle of the Middle Class: Oneida County, New York, 1790–1865* (Cambridge: Cambridge University Press, 1981), 105–44.

49. Stuart M. Blumin, *The Emergence of the Middle Class: Social Experience in the American City, 1760–1900* (Cambridge: Cambridge University Press,

1989), 66–107; Alfred Dupont Chandler, *The Visible Hand: The Managerial Revolution in American Business* (Cambridge: Belknap Press, 1977), 15.

50. Blumin, *The Emergence of the Middle Class,* 76. As Blumin explains it, nonmanual workers in Jacksonian America were more likely to be tradesmen who became proprietors and/or shop foremen.

51. Bledstein, *Culture of Professionalism,* 173–75. In addition to the semantic shift in the term "career" and the rise of the pejorative "amateurish" noted by Bledstein, Haskell points out that the now-current sense of the noun "expert" dates from this period. See Thomas L. Haskell, *The Authority of Experts: Studies in History and Theory* (Bloomington: Indiana University Press, 1984), xii.

52. Peter Dobkin Hall, "The Social Foundations of Professional Credibility: Linking the Medical Profession to Higher Education in Connecticut and Massachusetts, 1700–1830," in *The Authority of Experts: Studies in History and Theory,* ed. Thomas L. Haskell (Bloomington: Indiana University Press, 1984).

53. The history of professionalism in Britain supports this general proposition; see Harold Perkin, *The Rise of Professional Society* (New York: Routledge, 1989).

54. Wiebe, *Search for Order,* 115.

55. Barbara Ehrenreich and Deirdre English, *Witches, Midwives, and Nurses: A History of Women Healers* (Old Westbury, N.Y.: The Feminist Press, 1973).

56. And whereas turn-of-the-century schools recruited business educators from industry, universities trained their own professors after World War I. See Daniel Nelson, "Scientific Management and the Transformation of University Business Education," in *A Mental Revolution: Scientific Management since Taylor,* ed. Daniel Nelson (Columbus: Ohio State University Press, 1992).

57. This is one of the lessons of the essays collected in Daniel Nelson, ed., *A Mental Revolution: Scientific Management since Taylor* (Columbus: Ohio State University Press, 1992).

58. Thomas L. Haskell, *The Emergence of Professional Social Science: The American Social Science Association and the Nineteenth-Century Crisis of Authority* (Urbana: University of Illinois Press, 1977). The classic account of the relationship between professional culture and the American higher education is Bledstein, *Culture of Professionalism.* Bledstein shows that the period between 1870 and 1900 was decisive in the formation of the American university as a distinct institution, although he traces the origins of professional culture back to mid-century. Since the publication of his argument, it has become somewhat easier to distinguish the problems of American national character, the middle class, and professional authority from one another.

59. Daniel J. Walkowitz, *Working with Class: Social Workers and the Politics of Middle-Class Identity* (Chapel Hill: University of North Carolina Press, 1999).

60. Gary John Previts and Barbara Dubis Merino, *A History of Accountan-*

cy in the United States: The Cultural Significance of Accounting (Columbus: Ohio State University Press, 1998), 175–234; Paul J. Miranti, *Accountancy Comes of Age: The Development of an American Profession, 1886–1940* (Chapel Hill: University of North Carolina Press, 1990).

61. See chapter 2.

62. These developments are discussed in many of the standard histories, but see especially Bordwell, Thompson, and Staiger, *Classical Hollywood Cinema*, 243–61.

63. See chapter 3.

64. In the middle of the nineteenth century, most successful businessmen could expect to pass on firms they owned to male relatives; by the middle of the twentieth, the reproduction of neither management nor ownership obeyed this logic. Businesses relied less and less on family apprenticeship, and family wealth depended more and more on management by outsiders. See Zunz, *Making America Corporate*; Nelson, "Scientific Management and the Transformation of University Business Education."

65. To a striking degree, the controversy is coextensive with the broader problems of defining class and periodizing capitalism. For instance, in order to understand the rise of the "new middle class" as merely the latest episode in a long process of embourgeoisement, Wallerstein is compelled to rethink the entire concept and history of the bourgeoisie. See Immanuel Wallerstein, "The Bourgeois(ie) as Concept and Reality," in *Race, Nation, Class: Ambiguous Identities,* ed. Étienne Balibar and Immanuel Wallerstein (New York: Verso, 1991). For a survey of the debate over the new class in American letters before and immediately after the Ehrenreichs, see Jean-Christophe Agnew, "A Touch of Class," *Democracy* 3 (1983).

66. Barbara Ehrenreich and John Ehrenreich, "The Professional-Managerial Class," in *Between Labor and Capital,* ed. Pat Walker (Boston: South End Press, 1979), 12.

67. Ibid., 25.

68. Chandler, *Visible Hand,* 3–4. Moreover, while slightly different versions of modern business enterprise developed in all technologically advanced capitalist economies, the United States set the pace of incorporation worldwide. See Alfred Dupont Chandler, *Scale and Scope: The Dynamics of Industrial Capitalism* (Cambridge: Harvard University Press, 1990).

69. James Livingston, *Origins of the Federal Reserve System: Money, Class, and Corporate Capitalism, 1890–1913* (Ithaca: Cornell University Press, 1986).

70. Paul A. Baran and Paul M. Sweezy, *Monopoly Capital* (New York: Monthly Review Press, 1966).

71. Karl Marx, *Capital,* ed. Fredrick Engels, vol. 3 (New York: Penguin Books, 1991), 569.

72. C. Wright Mills, *White Collar: The American Middle Classes* (New

York: Oxford University Press, 1951); David Riesman, *The Lonely Crowd: A Study of the Changing American Character* (New Haven: Yale University Press, 1950); William H. Whyte Jr., *The Organization Man* (New York: Simon and Schuster, 1956). Cf. Barbara Ehrenreich, *Fear of Falling: The Inner Life of the Middle Class* (New York: Pantheon Books, 1989).

73. Kevin Gaines, *Uplifting the Race: Black Leadership, Politics, and Culture in the Twentieth Century* (Chapel Hill: University of North Carolina Press, 1996); Barbara Melosh, *"The Physician's Hand": Work, Culture, and Conflict in American Nursing* (Philadelphia: Temple University Press, 1982); Ellen S. More, *Restoring the Balance: Women Physicians and the Profession of Medicine, 1850–1995* (Cambridge: Harvard University Press, 1999); Walkowitz, *Working with Class.*

74. Nancy Cott, *The Grounding of Modern Feminism* (New Haven: Yale University Press, 1987), 232. This makes the problem coeval with the growth of the American Bar Association (founded 1878). See also Rosalind Rosenberg, *Beyond Separate Spheres: The Intellectual Roots of Modern Feminism* (New Haven: Yale University Press, 1982).

75. See chapter 4.

76. *Fortune*, "Portrait of a Vertically Integrated Company: Metro-Goldwyn Mayer," in *The American Film Industry*, ed. Tino Balio (Madison: University of Wisconsin Press, 1985), 318–19.

77. As Bordwell would have it: "Classical narration's reliability habituates the viewer to accepting regulated impersonality and sourceless authority" (*Classical Hollywood Cinema*, 83). The authority is impersonal but to suggest that it is sourceless mystifies the very relations of production Bordwell, Thompson, and Staiger so aptly describe. Furthermore, I believe the habitual content of Hollywood cinema tells us more about the attributes of that authority than a technique-oriented account of its style can provide.

I. THE VISUAL LOVE STORY

1. David Bordwell, Kristin Thompson, and Janet Staiger, *The Classical Hollywood Cinema: Film Style and Mode of Production to 1960* (New York: Columbia University Press, 1985), 16. Cf. David Bordwell, *Narration in the Fiction Film* (Madison: University of Wisconsin Press, 1985), 159.

2. *After Many Years* (1908) and *Enoch Arden* (1911), mentioned here, were both directed by D. W. Griffith for Biograph. *Enoch Arden* (1914) was produced by Britain's Neptune Film Company.

3. Tom Gunning, *D. W. Griffith and the Origins of the American Narrative Film: The Early Years at Biograph* (Urbana: University of Illinois Press, 1991), 110. On the 1908 version as a landmark film, compare Robert Sklar, *Movie-Made America: A Social History of American Movies*, revised ed. (New York: Random House, 1994), 50. Eisenstein mentions that Griffith attributes the parallel montage of *After Many Years* to a Dickensian inspiration. Sergei Eisenstein, *Film Form*, trans. Jay Leyda (New York: Harcourt Brace Jovanovich, 1977), 200.

4. On stage adaptations of Tennyson's poem, see Rick Altman, "Dickens, Griffith, and Film Theory Today," *South Atlantic Quarterly* 88, no. 2 (1989): 322; Ben Brewster and Lea Jacobs, *Theater to Cinema* (Oxford: Oxford University Press, 1997), 72–77; Gunning, *D. W. Griffith,* 112–16; Nicholas Vardac, *Stage to Screen* (Cambridge: Harvard University Press, 1949), 70–72.

5. Cf. Bordwell, Thompson, and Staiger, *The Classical Hollywood Cinema,* 130; Eileen Bowser, *The Transformation of Cinema, 1907–1915* (Berkeley: University of California Press, 1990), 198.

6. This is a visual transposition of the opera's reprisal of their love duet.

7. Virginia Wright Wexman provides a comparable synopsis in *Creating the Couple: Love, Marriage, and Hollywood Performance* (Princeton: Princeton University Press, 1993), 16–19.

8. Laura Mulvey, "Visual Pleasure and Narrative Cinema," in *Visual and Other Pleasures* (Bloomington: Indiana University Press, 1989), 19.

9. Carol J. Clover, *Men, Women, and Chain Saws* (Princeton: Princeton University Press, 1992); Jonathan Crary, *Techniques of the Observer* (Cambridge: MIT Press, 1990); Teresa de Lauretis, "The Technology of Gender," in *Technologies of Gender* (Bloomington: Indiana University Press, 1987); Geoffrey Nowell-Smith, "A Note on History/Discourse," *Edinburgh Magazine* 1 (1976); Judith Mayne, *Cinema and Spectatorship* (New York: Routledge, 1993); Kaja Silverman, *The Threshold of the Visible World* (New York: Routledge, 1995); Chris Straayer, *Deviant Eyes, Deviant Bodies: Sexual Re-Orientations in Film and Video* (New York: Columbia University Press, 1996); Linda Williams, *Hard Core: Power, Pleasure, and the "Frenzy of the Visible"* (Berkeley: University of California Press, 1989); Linda Williams, ed., *Viewing Positions: Ways of Seeing Film* (New Brunswick: Rutgers University Press, 1995).

10. The supposition that the spectator will project his own desires onto this blank face only supports my claim. Such faces demand reading; as pure surface, they cannot but signify depth. See Roland Barthes, "The Face of Garbo," in *Mythologies* (New York: Hill and Wang, 1972).

11. Mary Ann Doane, *Femmes Fatales* (New York: Routledge, 1991), 46–47.

12. For Doane, this establishes the woman's face as a figure for a founding problem of appearance-essence in Western metaphysics. As such, the figure typically demonstrates that it will take a masculine knower to grapple with the problem.

13. As Williams describes it, the money shot is an "obsessive attempt of a phallic visual economy to represent and 'fix' the exact moment of the sexual act's involuntary convulsion of pleasure. The money shot utterly fails to represent the satisfaction of desire as involving desire for, or of, the other; it can only figure satisfaction as failing to do what masculine sexual ideology frequently claims that the man does to the woman: to occupy, penetrate, possess her." Williams, *Hard Core,* 114.

14. In light of these critiques, Mulvey's own account may be read against

the grain. In order to prompt the sadistic investigation that Mulvey finds at the root of all Hollywood narrative, the woman must have at least some of the properties of the subject—it would otherwise be pointless to establish her guilt. Similarly, one might revisit Teresa de Laurentis's account of the woman as the "figure of narrative closure" to, first, question the proposition that such a figure cannot also be a figure of narrative movement and, second, ask what difference it made, historically, when this figure was actualized in the face of a woman who returned the man's admiring look. See Teresa de Lauretis, *Alice Doesn't: Feminism, Semiotics, Cinema* (Bloomington: Indiana University Press, 1984).

15. Kern argues that this question organizes the late-Victorian novel as well. Stephen Kern, *Eyes of Love: The Gaze in English and French Culture, 1840–1900* (New York: New York University Press, 1996), 1.

16. Ibid., 29.

17. See Brewster and Jacobs, *Theater to Cinema*; Wexman, *Creating the Couple*, 39–66.

18. *Birth* has been reedited many times. I am working from a print in the archives of Brown University that closely resembles the Library of Congress print.

19. Similarly, the romance of the Professor and cousin Kate in that film might compete for attention with that of the main couple if not for the goofiness of the Professor, who chases butterflies and wears enormous glasses.

20. In fact, writes Vito Russo, the two men "have the only real love scene" in the film. Vito Russo, *The Celluloid Closet*, revised ed. (New York: Harper and Row, 1987), 72.

21. Indeed, those who invoke Manichaeanism typically pair that notion with the idea that there is something specifically American and modern about *Birth's* racial depiction. Cf. Mary Ann Doane, "Dark Continents," in *Femmes Fatales* (New York: Routledge, 1991); Michael Rogin, "'The Sword Became a Flashing Vision': D. W. Griffith's *The Birth of a Nation*," in *Ronald Reagan, the Movie and Other Episodes in Political Demonology* (Berkeley: University of California Press, 1987); Clyde Taylor, "The Re-Birth of the Aesthetic in Cinema," *Wide Angle* 13, no. 3–4 (1991); James Snead, *"Birth of a Nation,"* in *White Screens Black Images: Hollywood from the Dark Side* (New York: Routledge, 1994).

22. For a discussion of Linneaus's racial scheme as well as reproductions of the illustrations, see Mary Louise Pratt, *Imperial Eyes: Travel Writing and Transculturation* (New York: Routledge, 1992). For reasons that I hope will become clear, I believe that Pratt greatly overstates the similarity between eighteenth-century racial categories and twentieth-century ones.

23. Allan Sekula, "The Body and the Archive," *October,* no. 39 (1986): 55.

24. George W. Stocking Jr., "The Turn-of-the-Century Concept of Race," *Modernism/Modernity* 1, no. 1 (1993); George W. Stocking Jr., "The Critique of Racial Formalism," in *Race, Culture, and Evolution* (New York: The Free Press, 1968).

25. Peggy Pascoe, "Miscegenation Law, Court Cases, and Ideologies of 'Race' in Twentieth-Century America," *Journal of American History* 83, no. 1 (1996).

26. Matthew Frye Jacobson, *Whiteness of a Different Color: European Immigrants and the Alchemy of Race* (Cambridge: Harvard University Press, 1998); Michael Omi and Howard Winant, *Racial Formation in the United States: From the 1960s to the 1980s,* 2nd ed. (New York: Routledge, 1994).

27. I have placed "culture" in quotations not because I disagree with that description of race but to indicate my suspicion of the claim that race was not cultural when biology avowed it. I take up this issue along with the historical distinction between race and ethnicity in chapter 4.

28. Shawn Michelle Smith, *American Archives: Gender, Race, and Class in Visual Culture* (Princeton: Princeton University Press, 1999), 180–81.

29. This effort, concretely speaking, grounds the attempt to articulate a black aesthetic within and against white conventions that defines Micheaux's early oeuvre, but especially *Within Our Gates.* Cf. Jane M. Gaines, *Fire and Desire: Mixed-Race Movies in the Silent Era* (Chicago: University of Chicago Press, 2001).

30. Gregory Jay, "'White Man's Book No Good': D. W. Griffith and the American Indian," *Cinema Journal* 39, no. 4 (2000).

31. Stills and a description of filmmaking technique may be found in Gunning, *D. W. Griffith,* 75–81. For a survey of images of Hispanics in the silent period that makes plain the difficulties of that classification, see Gary D. Keller, *Hispanics and United States Film: An Overview and Handbook* (Tempe: Bilingual Press, 1994).

32. I am thinking of films ranging from *Pinky* (1949) to *Guess Who's Coming to Dinner* (1967), *La Bamba* (1987), *Jungle Fever* (1991), *Dragon: The Bruce Lee Story* (1993), and *Lone Star* (1996).

33. Richard Dyer, *White* (New York: Routledge, 1997).

34. That such description began before the film's release (by those who advocated censoring it) suggests how little it depends on *Birth*'s particular rendition of a scenario made familiar by other forms. See Janet Staiger, *"The Birth of a Nation*: Reconsidering Its Reception," in *Interpreting Films: Studies in the Historical Reception of American Cinema* (Princeton: Princeton University Press, 1992).

35. Although he does not focus on the problem of spatial difference per se, Russell Merritt also notes the importance of how the sequence is filmed to the threat it conveys. Russell Merritt, "D. W. Griffith's *The Birth of a Nation*: Going After Little Sister," in *Close Viewings,* ed. Peter Lehman (Tallahassee: Florida State University Press, 1990).

36. This point is made by numerous commentators, but perhaps most concretely by Rogin, "'The Sword Became a Flashing Vision'"; and Staiger, *"The Birth of a Nation."*

37. Although the claim that *Birth* was the first feature film has been debunked, it continues to be invoked as proof of the film's historical significance. The difference is that while a first generation of film scholars (e.g., Lewis Jacobs) bypassed or apologized for the film's racism in praising its formal and aesthetic contributions, recent work finds the film's racism to be its most American feature. See Doane, "Dark Continents"; Rogin, "'The Sword Became a Flashing Vision'"; Taylor, "Re-Birth"; Linda Williams, *Playing the Race Card: Melodramas of Black and White from Uncle Tom to O. J. Simpson* (Princeton: Princeton University Press, 2001).

38. Director Victor Seastrom and Lillian Gish apparently planned an alternative, unhappy ending in which Letty simply disappeared into the wind, but the film was altered before its release. Bengt Forslund, *Victor Sjöström: His Life and Work* (New York: Zoetrope, 1988), 214; Lillian Gish and Ann Pinchot, *The Movies, Mr. Griffith, and Me* (Englewood Cliffs, N.J.: Prentice-Hall, 1969), 295.

39. Lewis Jacobs, *The Rise of the American Film* (New York: Harcourt, Brace and Company, 1939).

40. Noël Burch, "Primitivism and the Avant-Gardes: A Dialectial Approach," in *Narrative, Apparatus, Ideology,* ed. Philip Rosen (New York: Columbia University Press, 1986); André Gaudreault, "Detours in Film Narrative: The Development of Cross-Cutting," in *Early Cinema: Space, Frame, Narrative,* ed. Thomas Elsaesser and Adam Barker (London: BFI, 1990); Charles Musser, "The Early Cinema of Edwin Porter," *Cinema Journal* 19, no. 1 (1979).

41. Burch, "Primitivism." See also Noël Burch, *Life to Those Shadows,* ed. and trans. Ben Brewster (Berkeley: University of California Press, 1990).

42. Jean-Louis Baudry, "Ideological Effects of the Basic Cinematographic Apparatus," in *Narrative, Apparatus, Ideology: A Film Theory Reader,* ed. Philip Rosen (New York: Columbia University Press, 1986); Jean-Louis Baudry, "The Apparatus: Metapsychological Approaches to the Impression of Reality in Cinema," in *Narrative, Apparatus, Ideology: A Film Theory Reader,* ed. Philip Rosen (New York: Columbia University Press, 1986); Christian Metz, *The Imaginary Signifier: Psychoanalysis and the Cinema,* trans. Annwyl Williams, Celia Britton, Ben Brewster, and Alfred Guzzetti (Bloomington: Indiana University Press, 1982).

43. Although Jean-Louis Comolli is more typically credited with this argument, I believe it is fully implicit in Burch's account. See Jean-Louis Comolli, "Machines of the Visible," in *The Cinematic Apparatus,* ed. Teresa de Lauretis and Stephen Heath (New York: St. Martin's Press, 1980); Jean-Louis Comolli, "Technique and Ideology: Camera, Perspective, Depth of Field," in *Narrative, Apparatus, Ideology: A Film Theory Reader,* ed. Philip Rosen (New York: Columbia University Press, 1986).

44. Bordwell, Thompson, and Staiger, *Classical Hollywood Cinema,* 162; Bowser, *Transformation of Cinema,* 53; Miriam Hansen, *Babel and Babylon:*

Spectatorship in American Silent Film (Cambridge: Harvard University Press, 1991), 306. Gunning updates Burch's argument by challenging the idea of a sharp break between Burch's "primitive" and "institutional" modes of representation. He nicely sums up his revision in Tom Gunning, "Aesthetic of Astonishment," in *Viewing Positions: Ways of Seeing Film,* ed. Linda Williams (New Brunswick: Rutgers University Press, 1995). Hansen develops the arguments of Burch and Gunning by relating them to the production of a national audience. Brewster and Jacobs revise Burch from a different direction by revealing a continuity between theater and early cinema. Brewster and Jacobs, *Theater to Cinema.*

45. Burch, "Primitivism," 493–94.

46. The theory of film narrative that goes the furthest toward displacing it is Stephen Heath, "Narrative Space," in *Questions of Cinema* (Bloomington: Indiana University Press, 1981). Hansen calls attention to exactly the problem I have in mind when she notes that the rich volume of work concerned with cinema's "modernity" has thus far privileged early cinema, comparing its mode of address to panoramas, amusement parks, and department stores, often under the sign of Baudelaire's *flâneur.* This leaves unresolved the question of the modernity of twentieth-century cinema, especially in its prevailing American form. Miriam Bratu Hansen, "America, Paris, the Alps: Kracauer (and Benjamin) on Cinema and Modernity," in *Cinema and the Invention of Modern Life,* ed. Leo Charney and Vanessa R. Schwartz (Berkeley: University of California Press, 1995).

47. These observations are indebted to Kristen Whissel, "Narrative Space and National Space in the Silent Cinema's Transitional Period," SCS Conference, West Palm Beach, Florida, April 1999.

48. While the emphasis on shots over spaces is mine, this point is indebted to André Gaudreault, "Film, Narrative, Narration: The Cinema of the Lumière Brothers," in *Early Cinema: Space, Frame, Narrative,* and especially to Gunning, *D. W. Griffith.*

49. Ibid., 10–30.

50. The pioneering statement of this analogy is Dziga Vertov, *Kino-Eye: The Writings of Dziga Vertov,* ed. Annette Michelson, trans. Kevin O'Brien (Berkeley: University of California Press, 1984). The pioneering statement of the paradox that results is Comolli: "The photograph stands as at once the triumph and the grave of the eye." Comolli, "Machines of the Visible," 123. Cf. Mary Ann Doane, "Technology's Body: Cinematic Vision in Modernity," *differences* 5, no. 2 (1993). For a discussion of how the camera-eye analogy led to a misappropriation of Lacan's concept of "the gaze" and a consequent misconstrual of ideological questions, see Silverman, *The Threshold of the Visible World,* 125–37.

51. Bordwell, Thompson, and Staiger, *Classical Hollywood Cinema*, 87–153.

52. This was not the industry's first stock issue, but it is considered a turning point because (1) it involved a bank with a reputation for conservatism in international and railroad financing, (2) earlier publicly owned filmmaking corporations had failed, and (3) it enabled vertical integration. A succinct summary of industrial development may be found in Bordwell, Thompson, and Staiger, *Classical Hollywood Cinema*, 397–400. On the details of the Famous Players–Lasky mergers and acquisitions, see Richard Koszarski, *The Age of the Silent Feature Picture, 1915–1928* (Berkeley: University of California Press, 1990), 69–80. For an account of the stock issue and of the role of finance capital in industrial development generally, see Janet Wasko, *Movies and Money: Financing the American Film Industry* (Norwood, N.J.: Ablex, 1982),

53. The breakup of the "central producer" system, for instance, partly decentralizes control but certainly does not restore the director's authority over all aspects of production. Similarly, the antitrust litigation that put an end to the vertically integrated studio at midcentury arguably increased the importance of finance capital and the prominence of a hierarchy of managers in coordinating the production processes. See Bordwell, Thompson, and Staiger, *Classical Hollywood Cinema*; Wasko, *Movies and Money.*

54. In her portion of the *The Classical Hollywood Cinema*, Janet Staiger writes: "Rather than considering Hollywood's mode [of production] only as the historical conditions allowing a group style to exist, we must also see production practices as an *effect* of the group style, as a function permitting those films to look and sound as they did while simultaneously adhering to a particular economic practice. The circularity needs concrete explanation." I could not agree more and would simply observe that Bordwell, Thompson, and Staiger's volume, with its separate chapters devoted to the histories of "style" and "mode of production," inhibits such an explanation from developing even as it demonstrates the necessity for it. The separation leads Staiger, for instance, to treat "group style" mainly as a way of standardizing and differentiating product (see p. 88).

55. Burton J. Bledstein, *The Culture of Professionalism: The Middle Class and the Development of Higher Education in America* (New York: Norton, 1976); Barbara Ehrenreich and John Ehrenreich, "The Professional-Managerial Class," in *Between Labor and Capital,* ed. Pat Walker (Boston: South End Press, 1979); Immanuel Wallerstein, "The Bourgeois(ie) as Concept and Reality," in *Race, Nation, Class: Ambiguous Identities,* ed. Étienne Balibar and Immanuel Wallerstein (New York: Verso, 1991).

56. Nancy Armstrong and Leonard Tennenhouse, "The American Origins of the English Novel," *American Literary History* 4, no. 3 (1992); Mary P. Ryan, *The Empire of the Mother: American Writing about Domesticity, 1830 to 1860* (New York: Institute for Research in History and Haworth Press, 1982); Lori

Merish, *Sentimental Materialism: Gender, Commodity Culture, and Nineteenth-Century American Literature* (Durham: Duke University Press, 2000).

2. THE PUBLIC

1. Jürgen Habermas, *The Structural Transformation of the Public Sphere,* trans. Thomas Burger (Cambridge: MIT Press, 1991), 4. The book first appeared in English translation in 1989 and has been controversial both for its historical analysis of the eighteenth-century public sphere and for its defense of "the public" as a normative idea. To survey the controversy, see Craig Calhoun, "Introduction: Habermas and the Public Sphere," in *Habermas and the Public Sphere,* ed. Craig Calhoun (Cambridge: MIT Press, 1992); Bruce Robbins, "Introduction: The Public as Phantom," in *The Phantom Public Sphere,* ed. Bruce Robbins (Minneapolis: University of Minnesota Press, 1993).

2. Jürgen Habermas, *The Structural Transformation of the Public Sphere,* trans. Thomas Burger (Cambridge: MIT Press, 1991), 160, 63.

3. On the relationship between Habermas's later work and his book on the public, see Calhoun, "Introduction"; Jürgen Habermas, "Further Reflections on the Public Sphere," in *Habermas and the Public Sphere,* ed. Craig Calhoun (Cambridge: MIT Press, 1992).

4. The claim to be alternative rests on recovering a dimension of experience not representable within the terms of the official public's discourse. Negt and Kluge's work on the proletarian public sphere rebuts Habermas thusly. Oskar Negt and Alexander Kluge, *Public Sphere and Experience: Toward an Analysis of the Bourgeois and Proletarian Public Sphere* (Minneapolis: University of Minnesota Press, 1993). Nonetheless, it is feminist work that has most effectively critiqued and supplemented Habermas's model. In cinema studies, Miriam Hansen, drawing on Negt and Kluge, makes the exemplary argument in favor of considering moviegoing an alternative public sphere for women in *Babel and Babylon.*

5. "What I have tried to emphasize is that the effect of disturbance in mass publicity is not a corruption introduced into the public sphere by its colonization through mass media. It is the legacy of the bourgeois public sphere's founding logic, the contradictions of which become visible whenever the public sphere can no longer turn a blind eye to its privileged bodies." Michael Warner, "The Mass Public and the Mass Subject," in *The Phantom Public Sphere,* 253. For a development of this notion in relation to film melodrama's representation of race and gender, see Lauren Berlant, "National Brands/National Body: *Imitation of Life*," in *The Phantom Public Sphere.*

6. Benedict Anderson, *Imagined Communities* (New York: Verso, 1991). See also Calhoun, "Introduction"; Robbins, "Introduction"; Michael Warner, *The Letters of the Republic: Publication and the Public Sphere in Eighteenth-Century America* (Cambridge: Harvard University Press, 1990).

7. Robbins, "Introduction," xii.

8. For instance, the movie audience might be described as "workingmen," "drudging mothers," or "cultivated folks." Hansen, *Babel and Babylon,* 84.

9. On periodization, compare Eileen Bowser, *The Transformation of Cinema, 1907–1915,* 1–20; and Charles Musser, *The Emergence of Cinema: The American Screen to 1907,* 449–89. According to one estimate, between 1915 and 1928 the feature film accounted for only 68 percent of a total "attraction." Richard Koszarski, *The Age of the Silent Feature Picture, 1915–1928* (Berkeley: University of California Press, 1990), 9.

10. The kind of narrative that developed, as Hansen explains, "makes it possible to anticipate a viewer through particular textual strategies, and thus to standardize empirically diverse and to some extent unpredictable acts of reception." Hansen, *Babel and Babylon,* 16.

11. Douglas Gomery, *Shared Pleasures: A History of Movie Presentation in the United States* (Madison: University of Wisconsin Press, 1992); Koszarski, *Age of the Silent Feature;* Gregory Waller, *Main Street Amusements: Movies and Commercial Entertainment in a Southern City, 1896–1930* (Washington, D.C.: Smithsonian Institution Press, 1995).

12. For concise summary of the controversy over the composition of early audiences, see Melvyn Stokes, "Introduction: Reconstructing American Cinema's Audiences," in *American Movie Audiences: From the Turn of the Century to the Early Sound Era,* ed. Melvyn Stokes and Richard Maltby (London: BFI, 1999).

13. Richard Abel, *The Red Rooster Scare: Making Cinema American, 1900–1910* (Berkeley: University of California Press, 1999); Hansen, *Babel and Babylon.*

14. Lippmann is perhaps best known as an editor, journalist, and political advisor; Dewey, as a philosopher and educational reformer. Both were prolific authors. For an intellectual biography of Lippmann, see Ronald Steel, *Water Lippmann and the American Century* (Boston: Little, Brown, 1980). For a biography of Dewey, see Robert B. Westbrook, *John Dewey and American Democracy* (Ithaca: Cornell University Press, 1991).

15. I am not the first to consider *The Crowd* descriptive of a broader social picture. Kevin Brownlow places the film among those that commented on contemporary social problems. Kevin Brownlow, *Behind the Mask of Innocence* (London: Jonathan Cape, 1990), 293–99. Robert Lang calls the film a "melodrama that resists being one." Robert Lang, *American Film Melodrama: Griffith, Vidor, Minnelli* (Princeton: Princeton University Press, 1989), 130. Lynne Kirby sees the film as an ideological demonstration that the alienation of mass culture can be overcome through consumption, thus alienating us all the more. Lynne Kirby, "Gender and Advertising in American Silent Film: From Early Cinema to the Crowd," *Discourse* 13, no. 2 (1991). Hansen finds the "programmatic optimism" of the film's plot to be in tension with its visual organization and argues that the ending provides "as bleak an allegory of American mass culture

as Horkheimer and Adorno's vision of the Culture Industry." Miriam Hansen, "Ambivalences of the 'Mass Ornament': King Vidor's *The Crowd*," *Qui-Parle* 5, no. 2 (1992): 115. For Gilles Deleuze, the film performs a telling variation on what he sees as American cinema's defining movement from a situation or milieu through an individual action to a similar situation or milieu: it provides an individual who "no longer knows what do to and at best finds himself in the same situation once more: the American nightmare." Gilles Deleuze, *Cinema 1: The Movement-Image*, trans. Hugh Tomlinson and Barbara Habberjam (London: Athlone Press, 1986), 144. Finally, Jackson Lears claims that the film dramatized "a growing fear that the thinking individual had been subsumed in the irrational mass" and in the same passage describes Lippmann and Dewey as intellectuals "haunted" by that fear. Jackson Lears, *Fables of Abundance: A Cultural History of Advertising in America* (New York: Basic Books, 1994), 223. As I will explain below, however, Lippmann and Dewey each critiqued the notion that "individual" and "society" could be opposed. I believe the film provides a similar demonstration.

16. "Peace-Time 'Big Parade'," in *New York Times Encyclopedia of Film 1896–1928* (New York: Times Books, 1984).

17. "Camera Expert Studies Old Masters for Effects," in *New York Times Encyclopedia of Film 1896–1928* (New York: Times Books, 1984). On the cliché of comparisons between cinematography and Rembrandt, see David Bordwell, Kristin Thompson, and Janet Staiger, *The Classical Hollywood Cinema: Film Style and Mode of Production to 1960* (New York: Columbia University Press, 1985), 50. But the more important point is Janet Staiger's: "We want to know more about Hollywood production practices primarily because of the films that group of filmmakers created" (87).

18. For more information on the complexities of production, see Brownlow, *Behind the Mask of Innocence,* 298.

19. Quoted in ibid., 299.

20. In my experience, the film spontaneously draws this reaction from many, although by no means all, viewers. Cf. Hansen, "Ambivalences of the 'Mass Ornament'."

21. Although she does not emphasize expertise, Paula Rabinowitz makes a similar point about documentary filmmaking, namely, that it has the capacity to redefine who counts as public even as it establishes that they cannot represent themselves, that it takes a movie to represent them. This allows her to redefine the problems of documentary realism and the "objectification" of persons therein in ways that inform my analysis. Paula Rabinowitz, *They Must Be Represented: The Politics of Documentary* (New York: Verso, 1994).

22. Walter Lippmann, *Public Opinion* (New York: Free Press, 1997 [1922]); John Dewey, Rev. of Lippmann, *Public Opinion,* in *The Middle Works, 1899–1924,* ed. Jo Ann Boydston (Carbondale: Southern Illinois University Press, 1983).

23. John Dewey, "Practical Democracy," Rev. of Lippmann, *The Phantom*

Public, in *The Later Works, 1925–1953,* ed. Jo Ann Boydston (Carbondale: Southern Illinois University Press, 1984); Walter Lippmann, *The Phantom Public: A Sequel to "Public Opinion"* (New York: Macmillan, 1930 [1925]).

24. John Dewey, *The Public and Its Problems* [1927], in *The Later Works, 1925–1953* (Carbondale: Southern Illinois University Press, 1984). The book is based on lectures Dewey gave at Kenyon College in Ohio in 1925.

25. Robert Wiebe and James Weinstein each made this point in the 1960s against the account provided by Richard Hofstadter in the 1950s. Wiebe, for example, notes that "bureaucratic thought and pragmatism met only after John Dewey had transformed it into a theory that made that individuals the plastic stuff of society." Robert H. Wiebe, *The Search for Order 1877–1920* (New York: Hill and Wang, 1967), 151; James Weinstein, *The Corporate Ideal in the Liberal State, 1900–1918* (Boston: Beacon Press, 1968); Richard Hofstadter, *The Age of Reform: From Bryan to FDR* (New York: Alfred A. Knopf, 1955). The argument is developed in T. J. Jackson Lears, *No Place of Grace: Antimodernism and the Transformation of American Culture 1880–1920* (New York: Pantheon, 1981); Lears, *Fables*; and Warren I. Susman, *Culture as History: The Transformation of American Society in the Twentieth Century* (New York: Pantheon, 1984).

26. Lears, *Fables,* 188; Cornel West, *The American Evasion of Philosophy: The Genealogy of Pragmatism* (Madison: University of Wisconsin Press, 1989), 104–105. Cf. Richard J. Bernstein, "Dewey, Democracy: The Task Ahead of Us," in *Post-analytic Philosophy,* ed. John Rajchman and Cornel West (New York: Columbia University Press, 1985).

27. Stanley Aronowitz, "Is a Democracy Possible? The Decline of the Public in the American Debate," in *The Phantom Public Sphere.*

28. Lippmann, *Public Opinion,* 54–55.

29. Ibid., 11.

30. Ibid., 111, emphasis added.

31. Ibid., 81–82.

32. Thus, "the history of the notion of privacy would be an entertaining tale." Ibid., 29.

33. The Freudian sense of the term is operative in Lippmann, whose first book, *A Preface to Politics* (1913) applied Freudian psychoanalysis to political questions.

34. Lippmann, *Public Opinion,* 112.

35. Lippmann makes reference to the classic eighteenth-century theorists of the state (especially Locke, Hume, and Rousseau) as well as to nineteenth-century liberals such as Mill. It seems clear enough that he also has in mind the ideology of democracy that remains present in high-school civics classes.

36. Lippmann, *Public Opinion,* 18.

37. Here Lippmann specifically refutes Gustave Le Bon.

38. Lippmann, *Public Opinion,* 178.

39. Ibid., 170.

40. Ibid., 164.

41. Ibid., 195.

42. Ibid., 201–02. "Truth" requires experts "to bring to light the hidden facts, to set them into relations with each other, and make a picture of reality on which men can act." The news functions simply to "signalize an event" (226).

43. Ibid., 241.

44. Ibid., 10.

45. A stereotype confirmed supplants the invisible environment, but a stereotype challenged and revised can bring the role of representation to the fore, provoking an awareness of its positivity in the production of facts. In his most grandiloquent gestures, Lippmann imagines that the institutionalization of expertise in government will ramify throughout the society in just this way, dislodging the prevailing stereotypes of democracy, including the fiction of Public Opinion (250–57). And throughout the book, Lippmann places a premium on the alteration of stereotypes. See especially pages 65–66, where he describes the unfortunate man who "knows in advance that the Japanese are cunning and has the bad luck to run across two dishonest Japanese."

46. Lippmann, *Public Opinion,* 239.

47. The rhetoric is disingenuous in any case. Elsewhere, Lippmann is more forthright in his insistence that the electorate's proper task should be to ratify that its interests have been known by others: "Only by insisting that problems shall not come up to him until they have passed through a procedure, can the busy citizen of a modern state hope to deal with them in a form that is intelligible" (*Public Opinion,* 252). However, it would be mistake to presume that "the busy citizen" both knows what "the problem" is and will recognize it as such after it has passed through the appropriate scientific procedure. The whole point of the intelligence bureau would be to redefine problems, effectively shaping the electorate's understanding of a world too large and complex to know.

48. *The Phantom Public,* Lippmann's sequel to *Public Opinion,* is explicitly concerned with nonexpert oversight and may be regarded as a reply to the problems the earlier volume posed for the theory of popular rule. In effect, it advocates a rationalization of the democratic process that will secure expert authority over even nonexpert decision making by carefully defining the form such decision making can take—by framing questions to allow for clear "yes" and "no" answers, for example. Dewey reviewed the book favorably, but reiterated the fundamental objection I am about to explain.

49. Dewey, Rev. of Lippmann, *Public Opinion,* 337.

50. Ibid., 344.

51. Dewey, *Public,* 308 n. 1.

52. For an account of Dewey's career as a lecturer in political philosophy, see Westbrook, *John Dewey.*

53. Dewey, *Public*, 250. Dewey goes on to debunk even this fantasy of a position "outside the universe."

54. Ibid., 278.

55. Ibid., 243–47. And more compactly: "The lasting, extensive and serious consequences of associated activity bring into existence a public. In itself it is unorganized and formless. By means of officials and their special powers it becomes a state. A public articulated and operating through representative officers is a state; there is no state without a government, but also there is none without a public" (277).

56. According to Dewey, those who strongly separate the state from the government inevitably end up idealizing the former. According to this all-too-familiar error, the state comes into being as the embodiment of a nebulous common will, which is then "delegated" to government officers. This invariably leads to the sanctification of the state, while the government appears to be in constant need of reform. On the other hand, collapsing the state into the government "involves an unaccountable separation between rulers and people. If a government exists by itself and on its own account, why should there be a government?" Dewey argues that those who make this mistake (e.g., Lippmann) cannot explain why people obey. Both errors are ultimately attributable to the failure to understand that transactions define individuals as members of a group. Ibid., 277.

57. "Singular persons are the foci of action, mental and moral, as well as overt. They are subject to all kinds of social influences which determine *what* they can think of, plan and choose" (ibid.). Dewey's individual too can be typologized according to the different kinds of groups to which he belongs. As in Lippmann, he also has an unconscious that makes it difficult, if not impossible, to understand what determines his thoughts and feelings.

58. Ibid., 295.

59. Ibid., 303.

60. Ibid., 283.

61. Ibid., 326, 28.

62. Ibid., 330. This is consistent with the definition of social science Lippmann and Dewey share, according to which conclusions are scientific not "in virtue of their correctness, but by reason of the apparatus which is employed in reaching them" (ibid., 337).

63. Ibid., 332.

64. There is a nature-culture opposition at work here, but not one Dewey, or we, can be too sure about, because part of what it means to have culture is to live according to a set of rules and ideas that radically separate one from nature. "Human nature," then, if it is not to be an oxymoron, designates the unknowable potentialities that inform human conduct through its continuous transformation.

65. One should note that this process does not, according to Dewey, put an end to particular interests or "forces." Rather, these are "transformed in use and direction by ideas and sentiments made possible by means of symbols" that are shared (*Public,* 331).

66. Susman provides a helpful account of the development of this sense of "communication" among Dewey and his contemporaries. Susman, *Culture as History,* 252–70.

67. Dewey, *Public,* 371.

68. For Dewey, this is the very definition of thinking, as opposed to "habit" or "absolutistic" education (e.g., memorization and the propagation of fixed categories or forms). Thinking in this sense cannot be regarded as an individual activity, since it is only through dialog that the categories of thought may be altered: "Knowledge cooped up in a private consciousness is a myth" (*Public,* 345).

69. Dewey, *Public,* 371.

70. On the inadequacy of Dewey's proposals, see Westbrook, *John Dewey.*

71. The metaphor is used but qualified in the text, which stresses that "the human mind is not a film which registers once and for all each impression that comes through its shutters and lenses" (Lippmann, *Public Opinion,* 103).

72. Lippmann writes, "There can be little doubt that the moving picture is steadily building up imagery which is then evoked by the words people read in the newspapers. In the whole experience of the [human] race there has been no aid to visualization comparable to the cinema" (*Public Opinion,* 60).

73. "The increase in the number, variety and cheapness of amusements represents a powerful diversion from political concern" (Dewey, *Public,* 321).

74. For example, see ibid., 304.

75. See Graham Wallas, *The Great Society: A Psychological Analysis* (New York: Macmillian Co., 1915), 236. Wallas dedicated *Great Society* to the young Lippmann.

76. Ibid., 241.

77. James Bryce, *The American Commonwealth,* 2 vols. (Indianapolis: Liberty Fund, 1995 [1888]), 914.

78. Alexis de Tocqueville, *Democracy in America,* vol. 1 (New York: Vintage Books, 1990 [1835]), 188.

79. Dewey, *Public,* 340.

80. A growing body of scholarship places Lippmann and Dewey in a transatlantic conversation that is still very much in progress. See Giles B. Gunn, *Thinking across the American Grain: Ideology, Intellect, and the New Pragmatism* (Chicago: University of Chicago Press, 1992); and James T. Kloppenberg, *Uncertain Victory: Social Democracy and Progressivism in European and American Thought, 1870–1920* (New York: Oxford University Press, 1986). This work provides a salutary corrective to the nativist Dewey produced by, for example,

Richard Rorty, *Achieving Our Country* (Cambridge: Harvard University Press, 1998).

81. On Marx's critique, see Habermas, *Structural Transformation,* 124–29.

82. Charles A. Beard and William Beard, *The American Leviathan* (New York: Macmillan, 1930), 103–4.

83. Ibid., 107–8.

84. Charles A. Beard, *American Government and Politics* (New York: Macmillan, 1911). The shift was gradual. Beard reorganized the chapters in the fourth edition (1924), and the preface to the sixth edition announces that "emphasis is here lain on the functions of government as distinguished from the forms . . . To make room for the new material a number of time-honored chapters on historical development and several passages pertaining to theory have been omitted—sorrowfully but firmly." See Charles A. Beard, *American Government and Politics,* 6th ed. (New York: Macmillan, 1931), vi.

85. Beard, *American Government and Politics,* 6th ed., xi. The epilogue was introduced in the fifth edition (1928) and revised for the sixth.

86. Ibid., 805.

87. A similar shift can been seen between the 1923 and 1933 editions of James T. Young's less prominent text, *The New American Government and Its Work.* James T. Young, *The New American Government and Its Work,* 2d revised ed. (New York: Macmillan, 1923); Young, *The New American Government and Its Work,* 3rd ed. (New York: Macmillan, 1933).

88. Stuart Ewen, *PR! A Social History of Spin* (New York: Basic Books, 1996), 3.

89. Ewen traces the problem of "the crowd" through these figures and tends to follow other scholars in collapsing Lippmann into the trajectory. *Public Opinion,* in contrast, makes plain that it is an argument against Le Bon.

90. George Creel, *How We Advertised America; The First Telling of the Amazing Story of the Committee on Public Information that Carried the Gospel of Americanism to Every Corner of the Globe* (New York: Harper and Brothers, 1920), 4.

91. The language of "pleading," "education," and "interpretation" may also be found in Bernays, who writes that public relations counsel "interprets the client to the public, which he is enabled to do in part because he interprets the public to the client." Edward L. Bernays, *Crystallizing Public Opinion,* new ed. (New York: Boni and Liveright, 1934), 14. A contemporary, approving account of the "research bureau" may be found in Young, *The New American Government and Its Work,* 2nd revised ed.

92. Something of the scope of activity claimed by early public relations can been seen in the difference between Ivy Lee's failure to persuade the Rockefellers to change corporate policies in the service of Standard Oil's image and Theodore Newton Vail's more successful effort to transform AT&T from a fearsome "Trust" into a desirable monopoly by shaping everything from how

operators answered the phone to rate schedules and advertising campaigns. See Ewen, *PR!*, 82–101.

93. Bernays, *Crystallizing*, 52–53.

94. Bernays writes as though the individual precedes the group but also posits a "gregarious instinct" that submits the individual to the authority of the group at the expense of "individual judgement": "The mental equipment of the average individual consists of a mass of judgements on most of the subjects which touch his daily physical or mental life. These judgements are the tools of his daily being and yet they are his judgements, not on a basis of research and logical deduction, but for the most part dogmatic expressions accepted on the authority of his parents, his teachers, his church, and of his social, his economic and other leaders" (ibid., 61–62).

95. Ibid., 122.

96. Mary Poovey, *A History of the Modern Fact* (Chicago: University of Chicago Press, 1998).

97. Jean M. Converse, *Survery Research in United States: Roots and Emergence 1890–1960* (Berkeley: University of California Press, 1987), 36. Schools were the most popular topic.

98. Ibid., 122–23.

99. Pierre Bourdieu mocks the poll's tabulation of opinion as a "science without a scientist." But of course for pollsters this is precisely its virtue. Pierre Bourdieu, *In Other Words: Essays Towards a Reflexive Sociology* (Stanford: Stanford University Press, 1990), 168–76. Compare Converse, whose book seeks to restore the importance of polling methods in the development of the social scientific survey research that later reviled them.

100. Habermas, *Structural Transformation*, 241, 36.

101. Ibid., 247.

102. I do not wish to imply that German and U.S. scholarship developed in isolation from one another—quite the contrary. Bruce Robbins notes a line of criticism parallel to the Lippmann-Dewey debate in Weimar Germany, which he associates with Ferdinand Tönnies and Carl Schmitt. See Robbins, "Introduction," xi. Habermas's final chapters, however, focus clearly on the American case, rather than the German, and references to Schmidt do not have the prominence of those to Mills.

103. David Riesman, *The Lonely Crowd: A Study of the Changing American Character* (New Haven: Yale University Press, 1950).

104. William H. Whyte Jr., *The Organization Man* (New York: Simon and Schuster, 1956).

105. Indeed, in failing to approve the *Habilitantionschrift* (postdoctoral qualification thesis) on which *Structural Transformation* is based, they seem to have found Habermas's argument "insufficiently critical of the illusions . . . of an Enlightenment conception of democratic public life." Calhoun, "Introduction," 4.

106. The champion of the early, progressive, Lippmann, that is. Mills's stance had little in common with Lippmann's Cold War politics. See Steel, *Walter Lippmann and the American Century.*

107. C. Wright Mills, *White Collar: The American Middle Classes* (New York: Oxford University Press, 1951), 325.

108. C. Wright Mills, *Images of Man: The Classic Tradition in Sociological Theory* (New York: George Braziller, 1960).

109. C. Wright Mills, *The Power Elite* (New York: Oxford University Press, 1956).

110. According to Mills, the transformation of "public" into "mass" begins in the nineteenth century with the rise of the "assumed need for experts to decide delicate and intricate issues." Equally fatal to the public were "the discovery—as by Freud—of the irrationality of the man in the street" and "the discovery—as by Marx—of the socially conditioned nature of what was once assumed to be autonomous reason" (*Power Elite*, 301). Mills offers no real account of why the public lives on a critical term in the wake of these critiques, perhaps because to do so would make plain that he occupies the position of the hated "expert" who purports to tell the difference between public and mass.

111. Mills, *Power,* 304.

112. Ibid., 299.

113. Ibid., 300.

114. Calhoun, "Introduction," 33.

115. Habermas, *Structural Transformation,* 88; emphasis added.

116. Karl Marx and Frederick Engels, *The German Ideology* (International Publishers, 1970), 51–52.

117. In contrast, Marx still argued that nonbourgeois strata might overcome a "false" public by appropriating the bourgeois machinery of voting rights, political parties, and access to print. Although Habermas's argument is plainly indebted to this conception, he also reveals its reproduction of contradictions immanent to the bourgeois public sphere. Habermas, *Structural Transformation,* 124–29.

118. Reisman, for instance, worries that the "other-directed" audience of "popular culture" has gone "soft," while Mills (*White Collar,* xviii) writes of "white-collar people" that "no one is enthusiastic about them and, like political eunuchs, they themselves are without potency and enthusiasm for the urgent political clash." See also Andreas Huyssen, "Mass Culture as Woman," in *After the Great Divide* (Bloomington: Indiana University Press, 1986).

119. Felski makes a similar qualification of her own argument that contemporary feminism functions as a counter-public sphere when she notes that "one can no longer postulate the ideal of a public sphere which can function outside existing commercial and state institutions and at the same time claim an influential and representative function as a forum for oppositional activity

and debate." To mount a "public" opposition, feminism must work within existing institutions. Rita Felski, *Beyond Feminist Aesthetics: Feminist Literature and Social Change* (Cambridge: Harvard University Press, 1989), 171.

120. On the traditional paradox of the woman citizen, see Joan Scott, *Only Paradoxes to Offer: French Feminists and the Rights of Man* (Cambridge: Harvard University Press, 1996). On the new problem of the woman professional, see Nancy Cott, *The Grounding of Modern Feminism.* Denise Riley describes what amounts to the same shift by focusing on the articulation of "woman" with the "the social" in the late nineteenth and early twentieth centuries: Denise Riley, *"Am I That Name?": Feminism and the Category of 'Women' in History* (Minneapolis: University of Minnesota Press, 1988).

121. Moishe Postone, "Political Theory and Historical Analysis," in *Habermas and the Public Sphere,* 173.

122. Cf. Pierre Bourdieu: "To throw some light on discussions about the 'people' and the 'popular' one need only bear in mind that the 'people' or the 'popular' . . . is first of all one of the things at stake in the struggle between intellectuals. The fact of being or feeling authorized to speak about the 'people' or speaking for (in both senses of the word) the 'people' may constitute, in itself, a force in the struggles within different fields" (*In Other Words,* 150).

3. THE INFLUENCE INDUSTRY

1. Will H. Hays, *Moving Pictures: An Outline of the History and Achievements of the Screen from Its Earliest Beginnings to the Present Day* (New York: Doubleday, Doran, 1929), 506.

2. I am grateful for Richard Maltby's observation that practices of market differentiation have been compatible with a rhetoric that described a universal audience and gendered it: "Tillie, Kevin, and the 19-Year-Old Male: Hollywood Looks at Its Audience," paper presented at the *Screen* conference, Glasgow, Scotland, June 1999.

3. I refer to the lines of argument begun by Ann Douglas in literary criticism and Mary Ryan in history and particularly to those who have corrected Douglas's picture of feminization by better historicizing gender. Ann Douglas, *The Feminization of American Culture* (New York: Alfred A. Knopf, Inc., 1977); Mary P. Ryan, *The Empire of the Mother: American Writing about Domesticity, 1830 to 1860* (New York: Institute for Research in History and Haworth Press, 1982). And for the corrective, see Lori Merish, *Sentimental Materialism: Gender, Commodity Culture, and Nineteenth-Century American Literature* (Durham: Duke University Press, 2000); Philip Gould, "Introduction. Revisiting the "Feminization" of American Culture," *differences* 11, no. 3 (1999/2000); Leonard Tennenhouse, "Libertine America," *differences* 11, no. 3 (1999/2000). As I argue in the previous chapter, it also behooves us to historicize "influence" and "mass culture." Douglas opposes the masculine discourse of the Puritan

jeremiad to the feminine "influence" of sentimental fiction and writes that "'influence' was ironically the mother of advertising, the only faith of a secularized society" (68). The irony, I would suggest, is purely an artifact of Douglas's argument, which collapses the difference between the nineteenth-century language of "influence" and twentieth-century discourses of psychoanalysis and sociology that supply her own theory of that concept (347, n. 11).

4. Max E. Prager, "Some Accounting Problems of the Motion Picture Industry," *Administration: The Journal of Business and Analysis and Control* 2 (1921): 72. I discuss this article later in the chapter.

5. This might be the place to make plain my debt to and departure from several recent studies of cinema's participation in changes to normative definitions of femininity, masculinity, and appropriate sexual behavior around the turn of the century. Taken at glance, work by Lee Grieveson, Lauren Rabinovitz, Janet Staiger, Shelly Stamp, Ben Singer, and Gaylyn Studlar might be said to demonstrate how an emerging cinematic culture: (1) distinguished an active, clever, public woman consumer not merely from the stogy Victorian lady, but also from the dangerous seductress and the hapless victim of vice; (2) set a vigorous fun-loving masculinity at odds with dissipation and sexual objectification; and (3) significantly dissociated the problem of sexual desire from the institution of marriage. Although they have very different emphases, these studies collectively make it impossible to maintain that cinema's mission was to conserve nineteenth-century gender arrangements. They also banish the proposition that contemporary writing about cinema's influence simply described that influence. Rather, they make movies and writing partners in a hotly contested and often contradictory effort to understand and regulate social change. Finally, many of these studies draw attention to importance of "woman" as an allegorical figure for the movie audience or for modernity in general. The precise role of the rising feature film in mediating historical change remains unclear in these accounts, however. Thanks in part to the peculiar split between considerations of cinematic form and content I describe in the introduction, these studies tend to find history in thematic connections among films and writing about their audiences, or to compare film as a visual apparatus with such nineteenth-century technologies as display windows and world's fairs. With the exception of Studlar, moreover, all these authors describe very early films and/or a "transitional" period before the corporate feature film reigned supreme. They thereby describe a process that had yet to be completed and suggest that it would take the feature film to complete it. We can begin to understand how it did so, I am arguing, through a twofold move. First, we should describe how the visual love story transformed the problem of feminine virtue. Second, we should historicize the rhetoric of influence itself, understand the distinct type of social authority it sanctioned, and grasp the dependency of this authority on cinematic mediation. Lee Grieveson, "Fighting Films: Race, Morality, and the Govern-

ing of Cinema, 1912–1915," *Cinema Journal* 38, no. 1 (1998); Lee Grieveson, "'A Kind of Recreative School for the Whole Family': Making Cinema Respectable, 1907–1909," *Screen* 42, no. 1 (2001); Lauren Rabinovitz, *For the Love of Pleasure: Women, Movies, and Culture in Turn-of-the-Century Chicago* (New Brunswick: Rutgers University Press, 1998); Ben Singer, *Melodrama and Modernity: Early Pulp Cinema and Its Contexts* (New York: Columbia University Press, 2001); Janet Staiger, *Bad Women: Regulating Sexuality in Early American Cinema* (Minneapolis: University of Minnesota Press, 1995); Stamp, *Movie-Struck Girls*; Gaylyn Studlar, *This Mad Masquerade* (New York: Columbia University Press, 1996).

6. Sklar focuses on two films vocally opposed by moralists—*Old Wives for New* (1918) and *Male and Female* (1919)—while May situates these films in a larger group that includes *Don't Change Your Husband* (1919), *Why Change Your Wife?* (1920), *Forbidden Fruit* (1921), and *The Affairs of Anatol* (1921). Sumiko Higashi supplies the most extensive account of DeMille's oeuvre to date. She identifies *Why Change Your Wife?* as the third film in a divorce-and-remarriage trilogy that begins with *Old Wives for New* and continues through *Don't Change Your Husband.*

7. Robert Sklar, *Movie-Made America: A Social History of American Movies,* revised ed. (New York: Random House, 1994), 94.

8. "To put it another way, genteel women who exchanged the supportive intimacy of homosocial ties in a sex-segregated Victorian culture to become sexual playmates were still not equal to men, not even in a companionate marriage." Lary May, *Screening Out the Past,* 211–13.

9. Sumiko Higashi, *Cecil B. DeMille and American Culture: The Silent Era* (Berkeley: University of California Press, 1994), 147.

10. Burns Mantle, "The Shadow Stage," *Photoplay* 17, no. 6 (May 1920): 64.

11. Adela Rogers St. Johns, "What Does Marriage Mean?" *Photoplay* 19, no. 1 (December 1920): 28–29. See also her follow-up article, Adela Rogers St. Johns, "More about Marriage," *Photoplay* 19, no. 6 (May 1921).

12. W. J. T. Mitchell, "Metapictures," in *Picture Theory: Essays on Verbal and Visual Representation* (Chicago: University of Chicago Press, 1994).

13. She also poses for him in an elaborate negligee. For a discussion, see Virginia Wright Wexman, *Creating the Couple: Love, Marriage, and Hollywood Performance* (Princeton: Princeton University Press, 1993), 55–56.

14. Nan Enstad, *Ladies of Labor, Girls of Adventure: Working Women, Popular Culture, and Labor Politics at the Turn of the Century* (New York: Columbia University Press, 1999); Kathryn H. Fuller, *At the Picture Show: Small-Town Audiences and the Creation of Movie Fan Culture* (Washington: Smithsonian Institution Press, 1996); Stamp, *Movie-Struck Girls*; Gaylyn Studlar, "The Perils of Pleasure? Fan Magazine Discourse as Women's Commodified Culture in the 1920s," in *Silent Film,* ed. Richard Abel (New Brunswick: Rutgers University Press, 1996); Staiger, *Bad Women.*

15. A. F. Harlow, "How They Did It: The Methods and Policies That Have Helped Two Businessmen Win Unusual Success—One Applied Business Principles to the Movies and the Other Built His Business by Talking about It on Paper, Everywhere," *System: The Magazine of Business* 32, no. 3 (1918): 374.

16. *System* began in 1900 as a journal primarily concerned with the introduction of new cost accounting procedures: it advocated replacing ledger bookkeeping with more efficient card file systems adaptable not only to manufacturing and retail sales but also to professional medicine, law, and education. While it retained this emphasis, by the late 1910s it had both expanded its purview to consider all aspects of professional management and narrowed it to business exclusively. In 1927, the monthly was retitled *A Magazine of Business*. Two years later, *A Magazine of Business* became *Business Week*.

17. On the objectives of university business education, see Daniel Nelson, "Scientific Management and the Transformation of University Business Education," in *A Mental Revolution: Scientific Management since Taylor*, ed. Daniel Nelson (Columbus: Ohio State University Press, 1992).

18. Joseph Kennedy, "General Introduction to the Course," in *The Story of the Films, as Told by Leaders of the Industry to the Students of the Graduate School of Business Administration, George F. Baker Foundation, Harvard University*, ed. Joseph Kennedy (Chicago and New York: A. W. Shaw, 1927), 5. The claim that motion pictures were the fourth largest industry was commonplace in the 1920s and is debunked by Mae Huettig, who finds that they ranked forty-fifth in gross income according the Bureau of Internal Revenue's 1937 data. Mae Huettig, *Economic Control of the Motion Picture Industry* (Philadelphia: University of Pennsylvania Press, 1944), 48.

19. On the history of public relations, see chapter 2. On the new regulatory importance of cost accounting in the United States and the United Kingdom after World War I, see Anne Loft, "Accountancy and the First World War," in *Accounting as Social and Institutional Practice*, ed. Anthony G. Hopwood and Peter Miller (London: Cambridge University Press, 1994); Peter Miller and Ted O'Leary, "Governing the Calculable Person," in *Accounting as Social and Institutional Practice*. On the diffusion of scientific management, see Daniel Nelson, ed., *A Mental Revolution: Scientific Management since Taylor* (Columbus: Ohio State University Press, 1992).

20. Halsey, Stuart, and Co., "The Motion Picture Industry as a Basis for Bond Financing (1927)," in *The American Film Industry*, ed. Tino Balio (Madison: University of Wisconsin Press, 1985).

21. Prager, "Some Accounting Problems."

22. In addition to the sources already cited, see William S. Holman, "Cost Accounting for the Motion Picture Industry," *Journal of Accountancy* 30 (1920); Attilio H. Giannini, "Financial Aspects," in *The Story of the Films*; Richard W. Saunders, "The Motion Picture Industry from a Banker's Standpoint; Things

to Consider in Financing in this Field; the Law of Averages in Estimating Returns; Stages of Production; Depreciation of Cost; Residual Value; Eccentricities in Earning Power; Dangers of the Unusually Expensive Film; Average Cost," *American Bankers Association Journal* 16 (1923).

23. Prager, "Some Accounting Problems," 71.

24. See, for example, Kennedy, "General Introduction to the Course," 22; Halsey, Stuart, and Co., "The Motion Picture Industry," 125; Sidney R. Kent, "Distributing the Product," in *The Story of the Films,* 222–23.

25. Mary Poovey, *A History of the Modern Fact* (Chicago: University of Chicago Press, 1998).

26. Prager, "Some Accounting Problems," 71.

27. Ibid., 72.

28. Prager: "There is no strictly accurate and scientific basis for determining a periodical rate of depreciation" (ibid.).

29. The report was enough to persuade the investment bankers to back an issue of preferred stock, but not common stock as Famous Players had wanted. And they concealed their participation in the deal. The report's findings are summarized in Howard T. Lewis, "Gilmore, Field, and Company," in *Cases on the Motion Picture Industry* (New York: McGraw Hill, 1930). For an account of the production of the report, which uses fictitious names, see Janet Wasko, *Movies and Money.*

30. Halsey, Stuart, and Co., "The Motion Picture Industry," 215.

31. James A. Payant, "Why These Costs Agree with Estimates," *System* 31 (January 1917): 94.

32. Samuel Katz, "Theater Management," in *The Story of the Films,* 272.

33. Ibid., 277–78.

34. The regular "How They Did It" column offers an especially good comparative vantage on desirable management practices. See, for example, Irving S. Sayford, "How They Did It: The Ideas and Methods That Have Enabled Three Men to Attain More than Ordinary Success in Three Widely Different Lines of Business," *System: The Magazine of Business* 33, no. 2 (1918). The article includes a profile of John R. Frueler, president of Mutual Film Corporation.

35. Milton Sills, a star at First National who had been one of the founders of Actor's Equity in New York, ranked five different kinds of actors: from extras, the "nursery" of the profession, through "rank and file actors," "the respectable bourgeoisie of the motion picture community," to stars and "actor-producers," whom he likened to executives, "employers as well as employees." Milton Sills, "The Actor's Part," in *The Story of the Films,* 176–81.

36. Halsey, Stuart, and Co., "The Motion Picture Industry," 204. The earlier report on Famous Players–Lasky also addressed the question of star salaries. Lewis, "Gilmore, Field, and Company," 68.

37. Adolph Zukor, "Pleasing Most of the People Most of the Time," *System: The Magazine of Business* 34, no. 4 (1918): 481.

38. Richard DeCordova, *Picture Personalities: The Emergence of the Star System in America* (Urbana: University of Illinois Press, 1990).

39. Zukor writes: "In 1916 Mary was twenty-three, had been married for several years, and was being payed more money than the President of the United States. Yet to the public she was a little girl somewhere between the ages of twelve and eighteen. We did nothing to discourage the illusion." Indeed, Zukor and his staff guaranteed it. They arranged to include her mother in public appearances while excluding her husband Owen Moore, whose "name did not creep into Mary's copy." She was not allowed to smoke or drink in public, and "she could not be permitted to toy with a lipstick, a pencil, or a bit of paper. From a distance it might be taken for a cigarette." And her wardrobe was closely watched: "It was understandable that Mary wished to dress her age and in the height of fashion. But neither of us could afford it. As a customary member of her entourage on personal appearances, I cast an appraising eye, I must confess, on her mode of dress." Adolph Zukor, *The Public Is Never Wrong* (New York: G. P. Putnam's Sons, 1953), 175–76.

40. Halsey, "The Motion Picture Industry," 205. "Stardom is a matter over which only audiences have any real control. Something in a player's personality which they like is transmitted via the screen." Zukor, *The Public Is Never Wrong*, 183.

41. Sills, "The Actor's Part," 189.

42. Hays, *Moving Pictures*, 505.

43. Ibid., 506.

44. Miriam Hansen, *Babel and Babylon: Spectatorship in American Silent Film* (Cambridge: Harvard University Press, 1991), 76–89.

45. Hays, *Moving Pictures*, 506.

46. I discuss these materials in chapter 4.

47. Kennedy, "General Introduction to the Course," 20.

48. Adolph Zukor and Peter F. O'Shea, "Looking Ahead a Decade or Two," *Magazine of Business* 55, no. 1 (1929): 24.

49. Ibid.

50. Ibid., 25.

51. Julius Klein, "What Are Motion Pictures Doing for Industry?" *Annals of the American Academy of Political and Social Science* 128, no. 217 (1926): 79.

52. Samuel R. McKelvie, "What the Movies Mean to the Farmer," *Annals of the American Academy of Political and Social Science* 128, no. 217 (1926): 131.

53. On the rural–urban divide, compare Joseph Kennedy, "Preface," in *The Story of the Films*.

54. Halsey, Stuart, and Co., "The Motion Picture Industry," 213. Similarly, William Fox recounted to Upton Sinclair his dispute with the attorney gen-

eral's office over whether a merger with Loew's was in possible violation of the Sherman Anti-Trust Act: "I tried to bring these Government officials to realize that American trade follows American pictures, and not the American flag; that the Government's duty was to try to retain the supremacy of picture making in this country; that even if this consolidation did not entirely conform to laws on our books, that if a condition of this kind arose, it was their duty to help retain this industry for America." Upton Sinclair, *Upton Sinclair Presents William Fox* (Los Angeles: Author, 1933), 83. According to Ruth Vasey, the U.S. Department of Commerce coined the phrase "trade follows the motion pictures" in 1922. Ruth Vasey, *The World According to Hollywood, 1918–1939* (Exeter: University of Exeter Press, 1997), 42.

55. Jesse L. Lasky, "Production Problems," in *The Story of the Films,* 116.

56. In addition to the quoted article, see Adolph Zukor, "What the Movies Have Taught Me about Business," *Magazine of Business (System)* 53 (1928). One finds similar rhetoric in fictional as well as nonfictional biographies of early movie executives: Budd Schulberg, *What Makes Sammy Run?* (New York: Random House, 1952 [1941]); Sinclair, *Upton Sinclair Presents William Fox*; F. Scott Fitzgerald, *The Last Tycoon,* ed. Edmund Wilson (New York: Penguin Books, 1960 [1941]).

57. Zukor and O'Shea, "Looking Ahead," 24–25.

58. Kennedy, "Preface," ix.

59. May is describing reformers of the 1910s. May, *Screening Out the Past,* 46.

60. Richard Maltby, "The Genesis of the Production Code," *Quarterly Review of Film and Video* 15, no. 4 (1995); Ruth Vasey, "Beyond Sex and Violence: 'Industry Policy' and the Regulation of Hollywood Movies, 1922–1939," *Quarterly Review of Film and Video* 15, no. 4 (1995); Vasey, *The World According to Hollywood.*

61. Broadly speaking, the formation of American social associations occurs in two great waves, one in the mid-nineteenth century and the other in the early twentieth century. Many of the associations mentioned below were founded during the second period. I am grateful to Ruth Vasey for culling the following list of member organizations from a memo ("Committee on Public Relations," June 1922) in the Civic Committee file, reel 1, MPPDA Archive. Ruth Vasey, e-mail, 15 July 1996. Note that an asterisk indicates two representatives.

The Committee on Public Relations included representatives from: Academy of Political Science, Actors' Equity Association, American City Bureau, American Civic Association, American Federation of Labor, American Home Economics Association, American Legion,* American Library Association, American Museum of Natural History, American Sunday School Union, Associated Advertising Clubs of the World, Boy Scouts, Boys' Club Federation, Camp Fire Girls, Chamber of Commerce of United States,* Chautauqua Institution, Child Health Organization of America, Child Welfare League of America,

Colonial Dames of America, Commonwealth Club of California, Communi-
ty Service, Cooper Union for the Advancement of Science and Art, Council for
Jewish Women,* Dairymen's League Co-operative Association, Daughters of
the American Revolution, Federal Council of Churches of Christ in America,
General Federation of Women's Clubs, Girl Scouts,* Girls' Friendly Society in
America, International Federation of Catholic Alumnae, Jewish Welfare Board,
National Association of Civic Secretaries, National Catholic Welfare Council, National Child Labor Committee, National Civic Federation, National
Community Center Association, National Council of Catholic Men, Nation-
al Council of Catholic Women, National Health Council, National Congress
of Mother and Parent-Teachers Associations,* National Education Association,
National Safety Council, National Security League, National Society for Pre-
vention of Blindness, National Tuberculosis Association,* New York Child Welfare Committee,* New York City Federation of Women's Clubs, Russell Sage
Foundation, Safety Institute of America, Salvation Army, Sons of the American
Revolution, United Society of Christian Endeavor, War Department, Wood-
craft League of America, Women's Trade Union League, YMCA,* Young Men's
Hebrew Association, YWCA,* and Young Women's Hebrew Association. Mrs.
Frank H. Percells, Mrs. Charles S. Whitman, and Mrs. Charles Bull were on
the committee without institutional affiliation.

Organizations represented on the more selective Committee of Twen-
ty were: American Federation of Labor, American Legion, Boy Scouts, Camp
Fire Girls, Community Service, Daughters of the American Revolution, Feder-
al Council of Churches of Christ in America, General Federation of Women's
Clubs, Girl Scouts, National Catholic Welfare Council, National Congress of
Mothers and Parent-Teacher Associations, Russell Sage Foundation, Women's
Trade Union League, YMCA, and YWCA.

62. Frank Walsh, *Sin and Censorship: The Catholic Church and the Motion
Picture Industry* (New Haven: Yale University Press, 1996).

63. In 1923, the Russell Sage Foundation sponsored the first major survey.
The Payne Fund Studies followed a decade later. The emergence of social survey research more generally is described in chapter 2.

64. William Sheafe Chase, *Catechism on Motion Pictures in Inter-State Commerce,* 3rd ed. (Albany: New York Civic League, 1922), 5. The volume was first
published in 1921.

65. Ellis Paxson Oberholtzer, *The Morals of the Movie* (Philadelphia: The
Penn Publishing, 1922), 27.

66. Thanks to Michel Foucault, these are now commonplace assertions
in writing about motion picture censorship. Michel Foucault, *The History of
Sexuality Volume 1: An Introduction* (New York: Random House, 1978); Francis G. Couvares, ed., *Movie Censorship and American Culture* (Washington,
D.C.: Smithsonian Institution Press, 1996); Lea Jacobs, *The Wages of Sin: Censorship and the Fallen Woman Film, 1928–1942* (Madison: University of Wiscon-

sin Press, 1991); Annette Kuhn, *Cinema, Censorship, and Sexuality, 1909–1925* (New York: Routledge, 1988); Staiger, *Bad Women*; Vasey, *The World According to Hollywood.*

67. This was the approach eventually formalized in the "Dos, Don'ts, and Be Carefuls" of the 1930 Production Code. See Maltby, "The Genesis of the Production Code." One finds a similar logic at work in the writings of Oberholtzer and Chase, despite their insistence on prohibiting certain topics and scenes (see, for instance, Oberholtzer, 123–24).

68. Terry Ramsaye, "The Motion Picture," *Annals of the American Academy of Political and Social Science* 128, no. 217 (1926): 19.

69. Charlotte Perkins Gilman, "Public Library Motion Pictures," *Annals of the American Academy of Political and Social Science* 128, no. 217 (1926): 143.

70. See also Harmon R. Stephens, "The Relation of the Motion Picture to Changing Moral Standards," *Annals of the American Academy of Political and Social Science* 128, no. 217 (1926).

71. Arthur Edwin Krows, "Literature and the Motion Picture," *Annals of the American Academy of Political and Social Science* 128, no. 217 (1926): 73.

72. Ernst is the author of several books on censorship. Lorentz was at the time a well-known movie critic in New York City. He was later asked to set up a film unit for the U.S. Department of Agriculture and in 1936 produced the documentary classic *The Plow That Broke the Plains.* For an account of how Lorentz's filmmaking was part of a redefinition of the public during the New Deal, see Paula Rabinowitz, *They Must Be Represented: The Politics of Documentary* (New York: Verso, 1994).

73. Morris L. Ernst and Pare Lorentz, *Censored: The Private Life of the Movie* (New York: Jonathan Cape and Harrison Smith, 1930), 3. Writing eight years earlier, Oberholtzer had already found it necessary to counter this type of charge. See Oberholtzer, *The Morals of the Movie,* 7.

74. Ernst and Lorentz, *Censored: The Private Life of the Movie,* 16a.

75. Gilman, "Public Library Motion Pictures," 155.

76. Chase, *Catechism on Motion Pictures in Inter-State Commerce,* 8.

77. Gilman, "Public Library Motion Pictures," 145.

78. Donald Young, "Social Standards and the Motion Picture," *Annals of the American Academy of Political and Social Science* 128, no. 217 (1926): 149.

79. Ernest L. Crandall, "Possibilities of the Cinema in Education," *Annals of the American Academy of Political and Social Science* 128, no. 217 (1926): 110.

80. Nelson L. Greene, "Motion Pictures in the Classroom," *Annals of the American Academy of Political and Social Science* 128, no. 217 (1926): 124.

81. Ibid.

82. Alison M. Parker, "Mothering the Movies: Women Reformers and Popular Culture," in *Movie Censorship and American Culture,* ed. Francis G. Couvares (Washington, D.C.: Smithsonian Institution Press, 1996), 90.

83. Walkowitz specifically mentions the Russell Sage foundation in his

study of the emergence of the professional woman social worker. Daniel J. Walkowitz, *Working with Class: Social Workers and the Politics of Middle-Class Identity* (Chapel Hill: University of North Carolina Press, 1999).

84. Although focus on mass mediation produces a somewhat different account than a focus on arguments for suffrage or women's rights, my thinking here is indebted to Denise Riley, *"Am I That Name?"*

85. Richard Koszarski, *The Age of the Silent Feature Picture, 1915–1928* (Berkeley: University of California Press, 1990), 208.

86. Young, "Social Standards and the Motion Picture," 150, 49. Young mentions specifically: "The Institute of Religious and Social Surveys, the Knights of Columbus, the Young Men's Christian Association and the Young Men's Hebrew Association, the Federation of Women's Clubs, the Russell Sage, Carnegie and Rockefeller foundations, the Institute of International Education, and innumerable other projects." See note 61 for groups actually included on the industry's Public Relations Committee four years earlier.

87. Chase, *Catechism on Motion Pictures in Inter-State Commerce,* 124. Such legislation was introduced, and failed, several times during the decade. A contemporary chronicle of these attempts may be found in Chase and, later, Ford H. MacGregor, "Official Censorship Legislation," *Annals of the American Academy of Political and Social Science* 128, no. 217 (1926).

88. Cf. Steven J. Ross, "The Revolt of the Audience: Reconsidering Audiences and Reception During the Silent Era," in *American Movie Audiences: From the Turn of the Century to the Early Sound Era,* ed. Melvyn Stokes and Richard Maltby (London: BFI, 1999). Ross explains how the rising importance of "reactive pressure groups" skewed the representation of class on screen.

4. ETHNIC MANAGEMENT

1. Kevin Brownlow, *Behind the Mask of Innocence* (London: Jonathan Cape, 1990); Patricia Erens, *The Jew in American Cinema* (Bloomington: Indiana University Press, 1984); Lester Friedman, *Hollywood's Image of the Jew* (New York: Frederick Ungar Publishing, 1982).

2. Erens, *The Jew in American Cinema,* 31.

3. Donald Crafton, *The Talkies: American Cinema's Transition to Sound, 1926–1931,* ed. Charles Harpole, vol. 4 of "History of the American Cinema" (Berkeley: University of California Press, 1997), 519.

4. The claim that *The Jazz Singer* was the first talkie belongs to popular lore rather than scholarly history. Among historians, the most persuasive claims for originality come from those who see the film as pioneering the particular combination of singing, speech, music, and images that characterizes the musical film. See Rick Altman, "Introduction: Sound/History," in *Sound Theory/ Sound Practice,* AFI Film Readers (New York: Routledge, 1992); Andrew Sarris, *You Ain't Heard Nothin' Yet: The American Talking Film, History and Memory,*

1927–1949 (New York: Oxford University Press, 1998). For a detailed accounting of *The Jazz Singer's* synchronized sound sequences and the debt they owe to earlier Vitaphone shorts, see Charles Wolfe, "Vitaphone Shorts and *The Jazz Singer*," *Wide Angle* 12, no. 3 (1990).

5. Oland portrays Cantor Rabinowitz's body, but his voice was played by Hungarian Joseph Diskay. Wolfe, "Vitaphone Shorts," 71. Cantor Rosenblatt performs "Yahrzeit," the anniversary song for the dead.

6. James Lastra, "Reading, Writing, and Representing Sound," in *Sound Theory/Sound Practice*, AFI Film Readers (New York: Routledge, 1992), 75.

7. These claims derive from long-standing arguments over, first, whether or not the addition of synchronized sound substantially changed the conventions of the feature film and, second, the nature of the spatial relationship between audio and visual signifiers. For an introduction to the problems entailed by the historical consensus that sound did not much change "classical" Hollywood form, see Rick Altman, "Introduction: Four and a Half Film Fallacies," in *Sound Theory/Sound Practice*; Altman, "Introduction: Sound/History"; Crafton, *The Talkies*. From my perspective, sound films continue to reproduce the visual logic of the love story, but vocal sound supplements that logic in a decisive fashion. Here I am in full agreement with Michel Chion, who proposes that "there is no soundtrack" and thus no image-track either, insofar as the meaning of the one depends on the other. "It's like a recipe," he writes, "even if you mix the audio ingredients separately before pouring them into the image, a chemical reaction will occur to separate out the sounds and make each react on its own with the field of vision." Chion aptly terms the result a "*place* of images, plus sounds." Michel Chion, *Audio-Vision: Sound on Screen,* trans. Claudia Gorbman (New York: Columbia University Press, 1994), 40. I would point out, however, that Chion's continued reliance on the shot as a unit of analysis tends to undermine this emphasis on the signification of spatial relationships and to restore a merely technical conception of mixed visual and audio components. Finally, I do not wish the distinction between vocal sound and musical score (or what Chion calls "pit sound") to be understood as a reprisal of the customary distinction between "nondiegetic" and "diegetic" sound. That distinction is not supple enough to explain how various sounds contribute to the spatial distinctions that compose feature film narrative. Criticism acknowledges as much wherever it observes that sound helps to establish a particular locale, to define its limits or volume, and to juxtapose it with another, visible one. How sound could and should be used to these ends—as opposed to reproducing theatrical dialog—was a common concern among the first generation of film theorists. For an overview see Elizabeth Weis and John Belton, eds., *Film Sound: Theory and Practice* (New York: Columbia University Press, 1985). Among the selections included by Weis and Belton, the one from Bela Balazs (116–25) is particular revealing of early concern with spatial issues.

8. This ability distinguishes embodied sound, but as Christian Metz argues, it never makes sense, strictly speaking, to define sound in relationship to the frame: "either [a sound] is audible or it doesn't exist. When it exists, it could not possibly be situated within the interior of the rectangle or outside of it . . . sound is simultaneously 'in' the screen, in front, behind, around, and throughout the entire movie theater." Christian Metz, "Aural Objects," in *Film Sound: Theory and Practice,* ed. Elizabeth and John Belton Weis (New York: Columbia University Press, 1985), 157–58.

9. Rick Altman, "Sound Space," in *Sound Theory/Sound Practice.* Altman focuses on those practices that ensure the clarity of spoken dialog for the spectator at the expense of an "accurate" representation of the space in which the voice is placed, or of a perspective corresponding to that of the camera. As Altman explains, microphone placement techniques were developed during the thirties to ensure that the voice would be heard—and remain intelligible—as part of a particular location at the expense of techniques that would have made it subordinate to the camera's or character's perspective. Only when films need signal to spatial difference do they resort to strongly perspectival sounds.

10. Mary Ann Doane, "The Voice in the Cinema: The Articulation of Body and Space," in *Narrative, Apparatus, Ideology: A Film Theory Reader,* ed. Philip Rosen (New York: Columbia University Press, 1986); Pascal Bonitzer, "The Silences of the Voice," in *Narrative, Apparatus, Ideology,* ed. Philip Rosen (New York: Columbia University Press, 1986). Even in those flashback sequences where a voice has narrative power, some image is sure to lodge that body in a visible space on screen, and thus subsume it to another, audiovisual narrative. *Sunset Boulevard* provides the limit case.

11. All of these films were planned as silent features, with soundtracks added later. Kevin Brownlow reports that *Abie's Irish Rose* was withdrawn from circulation, cut from twelve to seven reels, and re-released with an added soundtrack. Brownlow, *Behind the Mask of Innocence,* 422–23.

12. Lastra, "Reading, Writing, and Representing Sound," 80–81.

13. Roland Barthes, "The Grain of the Voice," in *Image Music Text* (New York: Noonday Press, 1977). With Barthes, I claim that certain voices have a dimension of embodiment that exceeds adjectival description and that nonetheless emerges within signification. Unlike Barthes, I am not here concerned with the question of whether Jolson's voice provokes *jouissance* in its listeners. However, the combination of Jack's speech with his song is often said to have thrilled audiences with its apparent spontaneity and intimacy. Lewis Jacobs, *The Rise of the American Film* (New York: Harcourt, Brace, 1939), 298. To render this combination required the film's most technically ambitious recording efforts. See Wolfe, "Vitaphone Shorts," for a detailed accounting of the differences.

14. Herbert G. Goldman, *Jolson: The Legend Comes to Life* (New York: Oxford University Press, 1988); Larry F. Kiner and Philip R. Evans, *Al Jolson: A Bio-Discography* (Metuchen, N.J.: The Scarecrow Press, 1992).

15. *A Gesture Fight in Hester Street* may be seen on the web as part of the American Memory Collection of the Library of Congress: http://memory. loc.gov.

16. Miriam Hansen, *Babel and Babylon: Spectatorship in American Silent Film* (Cambridge: Harvard University Press, 1991), 73.

17. By the late 1910s the turn-of-the-century Jewish type had left the stage as well as the screen. This development is consonant with a general waning of nineteenth-century theatrical typification, whether of the Irishman, Dutchman, or the blackface minstrel; see Harley Erdman, *Staging the Jew: The Performance of an American Ethnicity, 1860–1920* (New Brunswick: Rutgers University Press, 1997). The minstrel show proper disappears in the 1920s, see Eric Lott, *Love and Theft* (Oxford: Oxford University Press, 1993). And the representation of blackface within *The Jazz Singer* differs markedly from the mid-nineteenth-century practices described by Lott. The contrasting white ring that calls attention to Jolson's mouth would not have been conventional in an earlier period, nor would audiences have been shown the application of burnt cork as part of the performance.

18. Friedman, for instances, writes that *The Jazz Singer* is typical of silent features in its emphasis on "economic success, intermarriage, freedom, and accommodation to American middle-class values." Friedman, *Hollywood's Image of the Jew,* 52. Cf. Brownlow, *Behind the Mask of Innocence*; Erens, *The Jew in American Cinema.*

19. As Eren's survey indicates, one finds the father in films before 1910 and mama throughout the 1920s, but neither appears in the racial caricatures of 1903 (ibid., 1–124).

20. Matthew Jacobson's otherwise careful history provides perhaps the best example of the pitfalls involved in failing to attend to the iconographic tradition. Jacobson relies on the screenplay to describe the film's depiction of various racial types and thus exaggerates differences among what plainly appear to be a variety of white faces on screen. Matthew Frye Jacobson, *Whiteness of a Different Color: European Immigrants and the Alchemy of Race* (Cambridge: Harvard University Press, 1998), 120–21.

21. Michael Rogin, *Blackface, White Noise: Jewish Immigrants in the Hollywood Melting Pot* (Berkeley: University of California Press, 1996), 108; Friedman, *Hollywood's Image of the Jew,* 51.

22. Linda Williams considers the voice more carefully than most and, not coincidentally, also stresses the ambivalence of the ending. Linda Williams, *Playing the Race Card: Melodramas of Black and White from Uncle Tom to O. J. Simpson* (Princeton: Princeton University Press, 2001), 136–58.

23. On the strategies by which Yiddish language films and audiences were assimilated to national audiences, see Hansen, *Babel and Babylon,* 60–89. I would simply add that America was also redefined to include the Jew as a partly foreign element.

24. On financing the transition to sound, see Janet Wasko, *Movies and Money: Financing the American Film Industry* (Norwood, N.J.: Ablex, 1982), 47–102. For a survey of the new types of expertise it involved, see David Bordwell, Kristin Thompson, and Janet Staiger, *The Classical Hollywood Cinema,* 294–308.

25. I would add, however, that two layers of makeup are required to make the whiteness appear more fundamental: the contrasting white ring around the mouth accentuates the blackface mask, but elsewhere brilliant illumination combines with dark lipstick and eye shadow to ensure that Jack will be seen as a pale white man.

26. Rogin's argument has antecedents in Lott, *Love and Theft*; Friedman, *Hollywood's Image of the Jew,* 50. It has been repeated and amended in numerous sources, including Jacobson, *Whiteness of a Different Color*; Jeffrey Paul Melnick, *A Right to Sing the Blues: African Americans, Jews, and American Popular Song* (Cambridge: Harvard University Press, 1999); Williams, *Playing the Race Card.*

27. Williams, *Playing the Race Card,* 150.

28. Melnick, *A Right to Sing the Blues*; Ann Douglas, *Terrible Honesty: Mongrel Manhattan in the 1920s* (New York: Farrar, Straus and Giroux, 1995).

29. W. T. Lhamon Jr., *Raising Cain: Blackface Performance from Jim Crow to Hip Hop* (Cambridge: Harvard University Press, 1998), 106.

30. Ibid.

31. Kallen's "Democracy *versus* the Melting Pot" essay originally appeared in *The Nation* in 1915 and was reprinted in 1924 as part of Horace Kallen, *Culture and Democracy in The United States* (New York: Boni and Liveright, 1924). All citations are to this later version. On Kallen's importance to the intellectual history of American pluralism, see John Higham, *Send These to Me: Immigrants in Urban America,* revised ed. (Baltimore: The Johns Hopkins University Press, 1984), 196–230. On the relationship between this history and late-twentieth-century multiculturalism, see Avery F. Gordon and Christopher Newfield, "Multiculturalism's Unfinished Business," in *Mapping Multiculturalism,* ed. Avery F. Gordan and Christopher Newfield (Minneapolis: University of Minnesota Press, 1996). Hyphenated Americans were resoundingly denounced by Kallen's contemporaries, presidents Theodore Roosevelt and Woodrow Wilson, see John Higham, *Strangers in the Land,* 195–204.

32. Higham, *Send These to Me,* 138–273; Higham, *Strangers in the Land,* 278; Marcia Graham Synnott, "Anti-Semitism and American Universities: Did Quotas Follow the Jews?" in *Anti-Semitism in American History,* ed. David A. Gerber (Urbana: University of Illinois Press, 1986).

33. Higham, *Strangers in the Land,* 278.

34. For a recent summary of immigration statistics, see Jacobson, *Whiteness of a Different Color,* 49.

35. Higham, *Strangers in the Land,* 277. On the origins of racial Anglo-

Saxonism in the first half of the nineteenth century, see Reginald Horsman, *Race and Manifest Destiny: The Origins of American Racial Anglo-Saxonism* (Cambridge: Harvard University Press, 1981).

36. David A. Gerber, "Anti-Semitism and Jewish-Gentile Relations in American Historiography and the American Past," in *Anti-Semitism in American History,* 38–39 n. 1; Sander Gilman, *The Jew's Body* (New York: Routledge, 1991).

37. The argument that finds the antisemitism of the Gilded Age to be an exception in American history begins with Oscar Handlin's work in the early 1950s, was substantially modified by Higham's *Strangers in the Land,* and has more recently been challenged by revisionists who provide antisemitism with a much longer, more mainstream history. Yet even those who argue for a more continuous history point to the period between 1890 and 1950 as a high point, and most follow Higham in arguing that the articulation of antisemitism with racism and nativism made a qualitative difference in that period. On the historiography of American antisemitism, see Gerber, "Anti-Semitism"; Higham, *Send These to Me,* 116–37. Gerber puts the main criticism of Higham succinctly in noting his tendency to "to collapse anti-Semitism into a species of nativism; thus, it becomes not unlike other prejudices against American white ethnic groups. Anti-Semitism, however, seems to be better understood, in its content, history, and functions, as a unique phenomenon even in the United States, where it has not been an important feature of the nation's historical development. What is particularly striking and unique about it is its durability and similarity of ideas across the centuries and national boundaries." Gerber, "Anti-Semitism," 39–40 n. 3. In his discussion of the Jewish voice, Sander Gilman strikes a similar note when he writes, "'Racial' or 'scientific' anti-Semitism of the late nineteenth-century is thought to have formed a radical break with the 'medieval' religious tradition of Jew-hating . . . But this is not true. The basic model of the Jew found within 'religious' contexts is merely secularized in the course of the eighteenth and nineteenth centuries." Gilman, *The Jew's Body,* 19. I would suggest that no phenomena can be "merely" secularized and would argue, contra Gilman, that idea of a hidden Jewish language is distinct from the idea of a unique "too Jewish" sound, and that the *Jazz Singer's* Jewish voicing of distinctly American songs differs yet again from the parodies of Jewish voices Gilman finds in turn-of-the-century Germany and the United States.

38. George W. Stocking Jr., "The Turn-of-the-Century Concept of Race," *Modernism/Modernity* 1, no. 1 (1993); George W. Stocking Jr., "The Critique of Racial Formalism," in *Race, Culture, and Evolution* (New York: The Free Press, 1968); Donna J. Haraway, *Modest_Witness@Second_Millennium.FemaleMan© _Meets_OncoMouse^{TM}: Feminism and Technoscience* (New York: Routledge, 1997), 213–66.

39. That racial categories changed in this way is a contention shared by much of the more recent work cited here. For a broad historical survey of shifts

in racial categorization, see Jacobson, *Whiteness of a Different Color.* One telling example is the Supreme Court case *United States v. Bhagat Singh Thind* (1923), which established that "whereas Thind, as a native of India, might indeed be Aryan ethnographically, he was nonetheless not 'white.'" Several Asian Indians, including Thind, were stripped of their certificates of naturalized citizenship. Sucheng Chan, *Asian Americans: An Interpretive History* (Boston: Twayne Publishers, 1991), 94. The classic account of the difference between Asian and Irish inclusion in the category of "white" is Alexander Saxton, *The Indispensable Enemy: Labor and the Anti-Chinese Movement in California* (Berkeley: University of California Press, 1971). Equally interesting evidence, both of the critique of racial science and the reinvention of racial categories, comes from the legal battles surrounding antimiscegenation legislation, see Peggy Pascoe, "Miscegenation Law, Court Cases, and Ideologies of 'Race' in Twentieth-Century America," *Journal of American History* 83, no. 1 (1996).

40. Kwame Anthony Appiah, *In My Father's House: Africa in the Philosophy of Culture* (New York: Oxford University Press, 1992); Walter Benn Michaels, *Our America: Nativism, Modernism, and Pluralism* (Durham: Duke University Press, 1995); Werner Sollors, *Beyond Ethnicity: Consent and Descent in American Culture* (New York: Oxford University Press, 1986).

41. Robert Ezra Park, "Behind Our Masks," in *Race and Culture: Collected Papers of Robert Ezra Park* (Glencoe, Ill.: The Free Press, 1950 [1926]), 247.

42. Michael Omi and Howard Winant, *Racial Formation in the United States: From the 1960s to the 1980s,* 2nd ed. (New York: Routledge, 1994), 14–23. The authors point out that the line from Park through Myrdal and Glazer and Moynihan has an intellectual biography as well as a conceptual history; Park's student E. Franklin Frazier advised both those major books.

43. On "color blindness" as a legal and political ideology that conserves race in order to deny its importance in the eyes of the beholder, see Pascoe, "Miscegenation Law, Court Cases, and Ideologies of 'Race' in Twentieth-Century America." Kevin Gaines, *Uplifting the Race: Black Leadership, Politics, and Culture in the Twentieth Century* (Chapel Hill: University of North Carolina Press, 1996), xii.

44. Robert Ezra Park, "Human Migration and the Marginal Man," in *Race and Culture, Collected Papers of Robert Ezra Park* (Glencoe, Ill.: The Free Press, 1950 [1928]), 354–56. Sollors notes, contra Park, that Lewishon never lived in a ghetto. Sollors, *Beyond Ethnicity,* 9.

45. On racial heredity and visibility in the nineteenth century, see Stocking, "The Turn-of-the-Century Concept of Race"; Stocking, "The Critique of Racial Formalism"; Robyn Wiegman, *American Anatomies: Theorizing Race and Gender* (Durham: Duke University Press, 1995), 21–42.

46. Kallen identifies Zangwill as a "Jew . . . of London, England," Jacob Riis—who produced a famous account of the Lower East Side—as a "Dane," and Edward Steiner and Mary Antin as "two Jews intermarried, 'assimilated'

even in religion, and more excessively, self-consciously, flatteringly American than the Americans." Edward Bok was the son of Dutch immigrants, a prominent reformer, and the editor of *The Ladies Home Journal*. Kallen, *Culture and Democracy in the United States*, 86.

47. Ibid., 121.

48. Kallen himself played a major part in founding the Harvard Menorah Society while a graduate student there in 1906. Higham, *Send These to Me*, 204.

49. Higham, e.g., faults Kallen for a white, European bias (ibid., 208). Gordon and Newfield make this the chief liability of his pluralist vision ("Multiculturalism's Unfinished Business"). Appiah compares Kallen's and Du Bois's "antiracist racism" *(In My Father's House)*. Jacobson critiques Kallen's imperialism (*Whiteness of a Different Color*, 214–15).

50. Kallen, *Culture and Democracy in the United States*, 75–76, 100.

51. On the James connection, see Larry C. Miller, "William James and Twentieth-Century Ethnic Thought," *American Quarterly* 31, no. 4 (1979).

52. W. E. B. Du Bois, *The Souls of Black Folk: Essays and Sketches* (Chicago: A. C. McClurg, 1903), 45–56.

53. Appiah, *In My Father's House*, 40.

54. Ibid., 42–43. Sollors's distinction between consent and descent informs Appiah's argument. Although Sollors's title suggests that "ethnicity" may be outmoded, I believe that something like its difference from race remains operative throughout his volume. See especially Sollors, *Beyond Ethnicity*, 39.

55. See chapter 1.

56. Rogin, *Blackface, White Noise*.

57. In addition to the sources already cited, see Gilman, *The Jew's Body*, 234–43.

58. Jacobson, *Whiteness of a Different Color*; Chan, *Asian Americans*, 54–55.

59. It is important to note that, under pressure of nativism, the major national Jewish defense organizations represented immigrants as well as native Jews, Southern Jews and Northern, Russian Jews and German, Ashkenazim and Sephardim—populations that might otherwise have gone their separate ways in the United States.

60. On the double-bind faced by the African American "Talented Tenth" in its mission of racial uplift, see Gaines, *Uplifting the Race*; David Levering Lewis, "Parallels and Divergences: Assimilationist Strategies of Afro-American and Jewish Elites from 1910 to the Early 1930's," *Journal of American History* 71, no. 3 (1984). This also prompted a running argument over whether Jewish promotion of African American causes is self-serving, see Hasia R. Diner, *In the Almost Promised Land: American Jews and Blacks, 1915–1935* (Westport, Conn.: Greenwood Press, 1977); Lewis, "Parallels and Divergences"; and Melnick, *A Right to Sing the Blues*.

61. Du Bois pioneered this rhetoric when he addressed *Souls of Black Folk*

to the white liberal question, "How does it feel to be a problem?" He offers himself as a native informant just long enough to make plain that the "problem" resides not in his black body but in the national culture that asks the question. In this single stroke, he establishes his own authority to represent the interests of Negro America and to objectify "the color-line" as the central problem of the twentieth century. He wins the power to represent both sides of "the veil," but at the costs, first, of making it the only problem about which he can really speak and, second, of opening himself to the charge that as an elite, he does not really represent black folks. For a detailed examination of how Du Bois's rhetoric constitutes African Americans as Americans, see Priscilla Wald, *Constituting Americans: Cultural Anxiety and Narrative Form* (Durham: Duke University Press, 1995).

62. The Fifteenth Amendment gave the vote to men regardless of race in 1870; the Seventeenth Amendment provided for direct election of U.S. Senators in 1913; and the Nineteenth Amendment extended the vote to women in 1920. For Dewey's explanation of why "there is no sanctity in universal suffrage, frequent elections, majority rule, congressional and cabinet government," see John Dewey, *The Public and Its Problems* [1927], ed. Jo Ann Boydston, *The Later Works, 1925–1953* (Carbondale: Southern Illinois University Press, 1984), 326.

63. See chapter 2.

64. Irving Howe, *World of Our Fathers* (New York: Harcourt Brace Javonovich, 1976), 164.

65. Sklar dates the first use of "movie mogul" to "around 1915." Robert Sklar, *Movie-Made America: A Social History of American Movies,* revised ed. (New York: Random House, 1994), 46.

66. Isaac F. Marcosson, "The Magnates of the Motion Pictures," *Munsey's Magazine* 48 (1912): 211.

67. Ibid., 212–21.

68. Ibid., 210.

69. Higham describes the paper as "the standard-bearer" of post-war nativism (*Strangers in the Land,* 282).

70. These articles were republished as books, appearing in four volumes between 1920 and 1922. *The International Jew, the World's Foremost Problem, Being a Reprint of a Series of Articles Appearing in the* Dearborn Independent *from May 22 to October 2, 1920* (Dearborn, Mich.: Dearborn Publishing, 1920). *Jewish Activities in the United States; Volume II of the International Jew, Being a Reprint of a Second Selection from Articles Appearing in the* Dearborn Independent *from Oct. 9, 1920, to March 19, 1921.* (Dearborn, Mich.: Dearborn Publishing, 1921). *Jewish Influences in American Life; Volume III of the International Jew, the World's Foremost Problem; Being a Reprint of a Third Selection from Articles Appearing in the* Dearborn Independent (Dearborn, Mich.: Dearborn Publishing, 1921). *Aspects of Jewish Power in the United States; Volume IV of the International Jew, the World's Foremost Problem; Being a Reprint of a Fourth Selection of*

Articles from the Dearborn Independent (Dearborn, Mich.: Dearborn Publishing, 1922). For a detailed accounting of the *Independent* and the "International Jew" series, see Leo P. Ribuffo, "Henry Ford and *The International Jew*," *American Jewish History* 69, no. 4 (1980).

71. *Jewish Activities, Volume II,* 117–18, 25.

72. See chapter 3.

73. As if to make plain that its attack has little to do with actual films, the article cites as a film with real feeling for rural America Griffith's *Way Down East* (1920)—a tale of seduction, unwed motherhood, and near fatal exposure. *Jewish Activities, Volume II,* 125–26.

74. Ibid., 127.

75. The document began to circulate in U.S. diplomatic circles at the end of World War I and was published in the United States as *The Protocols and World Revolution* in 1920, but the *Dearborn Independent* was apparently the main vehicle for the mass-distribution of its claims. For an exhaustive account of how the *Protocols* circulated in the United States, see Robert Singerman, "The American Career of the *Protocols of the Elders of Zion*," *American Jewish History* 71, no. 1 (1981). Higham points out that "Though the 'Protocols' served to substantiate the menace of the 'International Jew,' his entry into the stream of American nativism was largely independent of such exotic documents." Higham, *Strangers in the Land,* 281. Ribuffo confirms this point (448–49). Certainly the notion that Jews possess a special business acumen was not new. And late-nineteenth-century denunciations of Jewish control over the theater and press were common; see Erdman, *Staging the Jew: The Performance of an American Ethnicity, 1860–1920*; Steven Alan Carr, "The Hollywood Question: America and the Belief in Jewish Control over Motion Pictures before 1941" (Ph.D. diss., University of Texas at Austin, 1994), 126–39. Subsequent to the writing of this chapter, Carr's book was published. See Steven Alan Carr, *Hollywood Anti-Semitism: A Cultural History Up to World War II* (New York: Cambridge University Press, 2001). Tropes of Jewish control took a distinct, if not wholly novel turn, I am arguing, once combined with the rhetoric of motion picture influence discussed in the previous chapter.

76. The great rhetorical advantage of a conspiracy narrative is its ability to define those who denounce it as agents of the conspiracy, if only as unwitting accomplices. Just so, Ford's paper appropriated anticensorship arguments and denunciations of its own antisemitism as further confirmation of Jewish control: "Reader, beware! if you so much as resent the filth of the mass of movies, you will fall under the judgment of anti-Semitism. The movies are under Jewish protection." *Jewish Activities, Volume II,* 119. Similarly, the *Dearborn Independent* represented the selection of protestant and former postmaster general Will Hays to head the MPPDA as an attempt to conceal Jewish control—that is, as a response to their accusations and a proof of them.

77. Ibid., 130.

78. Ibid., 120.

79. Oliver Zunz notes Ford's hostility to corporate organization and financing, offering it as one explanation for why his company fell on hard times in 1919–20, just before the *Independent* series began. He also notes the irony, when seen from this perspective, that political economists have used "Fordist" production to exemplify early-twentieth-century capitalism. Olivier Zunz, *Making America Corporate, 1870–1920* (Chicago: University of Chicago Press, 1990), 79–90.

80. Higham, *Strangers in the Land,* 285.

81. Carr, "The Hollywood Question," 272–73; Carr, *Hollywood Anti-Semitism.*

82. See chapter 3.

83. William Sheafe Chase, *Catechism on Motion Pictures in Inter-State Commerce,* 13, 32, 119, 16. The *Independent* employed a similar rhetoric of disavowal in its writing on other aspects of the "Jewish question." For a discussion, see Ribuffo, "Henry Ford and *The International Jew,*" 474.

84. See, e.g., "Menace of Motion Picture Censorship," *American Hebrew* 108, 8 April 1921; "A Popular Executive Advocates Clean Pictures and Scrupulous Business Methods as Basis for Building Permanent Film Industry," *American Hebrew* 122, 16 March 1928; "Who Is Who in Motion Pictures—1927," *American Hebrew* 122, 2 December 1927.

85. Including, according to Carr ("The Hollywood Question," 161): Lucien Wolf, *The Jewish Bogey and the Forged Protocols of the Learned Elders of Zion* (1920); Israel Zangwill, "The Legend of the Conquering Jew" (1920); John Spargo, *The Jew and American Ideas* (1921); and Herman Bernstein, *The History of a Lie* (1921). In a similar vein, Walter Lippmann writes: "If you go stark, staring mad looking for plots, you see all strikes, the Plumb plan, Irish rebellion, Mohammedan unrest, the restoration of King Constantine, the League of Nations, Mexican disorder, the movement to reduce armaments, Sunday movies, short skirts, evasion of the liquor laws, Negro self-assertions, as sub-plots under some grandiose plot engineered either by Moscow, Rome, the Free Masons, the Japanese, or the Elders of Zion." Walter Lippmann, *Public Opinion,* 84.

86. Higham, *Strangers in the Land,* 285; Ribuffo, "Henry Ford and *The International Jew*"; Carr, "The Hollywood Question," 161–62.

87. "Ford Scenes in News Reel Cut When St. Louis Jews Protest," *Moving Picture World,* 30 July 1927, 305.

88. Terry Ramsaye, *A Million and One Nights: A History of the Motion Picture Through 1925* (New York: Simon and Schuster, 1964 [1926]), 482–85.

89. Ibid., 823. Underscoring the logic by which the Jewish executive now functioned as the model immigrant, this passage is followed by one noting the prominence of Greeks among theater owners. The Greeks were clearly at a different level of authority, and implicitly, success in assimilation.

90. This explanation survives in Lary May and Eliane Tyler May, "The Jewish Movie Moguls: An Explanation in American Culture," *American Jewish History* 72, no. 1 (1982).

91. *Jewish Activities, Volume II,* 130.

92. Upton Sinclair, *Upton Sinclair Presents William Fox,* xv.

93. *Fortune* made a related revision of the *Dearborn Independent* in February 1936. It ran a lengthy article entitled "The Jews in America" that aimed, first, to refute the notion of a Jewish race by describing Jews in ethnic terms, and second, to identify antisemitism as un-American by associating it with German nationalism. The article directly confronted the issue of Jewish control of industry and opinion by asking, "What difference does it make even if Jews do run away with the system? . . . A man's job should not be determined by his parentage." Despite this distinction between "job" and "parentage," however, *Fortune* proceeds to conduct a survey of industry as if the question of control could be decided by identifying the number of Jews in positions of authority. And while the article concludes that "there is no basis whatever for the suggestion that Jews monopolize U.S. business and industry" in general, it concedes that Jews "exert pretty complete control over the production of [motion] pictures," and that the movies have a "great power . . . in the influencing of modern society." In this way, the article seeks to mediate between the acknowledgement that Jews are prominent in the motion picture industry and the observation that "Jewish control" has been a racist claim. "Jews in America," *Fortune,* February 1936, 130, 36.

94. Sklar, *Movie-Made America,* 46–47. Cf. Neal Gabler, *An Empire of Their Own: How the Jews Invented Hollywood* (New York: Doubleday, 1988).

95. Lary May, *Screening Out the Past: The Motion Picture and the Birth of Consumer Society, 1900–1929* (New York: Oxford University Press, 1980), 175. Cf. May and May, "The Jewish Movie Moguls."

96. Gabler, *An Empire of Their Own,* 46. Cf. Ramsaye, *A Million and One Nights,* 823.

97. These novels drew from the story that made Jewishness an explanation for cinema's success the logical inference that the mogul's personal success could only alienate him from America, and they made that alienation readily intelligible as problem of insufficient, excessive, or inauthentic masculinity.

98. William Fox, "Reminiscences and Observations," in *The Story of the Films.*

99. Micheal Rogin writes "*The Jazz Singer* retains its magic because, like no picture before or since, it is a liminal movie. It goes back and forth not only between sound and silence, music and intertitles, blackface and white, but also between Kol Nidre and 'The *Robert E. Lee,*' Jew and gentile, street and stage, male and female." Rogin, *Blackface, White Noise,* 116. I agree that the film is an exceptional one, marks a transitional moment, and conjoins the terms Rogin

lists. I think its distinctiveness has less to do with alternation per se than with productive recombination.

100. Donald Bogel writes that "For blacks in films, the talkie era proved to be a major breakthrough." Donald Bogle, *Toms, Coons, Mulattoes, Mammies, and Bucks: An Interpretive History of Blacks in American Film*, new expanded ed. (New York: Continuum, 1989), 27. Linda Williams describes a "historic transformation of blackface into black performance" Williams, *Playing the Race Card*, 172. Compare Thomas Cripps's discussion of the "all-black celebrations of life, *Hearts of Dixie* and *Hallelujah!*" Thomas Cripps, *Slow Fade to Black* (New York: Oxford University Press, 1993), 236–62.

101. The classic account of how Hollywood studios employed black talent at the expense of independent black producers during the transition to sound is Cripps, *Slow Fade to Black*. Mark Reid carries forward that argument. Mark A. Reid, *Redefining Black Film* (Berkeley: University of California Press, 1993). I would add that this shift needs to be understood in the context of the conglomeration of the industry and its "public" ownership by shareholders. As an alternative to the problematic of "white ownership," I propose a more explicit focus on the problematic of white management, with the distinction between the racial mission and the racial composition of the managerial class that problematic entails. I am indebted to Wahneema Lubiano's theorization of this distinction. See Wahneema Lubiano, "Like Being Mugged by a Metaphor: Multiculturalism and State Narratives" in *Mapping Mulitculturalism*.

CONCLUSION

1. Three recent, but very different, accounts of the relationship between professional management and U.S. hegemony may be found in Giovanni Arrighi, *The Long Twentieth Century* (New York: Verso, 1994); Alfred Dupont Chandler, *Scale and Scope: The Dynamics of Industrial Capitalism* (Cambridge: Harvard University Press, 1990); Harold Perkin, *The Third Revolution: Professional Elites in the Modern World* (New York: Routledge, 1996).

2. Kristin Thompson, *Exporting Entertainment: America in the World Film Market, 1907–1934* (London: BFI, 1985).

3. Ruth Vasey, *The World According to Hollywood, 1918–1939*.

4. Indeed, I can think of no recent study of early feature films produced outside the United States that seriously considers those films either to have simply mimicked Hollywood or to have ignored it entirely—although authors often find themselves obliged to critique both positions. See, for example, Richard Abel, *French Cinema: The First Wave, 1915–1929* (Princeton: Princeton University Press, 1984); Thomas Elsaesser, *Weimar Cinema and After: Germany's Historical Imaginary* (New York: Routledge, 2000); Patrice Petro, *Joyless Streets: Women and Melodramtic Representation in Weimar Germany* (Princeton: Princeton University Press, 1989); Yuri Tsivian, "Between the Old and the New: So-

viet Film Culture in 1918–1924," *Griffithiana,* no. 55/56 (1996); Miriam Bratu Hansen, "Fallen Women, Rising Stars, New Horizons," *Film Quarterly* 54, no. 1 (2000); Zhen Zhang, "Teahouse, Shadowplay, Bricolage: *Laborer's Love* and the Question of Early Chinese Cinema," in *Cinema and Urban Culture in Shanghai, 1922–1943,* ed. Yingjin Zhang (Stanford: Stanford University Press, 1999); Paul G. Pickowicz, "Melodramatic Representation and the 'May Fourth' Tradition of Chinese Cinema," in *From May Fourth to June Fourth,* ed. Ellen Widmer and David Der-wei Wang (Cambridge: Harvard University Press, 1993). I acknowledge that "nation" is not necessarily the best concept to describe the audience addressed by every alternative. But no alternative, it seems to me, can entirely escape the problematic of nationalism. For a discussion, see Philip Rosen, "Making a Nation in Sembene's *Ceddo,*" *Quarterly Review of Film and Video* 13, no. 1–3 (1991).

5. Hansen makes this point concisely in "Fallen Women." The pioneering demonstration, however, comes from Stephen Heath, who cautions that one ought not use Ozu's rejection of Hollywood's "180 degree rule" to equate modernist aesthetics with anti-Western aesthetics. This problem runs throughout the Ozu debates. See Stephen Heath, "Narrative Space," in *Questions of Cinema* (Bloomington: Indiana University Press, 1981), 61–62; Edward Branigan, "The Space of *Equinox Flower,*" in *Close Viewings,* ed. Peter Lehman (Tallahassee: Florida State University Press, 1990); David Bordwell and Kristin Thompson, "Space and Narrative in the Films of Ozu," *Screen* 17, no. 2 (1976); David Bordwell, *Ozu and the Poetics of Cinema* (Princeton: Princeton University Press, 1988); Noël Burch, *To the Distant Observer: Form and Meaning in the Japanese Cinema* (Berkeley: University of California Press, 1979).

6. I discuss Lasky's phrase in chapter 3.

7. Although it does not explicitly take up the problem of professional authority, Paul Smith's study describes how such a process revised the American genre of the Western: Paul Smith, *Clint Eastwood: A Cultural Production* (Minneapolis: University of Minnesota Press, 1993).

8. Abel, *French Cinema,* 359–60; Georges Sadoul, *French Film* (New York: Arno Press, 1972), 28–29.

9. Abel, *French Cinema,* 364. Cf. Gilles Deleuze, *Cinema 1: The Movement-Image,* trans. Hugh Tomlinson and Barbara Habberjam (London: The Athlone Press, 1986), 76–77.

10. Lotte H. Eisner, *The Haunted Screen: Expressionism in the German Cinema and the Influence of Max Reinhardt* (Berkeley: University of California Press, 1969).

11. Siegfried Kracauer, *From Caligari to Hitler: A Psychological History of the German Film* (Princeton: Princeton University Press, 1974 [1947]).

12. Petro, *Joyless Streets.*

13. Tom Gunning demonstrates in great detail that Death does not control

the narrative in the way a strictly allegorical reading would suggest. There is a narrative agent that constructs the allegory and governs its progression. Evoking the "narrator system" he finds in Griffith, Gunning refers to this agent as a Lang's "destiny-system." Tom Gunning, *The Films of Fritz Lang: Allegories of Vision and Modernity* (London: British Film Institute, 2000).

14. Kracauer, *From Caligari to Hitler*, 9, 11. Reading Kracauer against the grain, one can detect the rise of new strata of German managers and office workers both like and unlike an older petite bourgeoisie.

15. Elsaesser, *Weimar Cinema and After*, 7.

16. Eisenstein famously identifies this type of parallel editing with the ideological limitations of Anglo-American capitalism in "Dickens, Griffith, and the Film Today." Sergei Eisenstein, *Film Form*, trans. Jay Leyda (New York: Harcourt Brace Jovanovich, 1977), 195–255.

17. Denise Youngblood, *Movies for the Masses: Popular Cinema and Soviet Society in the 1920s* (Cambridge: Cambridge University Press, 1992).

18. Eisenstein uses the vocabulary of "harmonic overtones" to describe the film's montage more broadly in "The Filmic Fourth Dimension." Eisenstein, *Film Form*, 64–71.

19. This does not mean that filmmakers and party bureaucrats held identical positions, simply that we would do well to understand their arguments as competitions internal to a rising intellectual class, with all the contradictions that involves. For an account of the film's production, see Jay Leyda, *Kino: A History of the Russian and Soviet Film* (Princeton: Princeton University Press, 1983 [1960]), 262–70.

20. See Bordwell, Thompson, and Staiger, *Classical Hollywood Cinema*, 70–77.

21. Kracauer's observation dates to the 1920s. Siegfried Kracauer, *The Mass Ornament: Weimar Essays*, trans. Thomas Y. Levin (Cambridge: Harvard University Press, 1995), 76.

22. In the number, Toby Wing substitutes for Powell's love interest (Ruby Keeler). *Dames* (1934) hyperbolizes the lewd gesture in its titular number: there, the chorines' torsos appear between the inverted "V" of their legs, flipping up one by one to allow the camera to pass. On *Dames* as a film that "generates an image of woman as 'image' itself," see Lucy Fisher, "The Image of Woman as Image: The Optical Politics of *Dames*," in *Genre: Musical, A Reader*, ed. Rick Altman. (London: Routledge and Keegan Paul, 1981), 77.

23. Soviet montage was all the rage in Hollywood during the early 1930s; see Bordwell, Thompson, and Staiger, *Classical Hollywood Cinema*, 72–74. This does not refute Berkeley's debt to American theatrical forms as documented by Martin Rubin, *Showstoppers: Busby Berkeley and the Tradition of Spectacle* (New York: Columbia University Press, 1993).

24. Although Rick Altman does not explicitly attend to the different spa-

tial models at issue, I believe his argument about the musical as a "dual-focus" narrative could be read in support of this contention. See Rick Altman, *The American Film Musical* (Bloomington: Indiana University Press, 1987).

25. Although Blondell takes center stage in the number, her voice is plainly dubbed by a black woman (Etta Moten) who also appears in the scene.

26. On the film's connection to discourses of discipline and the Great Depression see Patricia Mellencamp, "The Sexual Economics of *Gold Diggers of 1933*," in *Close Viewings: An Anthology of New Film Criticism,* ed. Peter Lehman (Tallahassee: Florida State University Press, 1990).

27. Michael Denning, *The Cultural Front* (New York: Verso, 1997). Cf. Giuliana Muscio, *Hollywood's New Deal* (Philadelphia: Temple University Press, 1996); Paula Rabinowitz, *They Must Be Represented: The Politics of Documentary* (New York: Verso, 1994).

28. Karl Marx and Frederick Engels, *The German Ideology* (International Publishers, 1970), 64.

Index

Mark Garrett Cooper is assistant professor of English at Florida State University, where he teaches film and American studies.